DAWN TRADERS'
GUIDE TO
WORLD MARKETS

Dawn Traders
London is one of the world's leading financial centres. The wealth of its markets is greater than that of many nations. LBC, Europe's largest commercial news/talk radio station, has been broadcasting for almost two decades and reaches millions of listeners in London and South-east England every day, informing, commenting and entertaining. *Dawn Traders*, LBC's early morning financial news programme, reports every working day on the pulse of the world's financial markets, offering vital and timely information to London's financial decision-makers.

The Author
Robin A. Amlôt graduated in International Politics before becoming a journalist. Initially specializing in commodities before being instrumental in setting up a database on corporate risk analysis, he was appointed Financial Editor of LBC and Independent Radio News in 1991, after four years as Deputy Financial Editor and, as such, is a regular contributor to syndicated commercial radio news throughout the world. He has appeared on UK television, written for both UK national and foreign daily newspapers, and numerous periodicals, and has travelled widely throughout Europe and South-east Asia.

DAWN TRADERS'
GUIDE TO WORLD MARKETS

Robin Amlôt

BOXTREE

In association with **LBC**

First published in the UK in 1992
by BOXTREE LIMITED, 36 Tavistock Street,
London WC2E 7PB

1 3 5 7 9 10 8 6 4 2

© Photomotive Ltd 1992

Design by Robin Amlôt
Cover design by Design 23

Set in New Century Schoolbook
Typeset by Photomotive Ltd
Printed and bound in Great Britain by Richard Clay Ltd,
Bungay, Suffolk

Except in the United States of America, this book is sold subject to the condition that it shall not, by way of trade or otherwise, be lent, resold, hired out or otherwise circulated without the publisher's prior consent in any form of binding or cover other than that in which it is published and without a similar condition including this condition being imposed on a subsequent purchaser.

A catalogue record for this book is available from the British Library.

ISBN 1 85283 136 7

All rights reserved

Contents

Introduction   vii

PART ONE: TRADERS AND TRADING

Chapter 1:	Stock Markets	3
Chapter 2:	Commodity Futures	17
Chapter 3:	Bonds, Borrowings and the Euromarket	32
Chapter 4:	Foreign Exchange	44
Chapter 5:	Financial Futures and Options	59
Chapter 6:	Players and Referees	73
Chapter 7:	Treasuries, Central Banks and International Institutions	89

PART TWO: EXCHANGES AND CONTRACTS

Chapter 8:	New York	103
Chapter 9:	Chicago	117
Chapter 10:	Tokyo	128
Chapter 11:	London	135
Chapter 12:	Western Europe	153
Chapter 13:	Primary Producers	166
Chapter 14:	Tigers and Dragons	175
Chapter 15:	Developing Markets I	187
Chapter 16:	Developing Markets II	192

PART THREE: APPENDICES

Appendix I	Glossary of Terms	199
Appendix II	Abbreviations in Text	205
Appendix III	Tax and Commission in Stock Markets	209
Bibliography		212

Introduction

"Globalization" was one of the financial markets' catchphrases of the 1980s. Investment became international as a result of deregulation and improved computer and telecommunications technology. The markets in raw materials, by their very nature, were always international. The ending of fixed rates of exchange in the 1970s provided the spur to the development of currency trading on a massive scale. Hand in hand with the growth of the foreign exchange markets came international bond trading. Both currency and bond trading grew, at least in part, as a result of the growth of international trade in goods and services and the development of international and multinational corporations.

Cross-border share trading rose from 6 per cent of total global equity turnover in 1979 to 15 per cent by the end of the 1980s. The value of such cross-border investment rose from US$300 billion (£518 billion) in 1985 to US$1,600 billion (£2,752 billion) in 1990. British companies and British investors have led the way in the development of the international financial market-place. Some 18 per cent of all UK investments are held in foreign stocks, compared to 7 per cent in the USA, and 5 per cent in Japan. UK pension funds now have between a fifth and a quarter of their investments in foreign assets, compared to 10 per cent for Japanese institutions and 5 per cent for US institutions.

However, US interest in international markets is growing. US investors purchased a record net US$9.4 billion of foreign stocks in the second quarter of 1991, spending most of their money in the UK and Japan. In the same period, foreigners bought a net US$7.7 billion of US stocks with the largest purchases coming from Canada and Japan. The proportion of international investments held by the major financial institutions is likely to increase over the next decade. Such a strategy would underline one of the basic investment principles—diversification to reduce risk.

The other side of this coin has been the internationalization of corporate business. Today, any leading company anywhere in the world can turn to foreign investors for new equity capital, instead of relying

INTRODUCTION

solely on its domestic market. Companies want diversification of their shareholder base and liquidity outside their home market. They may also wish to list their equity in a given market to support any substantial dealings in the shares. A company's domestic capital market may be limited in size. The trading of shares abroad can assist in raising international awareness of a company's products and services. Furthermore, by placing shares around the world, a company may hope to make a hostile takeover more difficult, or add a further weapon to its armoury which will assist in future acquisitions.

Deregulation has played an important part in the development of international investment. UK exchange controls were lifted in 1979, but the rest of Europe has lagged behind. Many continental investment institutions are still restricted from investing overseas by second-tier exchange controls which have remained in place despite the lifting of primary controls through the 1980s. These restrictions are looking more and more untenable with the approach of the single European market and the harmonization of financial regulation in the EC.

However, investing in overseas markets takes some courage on the part of the investor. The potential for mistiming an investment decision, to buy or to sell, is much greater in foreign markets, and the best calculations may be ruined by adverse currency movements in the foreign exchanges.

Futures and options have already been a major growth area. Investors have turned to futures, swaps and options to reduce risk. These derivatives, so-called because they are derived from underlying commodities or financial instruments, are evolving rapidly. The volume of contracts traded is increasing and new products and trading techniques are being introduced. Product development in futures and options trading, together with increased awareness of the significance of derivatives, resulted in trading volume growth of more than 30 per cent in Europe in 1989/90. Across Europe, since the first financial futures exchange was established in 1978, the number of such marketplaces has risen to twenty-three.

One of the most notable examples of the use of derivatives was the move into currency futures by Japanese pension and insurance funds in the late 1980s. Since the middle of the decade, the Japanese institutions had acquired large amounts of US dollar-denominated assets. However, the value of the US dollar declined over the latter half of the 1980s. The Japanese, concerned that it would fall further, turned to derivatives, selling US dollars forward in the futures market, that is to say, making commitments to sell dollars at set prices in the future, guaranteeing protection against loss of value on their assets through a compensatory

INTRODUCTION

gain in profit when settling the forward position. It has been estimated that the Japanese institutions "hedged", that is insured, more than half of their overseas portfolios in this way.

Financial futures and options have become essential risk management tools for corporate treasurers in banking and industry as well as for investment fund managers. Running parallel to the development of exchange-traded financial futures and options contracts, a substantial "over-the-counter" market has established itself. There is a fast growing inter-bank market for interest rate and currency swaps, forward rate agreements, interest rate guarantees and foreign currency options.

The liberalization and integration of the world's financial markets through the 1980s was inspired by a combination of hope and necessity. The hope lay in the expectation of a more efficient allocation of savings and investment. The necessity came from the financial instability of the inflationary 1970s which created government deficits and external financial imbalances on a scale that exceeded the capacity of fragmented national markets to cover. The resulting financial innovations, such as the explosive growth in derivatives, helped to overwhelm the traditional regulatory segmentation of national markets and contributed much to the effective integration of financial markets globally. Borrowers and investors are now capable of exercizing a global freedom of choice in financing and portfolio strategies.

Dawn Traders' Guide to World Markets provides the reader with a basic introduction to the global financial system. No prior knowledge of financial matters is required! In Part One of the book, chapter by chapter, the different financial instruments are discussed and their markets explained and set in context.

Chapter One describes the origin of joint stock companies in the seventeenth century, the development of the equity markets themselves and the variety of shares and equity-based instruments traded on them. The chapter provides a basic guide to the operation of stock markets and their value measures, the stock indices.

Raw materials, known as primary commodities, and their markets are the subject of Chapter Two, which explains the development and operation of commodity futures contracts. The importance and purpose of these contracts in serving industry, both the raw material producers and consumers, together with the role of the speculator is supplying liquidity to the market-place is explained.

Having shown the development of corporate financing in equity and the management of raw material supply, we review the other markets to which companies may turn to raise money, the domestic and international bond markets.

Introduction

The development of the foreign exchange market is set in context through an explanation of the attempts to establish fixed exchange rate systems, from the gold standard through the post-Second World War Bretton Woods agreement to the Louvre Accord in support of the US dollar in the 1980s and EC proposals for European Monetary Union.

The evolution and growth of derivative markets following the maturation of the commodity futures markets is investigated. The development of interest rate futures, options and swaps, stock market index futures and traded options is traced and the operation of these instruments explained.

The players in the financial markets are defined: the banks; the brokers; and the investing institutions. Brief summaries of the regulatory regimes in the major markets are given together with the historical development of the regulating agencies. The roles of government and central banks in the global economy and the global financial system are explained with examples from the USA, the UK, Germany and Japan, the world's four largest financial arenas. The difference in power structure, culture and style of operation is explained. The political decision-making process as politics impinges on markets is discussed with reference to the impact on the European financial sector of the coming single European market.

In Part Two, each chapter describes the major established markets in given locations around the world, providing an overview of the importance of each market-place, what they are, how they trade and what limitations they operate under. The historical development of each market is briefly outlined, together with the types of instrument that they trade. Contact addresses and telephone numbers are given for each of the markets discussed for readers who wish to know more to follow up for themselves.

Finally, abbreviations and terms used in the book are explained in the appendices and there is a brief summary of broking charges and taxation as they pertain to the major stock markets of the world.

PART ONE: TRADERS AND TRADING

CHAPTER 1

STOCK MARKETS

Three stock markets dominate the financial headlines around the world now; the markets in London, New York and Tokyo. Both New York and Tokyo are relative newcomers, but even the London Stock Exchange cannot lay claim to being the world's oldest market. That accolade goes to the Amsterdam Stock Exchange in The Netherlands. In 1602, the Vereenigde Oost-Indische Compagnie (VOC), the United East India Company, became the first company in the world to be financed by the issue of shares to the general public.

Shares are exactly what the name implies, that is to say they are shares in the ownership of the business. The shareholder is a part-owner of the company and can expect to share in its profits, but should also be prepared to share in its losses.

Ordinary shares are known as equity and are the risk-sharing portion of a company's funds, as distinct from stocks, which represent long-term loans and do not necessarily confer any rights of ownership in the company to the holders. The ordinary share holders own the company, they can vote on company policy, appoint and dismiss directors and, if the company makes a profit, they can expect to share in that profit in the form of a dividend.

A company can raise money by expanding the amount of equity in the market through the issue of the new ordinary shares. In the London market, this is normally done through what is known as a rights issue. In a rights issue, shares are offered to the company's existing share holders in direct proportion to the current size of their holdings, for example one new share for every four shares already held. Such share issues will be underwritten by traders in the market, who commit themselves to purchasing the shares should any share holders decided not to exercise their right to purchase. Alternatively, the company may decide to "place" a new block of shares on the market, selling them to new investors. This is a far more popular device than the rights issue in the New York markets where rights issues have become progressively rarer over the last twenty years. Most of the world's markets require the company to seek the existing share holders' permission to proceed with a placing. One further technique that has developed in recent years is the bought deal, in which a trading firm in the market purchases the block of shares itself and then sells them on to investors at a premium. Although less democratic than the rights issue, the placing and the bought deal are cheaper, speedier and more efficient ways of increasing the amount of equity in the market-place.

Following financial deregulation in London in 1986, placings and bought deals were expected to supersede rights issues. This did not happen, largely because of pressure from the institutional share holders in London. In October 1987 the institutions, which own a majority of UK equity, formed a loose coalition, known as the "pre-emption group", with the express intent of defending the right of existing share holders to first refusal on any new shares issued. The power of the institutions in the London market is such that the guidelines laid down by the pre-emption group are still in place. Effectively, the issue of more than 5 per cent of a company's existing share capital must be either by way of a rights issue or through the unsatisfactory compromise of a placing with existing share holders who have the right to claw back their entitlement.

The company may also choose to make a bonus issue of shares. This does not result in the company raising more money but is essentially an accounting exercise, with the company's retained earnings being transformed into share holder capital. Again, share holders are given shares in proportion to their existing holdings. These capitalization issues generally take place at times when corporate profits are running at a high level.

As well as ordinary shares, there are several other ways a company can raise money in the market without immediately altering the structure of ownership—something which the issue of more "voting" shares may do. The company may choose to issue preference shares which usually have a fixed dividend level. The voting rights of these shares is usually limited but in return for this, the holder has first claim on the company's dividends, and on its assets should the company be liquidated.

There are several types of preference share: the cumulative preference share, in which the holder is entitled to be paid in arrears if the company misses a dividend payment; the redeemable preference share, which, as the name suggests, will be redeemed in full at a set date, thus resembling a fixed term loan; the participating preference share, which may have a lower fixed dividend but will benefit from a higher dividend declared for the ordinary share, allowing the holder to benefit from higher profits made by the company while offering a measure of protection against lower profits or losses; and the convertible preference share, which may at some set date in the future be converted into ordinary shares at a specified price.

Companies may also choose not to issue preference shares, but may issue bonds or debentures. These are long-term borrowings, generally with fixed rates of interest, and can be attractive to both the issuer and investor. In virtually all of the national tax regimes the company is able to set the interest charged on the debenture against its tax bill and may keep the option of early redemption available. For the investor the attraction lies in the high level of security of the debenture, which is issued with the backing of the company's assets. Debentures tend to be issued in the market of the country in which the company is domiciled, bonds in the international markets (*see Chapter Three*).

A relatively recent development in the types of instrument a company may choose to use to raise finance is the warrant. Warrants give investors the right but not the obligation to purchase shares at a fixed price on a fixed date in the future, normally several years hence. The investor will pay a relatively small amount to buy the rights to a number of shares at a certain premium above the prevailing market price. The main attraction of warrants to the investor lies in the potential for capital gain in the event that the company's share price exceeds the specified fixed price in the warrant. In addition to the introduction of warrants, in the late 1980s there was growing interest in the issue of so-called "hybrids" involving the issue of warrants linked to bonds. Such issues are especially favoured by Japanese companies.

It is sometimes easy to lose sight of the fact that the primary function of any market-place for equities is to provide companies with a place to raise money to invest in their businesses. However, the vast majority of trading on the world's equity markets is secondary trading. That is to say it is the trading of shares which have already been accepted or listed by the Exchange and previously held by one or more other investor. To function as an attractive arena for companies to come to the market in the first instance it is important that there be a ready secondary market-place, otherwise investors would be unwilling to have their funds tied up forever.

Brokers on the equity markets offer clients three basic types of service. There is the no-frills execution or dealing only; advisory, in which the broker will proffer advice to the client on a deal if requested; and discretionary, where the broker will manage a portfolio of shares at his own discretion on the investor's behalf in order to maximize capital growth or income, or a mix of the two.

There are four specific variables to be considered in equity investment. First is the actual price of the share itself, the volatility of which will depend on the liquidity of the market in the company's shares. Anything may move the share price, from the general health of the economy to news of improved sales or a strike among the work force. Some markets are more susceptible to news than others. In early March 1991, milk company shares leapt on the Tokyo Stock Exchange following the announcement that Japan's Princess Kiko was pregnant. Nor was this the first time that the market had reacted to news from the Imperial Household. Speculation about market reaction to any news of pregnancy had been rife, especially following the tripling in price of one major pearl company's shares in 1990 in the months leading up to Kiko's engagement to Emperor Akihito's second son Akishino, after the princess-to-be popularized pearl necklaces!

Apart from the share price, the other variables to be considered are dividend cover, yield and the company's price-to-earnings ratio (P/E). Dividend cover is the ratio of net profit to dividend payout (profit divided by the amount paid in dividends). It is a measure of the dividend's safety. That is, the lower the cover, the greater the likelihood the company might have to reduce or forego a future dividend payout should profits decline. Conversely, the higher the dividend cover, the greater the expectation that the level of dividend payments be maintained in a time of reduced profits. Yield is expressed as a percentage and is the income the investor can expect from the shares as a proportion of the current market price.

The P/E ratio is another way of measuring the value of the share. It is a useful yardstick by which to compare companies which pay out different proportions of their profits in dividends. Profit retained still belongs to the share holders but is being held in the business because the directors believe they can get a worthwhile return on re-investing the money in the business. Profits can be expressed in two ways, either in overall terms or in "earnings per share". This latter figure is arrived at by dividing the total amount of profits by the total number of shares issued or in circulation. The P/E ratio is the current market price (P) divided by the earnings (E) per share. In general the higher the P/E number the more highly valued is the company by the market and its share holders, usually on the expectation of above-average growth in profits and dividends in the future. Obviously were profits to double but the share price remain unchanged, the P/E would halve; were the market to continue to rate the share at the same P/E then the share price would double. In practice, the result would probably be somewhere between these two extremes.

Trading on the equity markets is dominated by the institutional investors. The increasing computerization of price quotations over the last ten years has found a parallel in the use of computer program trading. Program trading regularly accounts for around a fifth of all business transacted on the New York Stock Exchange. This program trading, in which large transactions are speedily carried out, was blamed in part for the global market crash in 1987 *(see below)* and has resulted in renewed interest in the use of margin requirements to curb violent price swings. In equity markets the margin requirement is the proportion of the share price paid to the broker when buying shares. Its function is to restrict the amount of credit that brokers and dealers can extend to their customers for the purpose of buying stocks and shares. The US Congress first imposed official margin requirements on the American markets in 1934 in the wake of the Wall Street crash *(see below)*. Although they fell into disuse in the 1970s and 1980s, following the crash of 1987 they are once more being considered as a tool of market management.

In addition to the variety of instruments available directly to the corporate issuer, the world's markets have developed other types of investment to improve market liquidity and increase interest in stocks and shares. Among these instruments are those known as "traditional options". An option gives the holder the right to purchase (a call option) or to sell (a put option) a set number of shares in a company at specified dates over the next three months at the price set when the option was purchased. Traditional options are in the form of a direct contract between the seller and the purchaser and are not otherwise tradeable instruments as distinct from "traded options" *(see Chapter Five)*.

It is common practice for governments and municipal authorities also to make use of the stock markets to raise money through the issue of fixed interest stock. US government issues are known as Treasuries, in the UK such government stocks are referred to as Gilts, in Japan they are JGBs (Japanese government bonds) and in Germany, Bunds, etc. There are three basic types of government issue, those with fixed interest, those whose return is linked to the rate of inflation and those which are convertible. The latter type tend to be "short", that is to say with a term of three- to- five years, giving the investor the option, at specified time intervals, of converting his investment into a "long" bond, with a term of fifteen to thirty years *(see Chapter Three)*.

As well as providing an arena for companies to raise money and a secondary market-place for shares issued, the world's stock markets have been the scene, most notably through the 1980s, of spectacular takeover battles. The lengthy period of rising share prices through the decade gave managements the confidence and the potential financial muscle to expand by merger and acquisition. The globalization of the financial markets coincided with the globalization of business and the desire to become a pre-eminent international player in a given industry sector underlies many of the billion dollar deals of the 1980s. At a lower level, takeover activity is fuelled by the belief that one's own management team can make a better job of running the target company's business than is the case under its existing management. However, this belief is not always borne out by later experience and two important human factors should not be discounted: managers like the excitement of the bid battle, it is more fun than the daily grind; fashion also plays a part–if one's competitors are making bids and deals, the urge to jump on the bandwagon can be overwhelming.

PRIVATIZATION

Political historians are already beginning to evaluate the leadership of Margaret Thatcher in the UK during the 1980s. If nothing else, of one thing we can already be certain, the influence of her governments' policies over three election victories and more than a decade in power has ensured the term "privatization" a place in the general usage of the English language. Her administrations were not the first in the UK to return state-owned enterprises to the public sector, nor indeed was the UK the first country to have an organized policy for the disposal of state assets; the first such programme was undertaken by Chile in the mid-1970s with the privatization of the state pension funds.

However, the UK privatization programme undertaken by successive Conservative governments through the course of the 1980s has become a role-model which is now being followed by governments of a variety of political hues throughout the world. Prior to the first Thatcher administration, privatization was a relatively obscure concept confined to economic theory. Its wide general acceptance is a phenomenon which can be directly attributed to Margaret Thatcher and her policies. In the first ten years of the the UK privatization programme, the total market capitalization of the companies sold into the market exceeded £60 billion and more than £29 billion in assets and over one million jobs had been transferred from the public to the private sector.

Among the stated goals of privatization are exposure to the disciplines and opportunities of the private sector markets for capital and other resources for the enterprises being sold off and widening share ownership. By how much the state share sales have resulted in significantly greater participation in the share markets by individuals is a moot point. However, we can say that there is now greater public interest in and desire for knowledge about the markets and their mechanisms.

Privatization has changed the shape of the UK stock market, given the sheer size of the companies sold. The privatized utilities now account for a major part of the market's leading indices and consist of more than 10 per cent of the overall market capitalization of all UK-listed shares. The UK's programme of state sales remains the largest so far seen in the world but is likely to be dwarfed in the 1990s, in the number of enterprises involved if not in absolute financial terms, by the return to the private sector of industries in the newly-unified Germany and many East European countries.

The Gaullist government in France headed by Jacques Chirac, which came to power in 1986, had planned to dispose of assets worth more than FFr 200 billion in a programme which would have vastly exceeded the UK government's sales. However, electoral defeat and the replacement of the Gaullist administration by a Socialist government halted the programme of state sales. Despite this suspension, the evidence of opinion polls suggests that privatization has become popularly established in France.

Privatization in Western Europe, as opposed to the wholesale restructuring taking place in the newly-democratic nations of Eastern Europe, is in its first phase, with governments tending to sell commercial operations which happen to be owned by the state. The USA has little to privatize, in that it is a country in which the role of the state has traditionally been kept to a minimum. In common with its neighbour Canada, the US government is now examining the services run by local municipalities to establish whether they can be operated by private companies. Privatization has been enthusiastically embraced by the newly-industrialized countries of Asia, and also in Japan, led by the massive flotation of the telecommunications utility Nippon Telephone & Telegraph. On a limited basis the concept was also embraced by left wing governments in Australia and New Zealand in the 1980s.

As well as increasing public interest in the market-place, privatization has also redefined the limits of private investment and what may be achieved by the private sector. In 1981, for example, plans for a gas-gathering pipeline in the North Sea were shelved because of failure to raise capital from the private sector. By the late 1980s this situation had changed completely with the far more ambitious and expensive Channel tunnel being built with private funds. Privatization is indelibly associated with the politics of Margaret Thatcher but as a concept is probably one of the most successful British exports of the 1980s. It has been taken up and adapted by governments of every

Risks and Rewards

Prior to the formal public incorporation of the VOC in Amsterdam in 1602, the practice of sharing the risk of commercial ventures had already become well established. For example, in 1553, some 240 merchants in the City of London had each subscribed the then princely sum of £25 for the outfitting of an expedition intended to search for a north-east passage to China. This was the first joint stock company. Two of the expedition's three ships foundered in Norwegian waters but the third reached Russia and its master signed a treaty with the Czar, Ivan the Terrible, out of which the Muscovy Company (more properly known as "the Mysterie and Companie of Merchant Adventurers for the Discoverie of Regions, Dominions, Islands and places Unknowen") was formed. The Muscovy Company's shareholders subscribed the working capital and appointed a Governor and Deputy Governor to oversee the management of the company. It was this separation of ownership from management which allowed the shares of the company to become tradeable instruments in their own right.

The development of joint stock companies and public companies went hand in hand with the growth of trade and the expansion of the European trading empires. Many of the great voyages of discovery were funded as risk ventures by the merchants of the European ports. Thus the early financial markets developed in the great trading ports of the European Atlantic coast, most notably in Amsterdam and London.

London's investors and merchant venturers congregated in the coffee houses surrounding the Royal Exchange. In 1673, a law was passed restricting the number of brokers to 100 and banning them from dealing on their own account. These brokers required licences from the Lord Mayor of the City of London in order to operate. By 1698, daily price lists were on sale recording the movement of share prices.

It is in the nature of the financial markets that their history is punctuated by cycles of boom and bust and that it is the disasters which provide the punctuation marks to the development of the exchanges of the world. The three most celebrated stock market collapses are the South Sea Bubble, the Wall Street Crash and Black Monday 1987.

The South Sea Bubble

The first such disaster was the South Sea Bubble, which burst in the summer of 1720. The South Sea Company, or to give it its full title "The

Governor and the Company of Merchants of Great Britain trading to the South Seas and other parts of America and for encouraging the fishery", had been given a monopoly of the British trade with South America and the Pacific. The company had been set up in 1711 by the then Chancellor of the Exchequer, Robert Harley, with the idea of turning the United Kingdom's national debt into shares in the company.

Unfortunately, Robert Harley's bright idea took on a ill-fated life of its own, but investors saw the company as being backed by the government and, therefore, a safe investment. The great and the good invested in the South Sea Company as it took on more and more of the national debt, which was growing speedily due to the expense of the war between Britain and Spain, this latter development also ensuring that very little actual trade came the company's way from the Spanish Americas.

By the summer of 1720, a rip-roaring bull market in South Sea shares had been responsible for the creation of close on 100 similar companies, with the founders offering more and more ridiculous schemes with which to part luckless investors from their money. Perhaps the most celebrated example of this being the enterprising fellow who advertized, "A company for carrying on an undertaking of great advantage but nobody to know what it is." He sold 1,000 shares in six hours and was, of course, never heard from again!

This frenetic activity panicked the directors of the South Sea Company into persuading the government to declare a number of its rivals illegal. The move backfired as the rush to unload shares spread to the South Sea Company itself. From a peak of 1,000 in July, the shares fell to 400 in September and to 135 in November. Fortunes were made, by those who had sold at the top, but as has been the case since, many more were lost by those who did not. As well as rocking the British government, the South Sea Bubble taught the authorities valuable lessons in market regulation.

THE WALL STREET CRASH

With hindsight, the portents of the crash which shook Wall Street in October 1929 and pitched the United States into a decade of depression should have been easy to read. Several times in previous months the market's information dissemination service, the "ticker" had been unable to keep up with the flow of rising prices. It proved equally incapable of keeping pace as the market went into free fall.

The Dow Jones Industrial Average Index (*see below*), the market's leading indicator, peaked at 381 on 3 September, a level it was to take nearly twenty years to reach once more. On Wednesday, 23 October, the

Dow fell 7 per cent with the ticker way behind the market by the close. The following day volume on the market at 12.9 million shares was more than twice levels ever previously seen. A major support operation led by Richard Witney, then floor broker with the bank J.P. Morgan, did little more than defer the worst of the falls and by the close of Black Tuesday, 29 October, the Dow was down to 230, a fall of almost 40 per cent from its peak. The market appeared to hit bottom on 13 November with the Dow at 198.

However, shares continued to slide despite several attempts to rise and the market "rollercoastered" its way down in five successive crashes, each as vicious as October 1929, eventually to touch bottom in mid-1932 some 89 per cent down from its high point. The panic on Wall Street transmitted itself to other markets around the world. However, despite heavy falls, the declines in financial centres across Europe were nowhere near as cataclysmic as the slump in New York. Only the market in Canada, which fell by 85 per cent in the same period, suffered as badly as the American market.

The world's financial markets did not really recover from the Wall Street Crash until the post-war era. The ensuing global depression, felt most heavily in the United States, lasted until the late 1930s and the beginnings of European re-armament leading to the Second World War. Most notable of the regulatory changes which followed the Crash of '29 was the separation of the US banking system into two sectors through the Glass-Steagall Act of 1933 whereby the commercial banks were prohibited from acting as investment banks and from owning a firm dealing in securities.

BLACK MONDAY 1987

On Monday, 19 October 1987, the Dow Jones Industrial Average collapsed 508 points, a fall of some 23 per cent. Once again the American market's downfall echoed round the world. The great global bull market of the 1980s came to a crunching halt. Shares around the world had been rising since the global economy came out of recession in the early 1980s but by the summer of 1987 the markets had peaked and started to move "sideways" as the stock market analysts say.

On Friday, 16 October, the Dow had fallen by 108 points, a heavy fall but one which in no way gave a hint of the ferocity to come. By contrast, trading in London that day had ground to a virtual standstill; the British capital's daily life was interrupted by bad weather without precedent in the history of a nation obsessed with the subject. The hurricane which hit south-east England brought London's transport systems to a halt and so severely disrupted the electricity supply that those traders who had been able to reach their offices could transact no business to speak of. The financial hurricane which hit the world's markets the following Monday was also without precedent.

The collapse in share prices in Wall Street began as investors sold out of high-priced equity and bought fixed interest stocks and bonds. But the move to liquidate holdings in equities became a self-fulfilling torrent as more and more investors saw the value of their shares dropping. The speed of the collapse owed much to technological change. The "ticker" which could not keep pace with the market in 1929 had been replaced by computer trading screens and computer program trading, and the simple telephone and telegram communications of the 1920s by complex telecommunications operations which allowed traders to deal simultaneously with open markets around the globe.

Although the crisis was born in the USA, it was nurtured and fed worldwide. The worsening US trade and budget deficits, the realization that the West Germans and the Japanese were reluctant to support the dollar and the seeming disintegration of international co-operation on world exchange rates and economic policies were sufficient to tip the US market over the precipice. Program trading aggravated, rather than, as some claimed, instigated the collapse in share prices.

The tidal wave of falling prices washed round the world but the "tsunami" of sell orders began to break against the uniquely Japanese bulwark of the Tokyo market. Japanese brokers, by and large, prefer not to issue sell recommendations on shares at any time, and the Japanese institutional investors stayed out of the market as it fell; the volume of trading on the Tokyo market was miniscule. A nod and a wink from the Ministry of Finance was all that was required for the big four brokerages which dominate Tokyo to buy on their own accounts. The market fell but strategic stocks held their values and the worst of the crisis was over.

INDICES

The first market index was produced by Charles Henry Dow, a financial journalist and co-founder of Dow Jones & Company. In 1884, Charles Henry Dow compiled the first average of US share prices. The antecedents of the present Dow Jones Industrial Average index are directly traceable back to Dow's first index. Dow's formula is recognized as an original contribution to stock market methodology. The index is the market player's barometer. It lets him know how the market as a whole is performing, offering a measure of overall price movements. Against this he may gauge his own performance as a fund manager if he is managing a portfolio or the relative movement of the price of his investment if he holds shares in an individual company.

For the index to be an accurate yardstick against which to measure performance it is important that it be representative of the companies whose shares are quoted on the market. This is not always the case, as the history of the Hang Seng Index on the Hong Kong Stock Exchange shows. The Hang Seng Index was introduced in 1964 and the thirty-three companies included in its calculation account for close on three-quarters of the Hong Kong market's total capitalization. However, consistent criticism has been levelled at the index, the complaint being that the property sector is too highly represented and the industrial sector under-represented. Furthermore, at thirty-three, the number of constituents in the index has puzzled many observers. The explanation for this and the Hang Seng Bank's apparent determination to hold the index's constituent companies at this number may be explained, not by any market logic, but by reference to older and perhaps more potent forces. The Hang Seng Bank was founded on the third day of the third month of 1933 ...and add to this the positive resonance in Chinese numerology of the number thirty-three, meaning "life after life" with connotations of prosperity and fortune. Other indices may be more precise but the brokers in Hong Kong are unlikely willingly to give up the Hang Seng Index!

There are three types of market index: the geometric index; the basic arithmetical index; and the weighted arithmetical index. The geometric index involves multiplying the share prices of the constituent companies together and then taking the nth root of the result where n is the number of companies. The Financial Times 30 Share Index, introduced in the London market in 1935, is a geometric index. It was the first index to be calculated on share price movements in London on an hourly intra-day basis. The calculation of the FT 30 thus involves the multiplication of the prices of the thirty constituent shares and, finally, the taking of the thirtieth root. The FT 30's base date, i.e. first calculation, remains 1935. The main drawback of the geometric index is that although in the short term it is a fair basis for measuring market behaviour, over long periods of time it imparts a downward bias.

Charles Henry Dow's original index was the first example of the basic arithmetical index. This index is arrived at by the simple addition of the constituent share prices and then multiplying the result of that calculation with a constant figure. The basic arithmetical index in which all constituents have an equal weighting is the simplest and most straightforward. However, this type of index is also easily distorted. A large swing in any one of the constituent share prices will have a disproportionate effect on the index, detracting from its representation of the market as a whole. Furthermore, the weighting or importance of each share to the index is arbitrary and may vary if the number of shares a company has in the market is increased through issues or decreased through buy-ins.

The weighted arithmetical index is believed to offer the most accurate reflection of general market performance. The first indices of this type were the Standard & Poors indices introduced in the US market in the 1920s. The introduction in 1962 of the FT Actuaries Share indices by the Financial Times and the UK's Institute of Actuaries provided for a more accurate measure of the general market in London. These indices were the first weighted arithmetical indices published on the London market.

In the weighted arithmetical index, the number of shares issued by the constituent companies is taken into account in the index calculation. That is to say, movement in the share price of a company with a high market capitalization, which is the share price multiplied by the number of shares in issue, will have a greater impact on the index than a price move in the shares of a company with a smaller capitalization.

Of the three most important domestic market indices, the Dow Jones Industrial Average in New York, the Nikkei-Dow Jones Average in Tokyo, and the Financial Times-Stock Exchange 100-Share index in London, the latter is the most recently introduced. The FT-SE 100, more commonly known as "footsie", was first published in January 1984 with an index base of 1,000. The footsie consists of a weighted arithmetical index of 100 leading UK equities, calculated on a minute-by-minute basis. The constituent companies of the FT-SE 100 are reviewed on a regular basis, qualification for entry into the index being market capitalization.

The current vogue for market indices, be they domestic market only, international or even global owes much to the relatively recent development of tradeable futures market contracts based on the movement in these indices. The increasing globalization and computerization of trading, together with the development of communications technology, assisted the development of a number of proprietary international indices through the 1980s, most notably those produced by Morgan Stanley Capital International, Datastream and the FT Actuaries.

More recently, into the 1990s a race developed to establish a real-time benchmark index for leading European shares. The catalyst for this development is the single European market in financial services and business being introduced by the European Economic Community in 1993. Exchanges in London and Amsterdam both introduced European-wide indices in 1990. The Amsterdam-based European Options Exchange's Euro Top 100 Index was launched in July 1990. The index includes UK shares as well as continental European shares, is quoted in European Currency Units (ECUs) and takes its components' share prices from the national markets. The Euro Top was followed in October 1990 by London's Financial Times-Stock Exchange Eurotrack 100 Index, this latter index excludes UK shares. The London market launched a Eurotrack 200 Index in February 1991 which combines the shares of the FT-SE 100 with those of the FT-SE Eurotrack 100.

The importance of these cross-border real-time indices lies in the development of so-called derivative instruments. The trading of futures contracts and options based on such indices allows portfolio managers to hedge their international investments. Futures contracts and options already exist based on many of the domestic market indices. Futures and options are to be traded in the Euro Top 100 index on the New York-based American Stock Exchange, France's MATIF and Soffex, the Swiss Futures and Options Exchange. However, the race to market, as far as the trading of a derivative product is concerned, was won by London's Eurotrack 100. In November 1990, Bankers Trust launched a call warrant against the index, to be denominated in German marks, listed in Frankfurt and traded in London, and in 1991 the London International Financial Futures Exchange and the London Traded Options Market launched futures and options contracts based on the Eurotrack 100.

The introduction of Eurotrack in London reflects the increasing interest in continental European shares and the growth in turnover of the London Stock Exchange's SEAQ International, which has, occasionally on a daily basis, exceeded turnover in domestic UK stocks and shares. All the Eurotrack 100 constituent shares are traded on SEAQ International and have proven liquidity in London, which accounts for around 80 per cent of all European cross-border share trading. The Eurotrack indices themselves are quoted in German marks. Real-time prices of the constituent shares are quoted in national currencies and converted into marks minute-by-minute using prevailing foreign exchange values and then weighted in terms of market capitalization.

CHAPTER 2

COMMODITY FUTURES

Many people got their first taste of commodity trading from the highly successful 1983 film *Trading Places* starring Dan Akroyd and Eddie Murphy. In the climax of the movie our two heroes succeed in both making a fortune and bankrupting the villains in frantic trading in frozen concentrated orange juice futures. However, commodity trading is a far more important part of the world financial system than the more familiar stock market share deals which regularly make headlines.

There are two basic types of commodity market—physical and futures—though often both functions are carried out on the one Exchange. However, in both types of market the first and perhaps most important function of the commodity market is demonstrated. This function is called price discovery. As the name suggests the market serves as the means to bring buyers and sellers together—supply and demand meeting head on—and providing certain conditions are met a price fairly reflecting both the supply of and the demand for a given commodity is arrived at. In the physical market, as the name suggests, trading is limited to the pricing and sale of commodities to be delivered to the buyer more or less immediately. The futures market is more complex and is reviewed in detail in this chapter. The developments of the last two decades in the form of financial futures and index futures, which now overshadow futures contracts in primary commodities, are the subject of Chapter Five. Although many of the basic tenets of trading and the formats of the markets are similar, the instruments themselves are different.

Primary commodities are, as the name suggests, products in their natural state which have undergone little, if any, processing. From ingots of metal and barrels of oil to foodstuff, they are the building blocks of the modern world. With the historical exception of crude oil, the size, weight and shape and so forth of the commodities traded are usually decided by the Exchanges in consultation with the producers. The accepted basic unit of crude oil is the 42 gallon barrel, appropriated by the oil producers of Pennsylvania in the 1860s. The dimensions of the barrel date back to an English law promulgated in 1482 by King Edward IV, who established it as a standard size for herring to put an end to "divers deceits" in fish packing. Oil is the world's largest cash commodity but futures in crude oil and related products are a relatively recent development. Energy futures trading commenced in 1974 in New York, but only began to take off in 1978 when the New York Mercantile Exchange restructured and relaunched its heating oil contract.

The volatility of commodity prices and the potential for huge rewards have produced their own records of spectacular crashes and attempts to corner or control markets. Indeed the first market crash of modern history occurred in commodities with the "Tulipmania" which swept Holland in the 1630s. Rather more recently the markets have witnessed the attempt by the Hunt brothers to corner the silver market in the early 1980s, the crash of the International Tin Council and OPEC's success in raising oil prices (*see Cartels below*).

The commodity markets in Chicago and London developed as true terminal markets, trading both physical or cash and futures deliveries in the middle of the nineteenth century. The history of modern futures trading begins on the American midwestern frontier in the early 1800s. It is tied closely to the development of commerce in Chicago and the grain trade. The city's strategic location at the base of the Great Lakes and close to massive fertile farmlands contributed to rapid growth as a grain terminal. However, problems of supply and demand, transportation and storage led to a chaotic marketing situation. As the grain trade expanded a centralized market-place—the Chicago Board of Trade—was formed in 1848 by eighty-two merchants. The CBOT is the world's oldest and largest structured commodity market. Growing use of contracts "to arrive" in which buyers and sellers specified delivery of a commodity at a pre-determined price and date led, in 1865, to the CBOT formalizing the trading by developing standardized agreements called futures contracts. Quality, quantity, time and location of delivery were all standardized, leaving price the only variable. At the same time the Chicago Board of Trade introduced a margining system requiring traders to deposit funds with the Exchange to guarantee contract performance. To all intents and purposes the basics of all futures trading had been established.

Futures trading in the UK developed initially in cotton in Liverpool with impetus provided by the American Civil War which disrupted supplies and led to dealings in cotton "yet to be shipped". However, the forward trading in cotton failed to develop into a structured futures market. The oldest of London's structured markets is the London Metal Exchange which is still the world's pre-eminent futures market for industrial metals. The LME's original three-month forward trading span was established with formal contracts in the 1870s. The reason behind this choice of period was that it was approximately the length of time it took to ship copper from Valparaiso in Chile and tin from peninsular Malaya to the ports of London and Liverpool.

The futures market takes the basic commodity market a stage further in that physical commodities themselves are not bought and sold but it is the promise to buy or sell at a given date in the future at a given price which is traded. A further refinement of this process over the last decade has been the addition of options to commodity futures trading in which the right to buy or sell the promise is itself a marketable instrument.

For a commodity futures market to operate successfully according to textbook economics tenets, three main conditions need to be fulfilled:
1. The commodity itself must be durable, or at least capable of storage for several months without deteriorating. To return briefly to the film *Trading Places*, the climactic action takes place on the market for frozen concentrated orange juice. It would, however, not be feasible to attempt to operate a commodity futures market in oranges themselves.
2. The commodity must be homogeneous, that is to say it must be relatively easily standardized and classified. This means that the units or lots traded on the market are interchangeable.
3. Both the supply and demand for the commodity should be international in character and free from external controls. That is to say, a significant majority of the commodity's production and consumption must be free from controls, both governmental and inter-governmental, and by blocks of producers or consumers. The international character of the market allows it to provide a true reflection of the supply and demand of the commodity.

The market itself does not in any sense fix the price of the commodity being traded but merely acts as a barometer. Providing the conditions laid out above are met it is feasible to trade virtually any commodity. However, to provide an accurate measure and a true price, the market also relies on a free flow of information about the state of supply and demand. This enables the market participants to take a view on the commodity's overall status and its potential price movements. It is worth noting that the trend to screen-based trading which has overtaken much of the world's equity and financial instruments has made fewer inroads in commodity futures markets. Business in many cases continues to be carried on through the practice of "open outcry" with traders in pits or rings on a physical trading floor. The traders or brokers are members of the Exchange and buy or sell on the orders of their clients.

A considerable body of opinion within the commodity futures trading industry believes this mode of operation, with people crowded together all shouting at each other and using hand signals, remains the best method. The reasoning behind this is the transparency of the market which is offered by open outcry. Such trading is close to the ideal of pure competition with dealing in given commodity futures contracts at set times of the day. The brokers operating on specific markets face each other and cry out their bids for purchase and offers for sale for all to hear.

Transparency is an important factor in market credibility for both producers and consumers, lending authority as it does to the commodity market's function of price discovery. Open outcry is a classic example of the age-old auction market at work with every trader acting as his or her own auctioneer. Together, the shouts and hand signals compose an intricate network of communications. The style of hand signals varies slightly from market to market. However, those of the Chicago Mercantile Exchange serve as an example. There are four basic hand signals:

Buying a contract: bids are signalled by holding the palm of the hand facing the body—when the palm is facing the trader he is indicating the desire to buy.

Selling a contract: offers are signalled by holding the palm away from the body—when the palm faces away from the trader he is indicating a desire to sell.

Indicating a price: price quotes, for either bids or offers, can be indicated by a series of hand signals made directly in front of the body. Numbers between one and five are quoted with vertically extended fingers, prices from six to nine are quoted with the fingers extended horizontally and zero is indicated by a closed fist (*see diagram opposite*). Numbers above twenty are indicated by rapid sequential hand signals. In this series, five is shown by crooking the fingers. For example twenty-five would be two upraised fingers followed by crooking the two fingers in rapid up and down movements.

Indicating a quantity: the number of contracts or lots to be either bought or sold may be quoted in the same way as indicating a price except that the signalling hand is held near the head.

Even the commodity markets are not wholly immune from the march of the computer chip and many Exchanges now offer screen-based trading on their contracts on an after-hours basis, complementing rather than competing with the existing open outcry trading. The most ambitious of the screen-based operations is GLOBEX, an electronic trading system being developed by Reuters Plc in conjunction with several major markets (*GLOBEX is discussed in more detail in Chapter Five*).

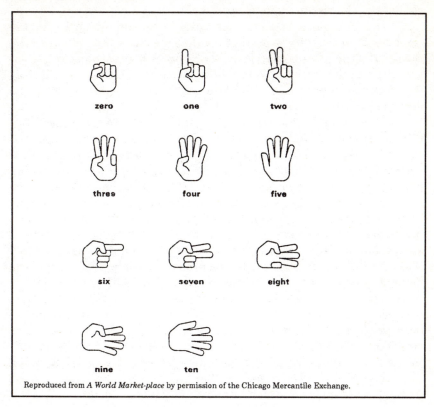

Reproduced from *A World Market-place* by permission of the Chicago Mercantile Exchange.

TRADING

The other main function of the commodity futures market is that of risk management through hedging. Hedging is the sale of a futures contract by a producer or the purchase of a futures contract by a consumer, each thereby ensuring respectively a market for the product and a steady supply of raw material at a known price. Although hedging is not a complete form of insurance against the risk of price fluctuation, to a large degree it lessens the risk of adverse price movements and allows forward planning on the basis of a known price.

In a selling or short hedge, a commodity producer or holder of physical stocks can protect the value of his output or stocks against the risk of a fall in price in the future by locking-in the current price. Selling forward is known as going short. If the cash price of the commodity falls, this loss in value is offset by the profit made on the futures contract. Conversely, if the cash price rises the loss made on the futures contract is offset by the profit inherent in the rise in the cash price the producer receives or the rise in value of stock held.

The difference between the cash price and the price of the commodity on the futures market is called the basis. In an ideal world, the price of the futures contract will always be higher than the cash or spot price of the commodity, the difference between the two reflecting the cost of financing, insuring and storing the commodity over the given forward period.

An example of short hedge would be that of a grain merchant constantly buying and selling grain. He may make forward commitments to sell grain, but frequently he will purchase grain that does not yet have a final destination. For such a purchase he would use a selling hedge to protect his eventual sale price. If he has grain under store, he may also use the selling hedge to earn storage income. Let us assume that the merchant has forward contracted for 20,000 bushels of wheat due to arrive in sixty days. He also anticipates selling the wheat in the same amount of time. He has forward contracted for the wheat at $4.00 and wants to sell at $4.04 to make a profit. It is 15 September and the December wheat futures contract is trading at $4.35 per bushel (the merchant uses the December contract because he plans to sell in November). His current basis, the difference between his anticipated cash price and the futures price, is thus $0.31 under the December contract. Because he believes prices may fall the merchant decides to hedge. Let us assume that the cash and futures prices do fall between September and November and, further, that the prices fall by the same amount. This is how our merchant fared with his hedge:

Cash	**Futures**	**Basis**
15 September		
anticipates sale of 20,000 bu wheat @ $4.04/bu cash	sells 4 Dec wheat contracts (20,000 bu) @ $4.35/bu	$0.31 under Dec.
15 November		
sells 20,000 bu wheat @ $3.85/bu	buys 4 Dec wheat contracts @ $4.16/bu	$0.31 under Dec.
Result		
$0.19/bu loss	$0.19/bu gain	change $0.00
cash price	$3.85/bu	
futures gain	+0.19	
actual sale price	$4.04/bu	

Although the merchant received only $3.85 per bushel when he sold the grain in the cash market, his futures market gain enabled him to receive his target price, the futures gain offsetting the cash loss. Another way to interpret the result is to look at the basis. In this example the basis was exactly the same when the hedge was placed and lifted. When this happens it is known as a perfect hedge, but this rarely occurs in the real world. However, even in situations where the basis has moved against the hedger (and it may also of course move to his benefit), he will have protected himself against the greater loss sustained on the cash position if he had not hedged. The same is true of the buying hedge.

The purpose of the buying or long hedge is to insure against a rise in price; a commodity consumer locks in the current price by buying forward for delivery in the future. Buying forward is known as going long. In this situation a rise in the cash price is covered by profit from the futures contract while losses incurred on the futures contract occasioned by a fall in the cash price are compensated for by the reduced costs of purchasing the physical commodity at a lower price.

Let us stay with the example of the grain merchant. This time, instead of selling wheat on 15 September, the merchant is planning to buy wheat in sixty days to fill a forward contract made with a customer. He has sold the wheat at $4.09 per bushel and will purchase at $4.04 to ensure his own profit margin. The December contract is trading at $4.35 per bushel and the basis is $0.31 under. Because he believes prices may rise over the next two months, he will attempt to protect his cash sale price by placing a long hedge in which the price risk already existing is assumed by another party in the market-place. Let us assume that both cash and futures prices rise and by the same amount. The merchant will

Cash	Futures	Basis
15 September		
anticipates purchase of 20,000 bu wheat @ $4.04/bu cash	buys 4 Dec wheat contracts (20,000 bu) @ $4.35/bu	$0.31 under Dec.
15 November		
buys 20,000 bu wheat @ $4.10/bu	sells 4 Dec wheat contracts @ $4.41/bu	$0.31 under Dec.
Result		
$0.06/bu loss	$0.06/bu gain	change $0.00
cash price	$4.10/bu	
futures gain	-0.06	
actual purchase price	$4.04/bu	

realize his price objective of $4.04 because the gain on the futures contract offsets the higher cash price he had to pay for the wheat.

As in our previous example this is a perfect hedge. The same general point holds true that, even though perfect hedges are rare in the real world, by hedging the merchant has significantly reduced his risk of loss. These examples are of a grain contract on the Chicago Board of Trade but they serve as a model for any futures contract. In both the selling and buying hedge, the end result is to lock in the price at the time the futures contract is taken out until the position in the market is closed, either by the sale of the contract or its falling due and delivery of the actual commodity taking place. Given that much of the activity on the world's commodity markets is of this kind of professional hedging or risk insurance, the proportion of contracts which are actually allowed to run through to physical delivery is far outweighed by those which are closed out before the due delivery date.

A refinement of hedging used both by producers and consumers as well as speculators is the spread or straddle in which risk is reduced through simultaneous sale of a contract for a given forward month at the same time as another contract for a different month is purchased.

The practice known as "cash and carry" is similar to taking a straddle position but refers specifically to the practice of buying a physical or spot commodity with a view to selling at a later date at a profit which, after the costs of holding the commodity are taken into account, represents a greater return than that available from investment in fixed-interest securities.

ORDERS AND PRICES

A variety of orders are used in futures markets, the most common is the market order, which states the quantity and delivery month of the contract to be purchased but specifies no price. It is implicit in the order for the broker to fill it at the best possible price at the earliest possible opportunity.

Stop orders are those in which a specified price is the trigger for the broker to buy or sell as instructed. When the commodity is traded at the trigger price it becomes a market order. A stop order to buy would be placed above the market and a stop order to sell would be placed below the market. A slight variation on the stop order is the stop-limit order. Stop-limit orders may be filled by the broker only at the stated stop price and are, therefore, not as easily fulfilled and less common.

Most futures markets now have daily trading limits above or below which the market may not trade during a given trading session. These are usually established by the exchange authorities and relate to volatility which may be typical for prices in the underlying cash market. However, there is a general provision for the expansion of daily price limits in periods of marked volatility. On the Chicago Board of Trade markets, for example, when three or more delivery months of a given commodity close at the higher or lower limit on a given day, the daily price limit is increased by 50 per cent and remains there for three consecutive business days. The expanded price limit remains in force for successive three-day periods until three delivery months fail to close at the higher or lower limit (known as limit-up and limit-down). At such a point, the daily price limit reverts to its previous level. Among the few exceptions to the practice of using price limits are the International Petroleum Exchange and the London Metal Exchange.

When the forward price is higher than the spot price, the commodity is said to be in a contango or forwardation. A backwardation or back describes the situation in which the spot price is higher than the forward price. In simple terms it reflects a short-term shortage in the supply of the commodity.

Most of the world's commodity markets offer options on futures contracts—in the case of the Chicago Board Options Exchange only options are traded. Traditional options in commodity futures have been virtually completely replaced by traded options (*see Chapter Five*).

Where contracts in the same commodity exist on more than one Exchange, the opportunity for arbitrage arises. Arbitrage consists simply of purchasing and selling the same commodity at the same time in two different markets to take advantage of the fluctuations in price which may exist between the markets.

Obviously the more transparent the market-place and the greater the similarity between the different contracts the smaller is the likelihood of such opportunities existing. In certain cases where Exchanges trade identical products a mutual offset arrangement has been set up between the markets. This linkage between two or more markets allows trading positions established on one Exchange to be offset or transferred on another Exchange. This means that the contracts are effectively interchangeable.

THE SPECULATOR

The position of the speculative investor on commodity futures markets has grown in importance in recent years. The speculator provides additional funds and liquidity to the market-place. The disadvantage of speculation in commodities is that dividends and interest are not payable on contracts, a factor which differentiates this activity from other forms of investment. The main attraction of commodity speculation is the potential for capital gain although it should be stressed that the risks involved are also much greater than in most other forms of investment due to the high gearing of futures trading. The apocryphal story told in the futures markets themselves suggests that when one is tired of standing on a street corner tearing up money then, and only then, should the individual contemplate investing in futures!

Typically, involvement in a forward transaction will mean a deposit or margin of around 10 per cent of the actual face value of the contract. However, the often violent price swings on the market may result in further and speedy "margin calls" on the investor's funds should the price move against his position. These price fluctuations are usually the result of unexpected and unpredictable events such as strikes, crop failure or mine disasters. Unlike the commodity producer himself who can, under certain circumstances, suspend delivery of commodities he is contractually bound to supply, there is no such thing as *force majeure* on the commodity markets.

One way of reducing the risk inherent in speculation in commodities is to spread the investment across a range of contracts rather than take a position in a single commodity. The simplest way for an investor to do this, rather than take these positions himself, is to place his money in an open-ended managed investment fund specializing in futures. Such a fund will retain at least half its assets in cash or fixed interest investments with the remainder invested in a diverse range of futures contracts. This diversification is itself a major factor in limiting risk.

Clearing

All the world's commodity exchanges now operate on a central clearing system. Prior to the collapse of the International Tin Council in 1985 (*see below*), the London Metal Exchange was the sole exception to this rule, operating as a principals' market. Following the Exchange's troubles with tin and alterations to UK financial legislation, the LME became a centrally cleared market in May 1987. The clearing entity operates as a third party in the transactions of the futures markets, standing as guarantor to both the buyer and the seller of the contract that it will be fulfilled if either of the two brokers involved in the transaction default. In the US markets the clearer is generally an association whose membership is comprised of the larger brokerages and trading firms acting jointly to guarantee the contract obligations of each clearing member. Under this mutual guarantee system the broker on the market, after executing a trade, deals exclusively with the clearing association which, in effect, acts as the seller to every buyer and the buyer to every seller.

The markets in London are cleared in the same way but the clearing entity is the International Commodities Clearing House, which celebrated its centenary in 1988. Originally set up as the London Produce Clearing House, the ICCH is backed financially by six leading UK banks to the tune of £100 million. The backing institutions are National Westminster, Barclays, Lloyds, Midland, Royal Bank of Scotland and Standard Chartered. To make use of the ICCH's facilities brokers on the exchanges merely pay a simple registration fee. The ICCH's reputation is such that several foreign commodity exchanges make use of its services for the clearing, though not necessarily the guaranteeing, of trades.

CARTELS

One feature of the markets for primary commodities has been the attempts by producers to impose some form of control on the price of their product. Most of the world's primary commodities are produced in less developed countries and governments have often felt cheated by the market. Without doubt the most famous and most successful such cartel has been the Organisation of Petroleum Exporting Countries (OPEC), which was originally formed in 1960 by five oil producers, Iraq, Iran, Kuwait, Saudi Arabia and Venezuela. At the time the cartel was formed, its member countries were responsible for over 80 per cent of the world's crude oil exports. Despite OPEC's apparent disarray in the early 1990s, the cartel has been demonstrably successful on more than one occasion in the unilateral raising of prices. However, as has been the case with other attempts at market regulation, OPEC's effectiveness decreased through the 1970s and 1980s as the proportion of world production that its members controlled fell.

The second oldest producers' cartel of recent times is the Council of Copper Exporting Countries (known by its French initials CIPEC). The copper cartel was formed in the 1960s by Chile, Peru, Zaire and Zambia. However, the organization was never able to have any meaningful impact on the copper price and through the 1970s dropped its stance of hostility towards consumers and broadened its membership.

While producer cartels, with the notable exception of OPEC, have been relatively ineffective at supporting the price of their commodity, those international commodity organizations established under United Nations mandate have had greater, and in one case unlooked-for, impact on the world's commodity markets. The United Nations Conference on Trade & Development was an early and consistent supporter of the theory of commodity agreements between producers and consumers to ensure equitable prices. In practice the commodity organizations set up under UNCTAD auspices operated a buffer stock scheme, buying the commodity and storing it in times of low prices and selling into the market at times of high prices. The buffer stock itself operates on a series of price bands, with a floor price below which it must buy in the market and a ceiling price above which it must sell. The original idea of smoothing out the peaks and the troughs of price swings within the market to ensure regular supply for consumers at a fair price for producers is an admirable if, as experience sadly showed, difficult theory to put into practice.

Were we to ignore events post-1985, then one could still look to the International Tin Council as a shining example of the kind of commodity organization first envisaged by UNCTAD shortly after the end of the Second World War. The ITC was established in 1953 under the first of six International Tin Agreements. For most of its life the ITC was successful in following its mandate for the simple reason that the producer members of the agreements controlled a large majority of the world's tin production capacity. This situation began to change in the 1960s with the entry into the market of a major seller—the US General Services Administration—following the US government's decision to reduce its strategic stockpile of tin. The ITC's hand was further weakened with the discovery and development of large tin resources in non-member countries, notably Brazil and China.

Despite these destabilizing developments the Council could conceivably have continued to operate successfully as an instrument of market regulation—its original reason for being—were it not for a change in Western cultural attitudes. Although outwardly nothing changed, through the 1970s it became apparent that the consumer member countries of the ITC, which were mainly highly developed and industrialized "Western" nations, tacitly viewed membership of the ITA and participation in the ITC as a form of aid to producer member countries, which were by and large less developed countries. Thus, rather than a tool of economic management, the ITC became a disguised form of aid to developing nations. Between January 1975 and October 1981, the ITC buffer stock price bands were revised upwards nine times, with the floor price virtually doubling. Each time the market price moved above the ceiling price the support prices were moved up. This sustained period of rising prices coincided with the peak of world demand for tin. As demand fell back and output from the new producers increased, the tin buffer stock manager found himself defending the indefensible. From February 1982 the buffer stock defended an increasingly unrealistic floor price. It did not, apparently, occur to anyone that the floor price should have been lowered—such a solution would have been unacceptable to the producer members of the ITC. The situation was compounded by the fact that the artificially high price of tin attracted yet more metal onto the market, increasing the scale of the buffer stock task.

Ultimately the ITC could not win but even so it was a major shock to all concerned when the buffer stock manager informed the London Metal Exchange on 24 October 1985, that he was withdrawing from the market as he had no further funds to commit. Tin trading was suspended and indeed there was no exchange trading tin for a period of four months, until physical trading resumed on the Kuala Lumpur Tin Market in Malaysia. Futures trading in tin did not recommence until October 1987 when the Kuala Lumpur Commodity Exchange introduced a contract. A tin contract did not return to the London Metal Exchange until June 1989. The collapse of the ITC's operations was followed by one of the more reprehensible episodes in diplomacy. The twenty-two sovereign governments which made up the supra-national organization were unable to agree a rescue package among themselves and the collapse into recriminations transferred to the courts. Almost five years of legal wrangling ensued over the responsibility for debts of around £520 million until agreement was reached and the ITC paid its creditors £182.5 million in an out-of-court settlement. The ITC débâcle badly shook the London Metal Exchange and it is to the credit of the exchange authorities and their handling of the matter that the chaos on the tin contract had little spill-over impact on the rest of the market. It would be safe to say, however, that the affair has meant that the prospects for the successful operation of any other commodity organization have been severely curtailed.

COMMODITY SWAPS

One relatively recent development in commodity futures trading is the booming market in commodity swaps and options. A swap is a device by which risks are exchanged. An oil company, for example, may agree to compensate a consumer should the oil price rise above a given ceiling, but in return would itself be compensated were the price to fall below a given floor. In an option, the consumer pays a fee for the option to pay for a product at an agreed price, exercisable should prices rise but leaving the option holder free to take advantage of lower prices in the future at the loss only of the option fee. The main difference between these options and those formally available on equity and commodity futures markets is the length of time over which they may be exercised.

Estimates of the size of this business vary but since 1986 when the first such deal was struck the volume of swaps has risen dramatically.

COMMODITY FUTURES

The first crude oil swaps emerged in 1986-87. The market for commodity swaps, of which oil has the lion's share, saw volume quadruple in the months following the Iraqi invasion of Kuwait in August 1990. Activity in oil swaps and options surged, driven by the violent price swings in crude oil which took place in the run-up to the Gulf War. One estimate of the value of commodity swaps and options in early 1991 put a value of US$40-50 billion on the market. Around 85 per cent of all these deals are in crude oil.

The banks and trading houses have adapted the techniques of the trillion dollar market in interest rate swaps to commodities. A typical commodity swap, in common with a standard interest rate swap (*see Chapter Four*), involves the exchange of fixed and floating rate payments. Among the earliest corporate users of these types of instruments were the airlines, attempting to fix the cost of their fuel. The aim of the swap is to provide producers and users with a fixed price, or a ceiling or a floor price, over a period of time far longer than anything available on the more traditional futures markets. The bank then lays off the risk with another client or through the structure of its own portfolio.

Interest is continuing to grow in the use of commodity swaps in non-oil commodities. A typical base metal swap might run as follows: a core swap for 50 per cent of the user's requirement, a zero-cost collar for 25 per cent and the remaining 25 per cent left open. A zero-cost collar allows the user a guaranteed ceiling price for a premium which is offset by the user guaranteeing a floor price to the bank.

The majority of swaps have a maturity of between two and three years, although some run up to fifteen years. This contrasts sharply with most futures markets where contracts tend to run no further than 18 months forward. Liquidity is provided by a string of commercial and investment banks along with a few insurance companies and some of the major oil producers themselves, notably British Petroleum and Elf Aquitaine. Swaps and options in oil are already beginning to have an influence on the cash oil price and on price movements in the futures markets. The decision taken in November 1990 by NYMEX, the New York Mercantile Exchange, to extend the delivery dates of its crude oil contracts out to thirty-six months following approval from the Commodity Futures Trading Commission may be interpreted as a move to claw back potential lost business from swaps.

The market for swaps, although dating back to the mid-1980s only began to develop seriously following a ruling by the US Commodity Futures Trading Commission in 1989 which exempted the products from regulation. As well as crude oil, market interest in swaps in aluminium and copper is growing, and a market for swaps in natural gas is also developing. A further refinement of these products was developed in 1990 with the offering of the first "synthetic oilfield"—a trust with a payout modeled on the depletion of a real oilfield with a ten-year life. Several of the financial institutions involved in the swaps market have already marketed "synthetic oil" in the form of bonds which pay a high rate of interest and which are redeemable on maturity according to the value of a number of barrels of oil. These issues are attractive to the financial institutions because of the potential differential between the future price of oil available in the market place and the much higher future oil price implied in the share prices of the oil companies. The banks involved believe they can obtain oil more cheaply through the markets than oil companies can by exploring for it and producing it.

The availability of these instruments also has broader implications for the companies which take advantage of them. Namely, the banks appear to be willing to raise lending limits and improve financing terms for investment projects in which the mineral exploration companies have offset risk through the use of such swaps and options. However, the swap providers, that is to say the financial institutions, may end up with large "unbalanced" risks on their books with the obligation to buy or sell at a given price without themselves having the ability to hedge the risk.

CHAPTER 3

BONDS, BORROWINGS AND THE EUROMARKET

International trading in bonds dwarfs the cross-border trading in shares. The 1980s saw exponential growth in international bond purchases. Total foreign portfolio bond holdings in the world's principal international investors, Japan, Germany, the United States and the UK, rose from less than US$100 billion in 1980 to over US$800 billion by the end of the decade. Much of the growth towards the end of the decade was driven by a wall of Japanese money. Between 1987 and 1990 net Japanese international bond purchases were running at an annual rate of US$80 billion.

Bonds are essentially debt, a way for companies and governments to borrow money on a structured basis. Governments issue bonds to fund shortfalls in revenue over expenditure, while companies borrow to expand, purchase new equipment and fund takeovers. Bonds, unlike a company overdraft, are tradeable instruments in their own right with a set lifespan. They are issued onto a market-place, in much the same way as shares, and may be traded in the same way.

The bond, like a banknote, will have a face or par value which is what the issuer will pay the holder of the bond when it matures. Bonds are issued with maturities ranging from a few days to thirty years. This means the bond may be traded until it matures, at which time the current holder will receive money equivalent to the face value. In some cases, bonds are undated, although few corporate issues are undated. Undated bonds are never redeemed but continue to pay a regular coupon. The coupon is the rate of interest payable on the debt which the bond represents and is so called because it was originally payable on the presentation of a physically detachable paper coupon from the bond certificate.

In the market-place, bond prices are often compared in terms of the yield the bond produces, that is the coupon, or rate of interest the bond pays, compared to the current market price as a percentage figure. For example, a bond with a par value of US$100, paying 5 per cent interest, purchased in the market for US$50 would have a yield of 10 per cent. Bonds may be issued at par value, discounted from par value, thus making the yield more attractive, or on a partly-paid basis. Partly-paid bonds offer investors the potential for a greater return if the price of the bond moves up or the prospect of a smaller payment for the remainder of the bond if the price falls.

Because bonds are borrowings they are often secured, that is to say backed, by some form of asset. In the industrial sector bonds may be secured against factories or plant and equipment. Usually there is a degree of over-collateralization, which means the value of the repackaged assets exceeds the face value of the debt, providing greater security for investors. In the financial sector, banks have securitized loans on their balance sheets, most often credit card debt and mortgages. In securitization the bank can take assets off its balance sheet by repackaging them as debt and selling them on to investors in the form of bonds.

Although bonds are issued with a par value, the price of a bond will fluctuate in the market, moving as interest rates change or as perceptions about the ability of the bond issuer to meet the interest and principal payments change. Obviously a bond issued with a fixed rate of interest will fall in price as interest rates rise because at par value it offers a poorer yield or rate of return. The price falls until the yield once more becomes competitive with market interest rates.

CREDIT RATINGS

Credit rating agencies have assumed an important role in the bond market-place. The two biggest agencies, Standard & Poors and Moody's, are both American. Before a bond issue takes place, the issuer may request a rating from an agency. This rating provides a basic guide as to how able the bond issuer is to meet the obligations he is taking on, both in terms of interest payments and repayment of principle. The highest grade given by Standard & Poors is AAA, which means the borrower has the very best ability to repay the bond. The grades range down to grade D, which means the bond is in default and that payment of interest or repayment of the principle is in arrears.

These ratings have a great impact on the pricing of the bond issue. Obviously the higher the rating, the less the issuer needs to do to make the bond attractive to potential investors because they are more sure of getting an actual return on their money. Furthermore, rating is not a one-off process. The agencies may, from time to time, re-rate an issue upwards or downwards or place it on "credit watch" in anticipation of a re-rating downwards. These moves will also affect the price at which the bond trades.

However, not all bonds are rated. The decision to apply for a rating is at the discretion of the issuer. Rating tends to be less formalized in bonds in domestic markets because it is assumed that investors will have enough knowledge about the issuer to make their investment decisions. Bonds on the international markets are more likely to have ratings than not, because of the need to attract investors to whom the issuing institution may only be a name they have heard rather than a company they know about. Bonds graded below BBB are not regarded as being of international investment grade and may not attract buyers from financial institutions because of their low credit rating.

So-called "junk bonds", pioneered by the US brokers Drexel Burnham Lambert in the mid-1970s, are corporate bonds below investment grade. By definition they are high risk, high yield issues. They allowed companies to borrow more than their credit ratings would otherwise have allowed them to do. Although potentially attractive to investors because of the high rate of return promised, these bonds also come with a much higher risk of default.

The US takeover boom of the mid-1980s was fuelled by junk bonds. Companies would borrow money to launch takeover bids of firms often much larger than themselves, gambling on paying the costs of the bonds from the sale of parts of the takeover target. This type of acquisition is known as a leveraged buy-out and several were successfully completed. However, the downturn in the markets at the end of the decade resulted in companies, which had expanded through the use of junk bonds, being unable to meet their payment obligations and several face bankruptcy. Drexel Burnham Lambert itself, having been the centre of a major financial scandal (*see Chapter Six*), is also struggling to survive.

DOMESTIC BOND MARKETS

Most domestic bonds have fixed interest rates. In the UK market, for example, some 60 per cent of the securities listed are non-governmental fixed interest stocks. In terms of their share of market capitalization, however, these stocks account for just 10 per cent of the market and they account for less than 2 per cent of the market's daily turnover. Domestic stocks are usually registered, so ownership is known, and they are often secured against tangible assets. Domestic bonds are usually those issued by companies based in the country of issue and by the regional and local government of that country.

A company wishing to issue bonds into the market will price the issue so that it is attractive enough to ensure a favourable market reception. Corporate bond issues tend to be priced more competitively than government bonds owing to the smaller size of the market in corporate issues and the corresponding lack of liquidity in secondary trading. The issue would be priced in such a way that the yield it provides will be greater than that offered by comparable government bonds. The yield can be amended by altering the interest payments offered on the bond or by issuing the bonds at a discount on the nominal face value.

Corporate bonds are issued in a similar fashion to share placings. A lead manager may be engaged to provide for the underwriting and distribution of the issue, or the bonds may be issued through an offer-for-sale, in which the general public would be invited to subscribe either at a fixed price or to tender an offer above a stated minimum price.

Corporate issues come in four basic types: debentures; unsecured loan stock; unsecured convertible loan stock; and preference shares. A new hybrid fund-raising technique is also growing in popularity; this is the convertible capital bond. A debenture is secured against the assets of the issuing company and may take the form of a charge against a specific asset or against such unspecified assets as would need to be sold for the debenture holder to realize the amount owed to him. If the issuer fails to meet the payments due on the debenture, the holder has legal recourse to recover his money. These rights and possible restrictions on the disposal of certain key corporate assets are laid out in the issuing terms.

Unsecured loan stocks are not secured against any specific assets and, in the event of default, the holders' claims are subordinate to those of debenture holders and settlement of such claims is only made from what remains after the secured creditors have been paid in full.

Unsecured convertible loan stocks may be considered as a form of deferred share capital rather than as debt. Although not secured against assets they offer the holder the option of conversion into a specified number of ordinary shares in the company. The option may be for a set period of time, and with some convertible stocks the number of shares, for which the option may be exercised, may reduce towards the end of this set period.

Preference shares are effectively share capital (*see Chapter One*) but may also be considered as a form of corporate debt, paying fixed dividends. They are in a class above ordinary shares in that no ordinary share dividend may be paid by the company until the preference dividend has been paid in full.

Convertible capital bonds take advantage of the combined characteristics of both bonds and shares. In the UK, for example, the interest payable by corporate issuers is deductible from corporation tax whereas interest on convertible preference shares is not. However, despite this tax treatment, these types of bonds are treated as equity by UK auditors. For a company planning to expand, this accounting practice has an important impact on gearing, the ratio of debt to equity. Funds raised through convertible capital bonds do not increase gearing, though at the expense of equity dilution. The bonds convert first into preference shares and then simultaneously into ordinary shares. By this sleight of hand, the financiers have been able to persuade auditors that these bonds should be treated as equity, as are convertible preference shares under current accounting practice. For the investor, the attraction of such bonds is similar to that of straightforward convertible loan stock.

Bonds issued by local and regional authorities are similar to those issued by the central government, but they are usually guaranteed only by the issuing authority and not by the government itself. In the UK market, for example, there are two basic types of local authority issues, local authority bonds, known as yearlings, and local authority stocks. Yearlings are bonds with maturities of less than one year, whereas local authority stocks have a full range of maturities.

International bond issues come in two forms: foreign bonds issued on the domestic market of another country and those issued on the Euromarket (*see below*). As well as being issued in only one country, foreign bonds are underwritten solely by institutions in the lending country and are denominated in the currency of the country of issue. Foreign bonds issued in the USA are known as Yankee bonds, in the UK they are Bulldog bonds, in Japan Samurai, in the Netherlands Rembrandt, etc. Historically the most important markets for foreign bond issues are those in the USA, Switzerland, Germany, Japan and the UK. The markets distinguish foreign bonds from external bonds, which are those placed on one domestic market but in another currency, for example, external bonds in Japan are known as Shogun bonds.

GOVERNMENT BONDS

Among the largest players in the bond markets, both international and domestic, are governments. The three largest issuers of government bonds on domestic markets are the USA, Japan and Italy, although unification could see Germany taking a place in the top three as the government there issues bonds to raise funds for the reconstruction of East Germany. In the UK, which has the longest tradition of government borrowings, such issues are known as "gilts" because the certificates themselves were originally edged with gold leaf.

These government bonds are sold onto the market-place in two basic ways: by tender and by auction. In the tender system the issuer, in the UK the Bank of England, announces the issue at a minimum price in line with prevailing market conditions. If the issue is oversubscribed, the highest bids are allocated in full and the lowest bids scaled back. If the issue is undersubscribed, the issuer will hold back some of the bonds to be sold onto the market by "tap". Tap issues are sold gradually into the market at whatever price the issuing authority believes will lead to the issue being exhausted.

Less common in the UK but standard practice in the US Treasury bond market is the sale of bonds by auction. There is no obligation on the market-makers and brokers to bid in an auction and the issue is not underwritten. The main difference between an auction and the tender system is that in a tender, bidders will receive their allotted amount at the minimum price necessary to exhaust the issue, whereas in an auction, they pay the actual price they bid for the issue.

In the late 1980s, the UK government's financial surpluses allowed the authorities to hold "reverse-auctions", reducing outstanding debt. There are three ways a government can reduce the number of its bonds in circulation. First, through the natural redemption of maturing bonds; second, by direct purchases in the market; and third, via a reverse auction. In a reverse auction, government bond-holders are invited to sell their bonds back to the authorities on a competitive offer price basis.

A government may also use "repurchase agreements" (repos) as a way of controlling funds in the market. Repos are money market transactions in which securities, usually government bonds, are sold with an agreement to repurchase them at a later date. A repo can be seen as a secured loan with the lender of the money receiving the securities as collateral to protect him against borrower default. These agreements were developed and remain most common in the US markets. A reverse repo is the mirror of a repo, involving the purchase of securities and an agreement to sell them at a later date. In fact, one man's repo is another man's reverse repo.

THE EUROMARKET

The Euromarket is distinguishable from domestic bond markets in that securities are sold internationally rather than in just one country and in most cases they will be sold outside the country of origin of the borrower. The prefix "Euro" is a historical one for which there are two explanations. The more prosaic suggests that it denotes simply the issue of securities in a currency or currencies other than that of the country of origin of the bond issuer. However, the market has its origins in the cold war of the late 1950s and, so the story goes, in the unwillingness of the Soviet Union to hold US dollar accounts in the United States for fear that they would be frozen in times of political tension. The Moscow government, still requiring access to dollars for international trade, began to borrow them in Europe through the Soviet-owned Banque Commerciale pour l'Europe du Nord whose telex code was Eurobank. Whatever the origins of the name, the first Eurocurrency was the Eurodollar—simply US dollar deposits held outside the United States. Now any internationally tradeable currency can be a Eurocurrency.

With the US dollar as the most important currency for international trade, and the USA running a current account deficit for most of the post-war period, both the demand for dollars and the supply grew apace. The impetus to the establishment of a thriving Euromarket came from the imposition by the US Treasury of two restrictions on the domestic US market-place. Regulation Q was originally drawn up in 1933 as one of the post-Wall Street crash measures introduced to bolster the faltering US financial industry. It set effective ceilings on the rates of interest which US banks could pay on deposits. However, the regulation did not begin to bite until after the Second World War. In 1970 and 1973 it was lifted on deposits of maturities of 30-90 days and over 90 days, respectively. Regulation Q meant that non-US banks could offer more attractive interest rates on dollar deposits than their US counterparts.

Furthermore, the US Treasury made it virtually impossible for US domestic banks to compete for these deposits. The Interest Equalization Tax, imposed in 1963, raised the costs to US investors of taking part in issues by foreigners on the US markets. The result of the tax, which was not withdrawn until 1974, was to discourage foreign borrowers from coming to the US market-place and encourage US borrowers to resort to foreign markets. Regulation Q itself was not withdrawn until the 1980s, under the ægis of the Monetary Control Act of 1980 which phased the regulation out over a six-year period.

With the dismantling of post-war currency controls in many countries, the liquidity of the market improved. The end of the fixed exchange rate system in 1971 (*see Chapter Four*) gave the market in short-term Eurocurrency deposits a major boost, offering a way to limit the risk of adverse currency movements against profits in export sales. Effectively, a company could hedge against these risks by borrowing the foreign currency and exchanging it into domestic currency, offsetting some of the costs of the transaction by placing the money on deposit to earn interest. The initial loan would then be repaid out of the monies received from abroad. Although such a transaction rules out the potential for windfall profits if exchange rates move favourably, it also negates the prospect of heavy losses if they move adversely.

These short-term borrowings take two forms: certificates of deposit, and notes or commercial paper. Euro-certificates of deposit (CD) are the oldest established money market instruments in the Euromarket. CDs are negotiable, interest-paying, bearer bonds with a maturity of generally less than one year. The CD is an acknowledgement from a bank of a deposit of funds with that bank for a set period at a specified rate of interest. It is this negotiable instrument which would form the basis of the transaction described above.

The Euronote and Eurocommercial Paper (ECP) are refinements of the CD. Once issued there is little to distinguish Euronotes and ECP. The difference between the two lies in the issuing process, in that Euronotes are underwritten by an investment bank or banks, ensuring the issuer will receive the funds if the issue is not fully taken up by investors, whereas ECP issues are not underwritten. Euronotes and ECP also have maturities of less than one year.

There are two basic types of Euronote facility: the revolving underwriting facility (RUF) and the note issuance facility (NIF). Both effectively offer the issuer/borrower short-term credit on a long-term basis. The RUF was more common in the early days of the market. Under an RUF, a bank or banks would agree to underwrite short-term Euronotes for an issuer over a period of several years, allowing the borrower the option of using the facility at his discretion, without having to make further underwriting arrangments. The NIF differs from the RUF in that the underwriting fee is not fixed in advance; a group of banks already guaranteeing a revolving credit facility to the issuer will bid to issue the notes. Such a bid may be below what the bank would otherwise have charged as a straightforward underwriting fee, if it believes it can make a profit on the onward sale of the notes to investors.

Longer-term borrowings on the Euromarket are known as Eurobonds. The Eurobond market is attractive to both borrower and investor for several reasons. The borrower can avoid complex national regulations, making the actual bond issue cheaper, and has access to a greater number of potential investors. For the investor the attractions of the market are interest paid gross, any withholding tax borne by the issuer, and anonymity. Eurobonds are issued as bearer bonds; ownership need not be registered and is evidenced by physical possession. Prior to the introduction of computerized clearing, interest on these bonds was paid through the presentation of a detachable coupon. The international nature and size of the market ensures a secondary market for the bonds.

Eurobonds are typically long-term instruments with maturities of up to thirty years, issued in relatively small denominations. The most important borrowers on the market tend to be supranational organizations, governments and the larger multinational companies—in other words, household names with high credit ratings. It is rare, given the quality of the borrowers, for these issues to be secured. Although it is not a requirement of the market, Eurobonds are usually listed on a stock exchange, the most popular for this purpose being the Luxemburg Stock Exchange and the London Stock Exchange. Listing makes the issue more attractive for investors because of the disclosure and reporting requirements imposed by the exchanges, and because in some countries it is illegal for investors to purchase unlisted foreign securities. However, although the bonds may be listed on these exchanges, only a small percentage of trading in listed Eurobonds takes place on them.

Among the factors distinguishing Eurobonds from ordinary foreign bonds is that the syndicate of banks which underwrites the bond, i.e. guarantees the sale of the issue, is itself multinational in make-up. The banks earn fees from underwriting these bonds and there is tough competition to underwrite Eurobond issues. Much prestige is associated with getting the bank's name onto the so-called "tombstone" advertisements announcing the issues, especially as the lead-manager, or organizer of the issue. Given the international nature of the Eurobond market, the credit rating agencies (*see above*) play an important role in the market-place. Indeed, without a credit rating the bond issue would be unlikely to attract sufficient international interest.

The secondary market in Eurobonds is regulated by the International Securities Market Association (ISMA), previously known as the Association of International Bond Dealers. The ISMA is a designated investment exchange under UK law, although the Association's authority and the adequacy of protection to investors given by the ISMA is being challenged by some national regulatory agencies in Europe. Trading in Eurobonds is carried out on an over-the-counter basis by dealers over the telephone rather than on any exchange floor. The market is dominated by the major dealers who act both as market makers and brokers. There are two clearing-houses operating in the Eurobond market, Euroclear and Cedel.

Historically, the classic Eurobond was a fixed interest rate, fixed maturity, unsecured loan. However, the explosive growth of the market led to the development of significant variations on this theme. The most important of these is the floating rate note (FRN). As the name suggests, the main feature distinguishing FRNs from other bonds is a floating interest rate. The coupon is refixed periodically by reference to an independent rate of interest. In the Euromarkets, the most common reference point is some fixed margin over the London Interbank Offered Rate (LIBOR). FRNs are usually long-dated bonds with interest rates linked to short-term money market indices with coupons refixed and interest paid every six months, whereas fixed rate Eurobonds more commonly pay interest on an annual basis.

The FRN was introduced to the Euromarket in 1970, the first issue coming from the Italian utility company ENEL. The success of FRNs lies in the linkage of the long-term borrowing to short-term interest rates. These types of bonds are attractive to investors at times when short-term interest rates are higher than long-term rates, i.e. when the yield curve is inverted. They are equally attractive to issuers in that they are not locked in to paying the prevailing high rate of interest.

BELLS, WHISTLES AND ROCKET SCIENTISTS

Throughout the 1980s the world's financial institutions continued to compete for Eurobond business. Part of this competition was a continuing refinement of the product through the addition of new features. These refinements became known as "bells and whistles", added by the financiers' tax and economics experts, so-called "rocket scientists", in a never-ending battle for market share. The aims of these refinements, some of which are described below, were two-fold, to continue to bring investors into the market while at the same time offering more attractive financing terms to borrowers.

The zero-coupon bond pays no interest but is issued at a deep discount to the face value, the investor thus realizing a capital gain on maturity but receiving no interim payments. The zero-coupon bond may be considered as an ordinary fixed rate bond with all the interest receivable paid in a lump sum at the end of the bond's life. This kind of issue is attractive to investors living in a tax regime where the tax on capital gains, if any, is lower than the tax on income.

There are several variations on the theme of floating rate notes. Among the more straightforward types, there are those which put a ceiling on the rate of interest payable (capped FRNs), those which put both a ceiling and a floor on the rate of interest payable (minimax FRNs) and those with a decreasing margin over the reference interest rate (step-down FRNs).

Other variations which have been offered include extendible notes, in which the interest rate is adjusted every two years to a rate linked to a two-year market index. The investor also has the option of selling the bond back to the issuer at par value every two years. Drop-lock FRNs automatically convert to fixed interest rate bonds when short-term interest rates fall below a previously specified level.

Perpetual floating rate notes (PFRNs) came into being in 1984 and for a time were highly popular with banks. As the name implies they have no redemption date but are otherwise similar to ordinary FRNs. The attractions of the PFRN to financial institutions are that many central banks allow such securities to rank as primary capital. They were a relatively cheap way to raise capital, enabling the banks to match their assets with "quasi-equity". However, the market in PFRNs hit a crisis of confidence in late 1986. The slump in secondary market prices and the ensuing evaporation of investor confidence in such issues has relegated them to a historical footnote, albeit a painful one for some of the market makers whose collective losses were put at around US$100 million.

The most successful and one of the oldest variations on the straightforward Eurobond is the convertible bond. Convertible bonds, as well as paying the usual coupon, are exchangeable for other assets at the investors' discretion.

Bonds have been issued which are asset convertible or currency convertible. The asset convertible bond may be exchangeable for other types of bond or even for tangible assets such as oil or gold. Currency convertible bonds are those which, having been issued in one currency, allow the investor the option of repayment of principal and/or interest in an alternative currency or currencies.

However, by far the most popular type of convertible bond, with both issuers and investors, is the equity convertible bond, allowing the Eurobond, on redemption or at any time during a stipulated conversion period, to be exchanged for ordinary shares in the company issuing the bonds at a stipulated exercise price. The company is obliged to issue new shares for the purpose.

Such bonds are attractive to corporate issuers because they can be made with lower interest rates than a comparable non-convertible bond and are a relatively cheap way of internationalizing the ownership of the company's stock. For the investor the attraction is two-fold, holding out the potential for capital gain if the price of the company's shares rises above the exercise price, while at the same time reducing the risk of a loss because even if the share price falls or fails to reach the exercise price, the investor still receives the coupon payment.

Eurowarrants have become increasingly popular since their inception in 1986. The warrant, as discussed in Chapter One, gives the investor the right to purchase shares at a set price at a set date in the future and is a form of call option. Eurowarrants are effectively two assets, the bond itself paying a fixed coupon at regular intervals, together with a warrant giving the investor the right to purchase the stock of the issuer at a pre-specified price over a given period, normally five years.

ECU BONDS

Perhaps the most important development for the future of the Eurobond markets has been the currency in which they are issued. The first Eurobond to be denominated in European Currency Units (ECUs) was issued in April 1981 by an Italian telecommunications group. The market for ECU Eurobonds is now the fifth largest Eurobond market with outstanding bonds of approximately ECU 55 billion and more than 500 issues. The ECU bond market took off towards the end of the 1980's with growth outstripping all the other major bond markets in the last three years of the decade.

Even though European Monetary Union (EMU) is some years away, borrowers, spurred by hopes for a single European currency and strong demand for fixed interest issues, came to the market in ever-increasing numbers, both in terms of borrowers and size of issues. Demand has been highest for long-dated issues with dealers pinning their hopes on the ambitious schedule for monetary union put forward by Brussels. The ECU could be the world's largest and most important currency by the turn of the century. Most of the issuers have been governments and supranational European bodies with high credit ratings, making the issues liquid enough in the secondary market to attract institutional investors. The ECU bond is being used as a political tool as well as a monetary one. The French government has vowed to meet at least 15 per cent of its borrowing requirement through ECU-denominated issues, and the new European Bank for Reconstruction and Development has also pledged to use the market.

However, the ECU bond is not being used solely by so-called European patriots. The more cynically-minded may interpret the UK government's massive ECU 2.5 billion issue in February 1991 merely as a strong send-off for the futures contract in ECU bonds launched by the London International Financial Futures Exchange the following month. The fate of the ECU bond market rests ultimately on the progress towards EMU. Only a small percentage of cross-border trade within Europe was denominated in ECUs at the start of the 1990s. The coming single European market should see firms increasingly turning to the ECU for transactions and financing requirements but significant private sector interest may only come towards the end of the decade with the agenda for EMU.

CHAPTER 4

FOREIGN EXCHANGE

The most up-to-date overview of the world's foreign exchange (forex) markets, a survey by the Bank for International Settlements (BIS), showed global turnover of US$650 billion a day in April 1989. That staggering figure is three times the size of that shown in the last survey, in 1986, and there is no reason to suppose that the market has not continued to grow since the BIS survey was carried out. Yet currency trading as we know it today is barely twenty years old.

To understand the background to the explosive growth of the forex markets we need to return to the nineteenth century and the growth of international trade. Gold has always played an important role in the world's currencies. It is the historical association of gold with the official sector which gives the metal its unique position among commodities; gold coinage appears to have been struck as long ago as 4000 BC. The currency system, the gold standard, which operated in the nineteenth century had evolved over several centuries. The world's leading economies all operated the gold standard under which exchange rates were fixed to the value of gold. Each country valued its own currency in terms of gold and arranged for its central bank to convert gold into currency and currency into gold as required. As all debts, both domestic and foreign, could be expressed in terms of gold, these debts could generally be offset against each other and few physical transfers actually took place. International trade was dominated by the British Empire and the Royal Navy kept the seas safe for merchant vessels. British dominance of world trade lasted into the early years of the twentieth century.

The First World War delivered a serious shock to the established economic order and the huge costs of the war wrecked the European economies. In common with other major nations, the UK came off the gold standard in 1914, being unable to prosecute the war and defend the value of sterling at the same time. In 1919, the UK formally abandoned the gold standard. An attempt to turn the clock back during the inter-war years failed. Between 1925 and 1931 the UK government attempted to hold a gold bullion standard, whereby the central bank had to buy and sell gold at a fixed price. However, the stock market crash of 1929 and the ensuing depression forced the government to abandon a fixed gold price.

With the abandonment of a direct link between gold and money, gold became a "safe haven" for investors to turn to in times of economic uncertainty. Gold's heyday was the era of high inflation around the world in the 1970s. The price also rose in 1980, following the Soviet invasion of Afghanistan, in 1982 with the beginning of the Mexican debt crisis, and again in 1984 following the collapse of the Continental Illinois bank in the USA. Because the return on gold does not correlate with paper assets it was viewed as an ideal investment at a time when paper assets were falling in value, that is, when inflation was running at a high level. However, the increasing globalization and openness of the world financial system appears to have made the notion of a safe haven a dated one. For example, the price of gold showed little reaction to the Gulf conflict in 1990/91.

Gold is now considered by many of the large institutional investors as just another commodity. As such there are several contracts trading gold bullion on futures markets around the world. Bonds, warrants and options in or linked to gold and gold mining companies are traded in various markets. So-called "gold loans" were developed as investment vehicles for gold mining companies to fund their mine production. A gold loan is a loan denominated in bullion, which the borrower repays through the delivery of gold to the lender.

Two of the international institutions we now accept as part of the global financial order came out of the United Nations Monetary and Financial Conference held at Bretton Woods, New Hampshire, in July 1944. The conference met to consider the post-war economic order and both the International Monetary Fund and the International Bank for Reconstruction and Development, better known as the World Bank, were established as a result. The conference also laid out a framework for foreign exchange, the Bretton Woods system, which became fully operational in 1958, and pegged the exchange rates of the world's major currencies to fixed levels against the US dollar. The system was merely a variation of the gold standard, substituting the dollar for gold and with the dollar itself convertible into gold. The end of the Second World War saw the world split into US dollar and sterling areas, with those currencies being used as the reserve currency in different regions. However, the UK's position in the world economy was no longer what it had been in the previous century and by the mid-1960s the dollar stood alone as the reserve currency of the world system. However, gold continued to play an important role in the Western World's foreign exchange reserves. At present, gold holdings by governments and the international financial institutions amount to over a third of all the gold that has ever been mined, and gold reserves account for more than 40 per cent of total official foreign exchange reserves.

The Bretton Woods system was itself doomed to fail in a similar fashion to the gold standard which it attempted to emulate. Between 1945 and the late 1960s, US gold reserves fell from more than 620 million ounces to less than 290 million ounces. Once again it was a war which forced the crisis. Unable to meet the costs of his "Great Society" reforms and pay for the war in Vietnam at the same time, the then US President Lyndon Johnson de-escalated the war and balanced his last budget to prevent a run on gold. However, the writing was on the wall, and by 1971 the pressure on the US gold reserves was critical once more. President Richard Nixon, with an eye to the presidential election the following year, refused proposals to restore fiscal balance which would have led to a contraction of the economy. The US government officially abandoned the dollar's link to gold on 15 August 1971, and allowed the currency to float.

The problem with the gold standard as a means of exchange rate management is that a country's internal purchasing power and prices are dependent on its balance of payments. A country running a current account deficit would actually have to pay out gold, resulting in the internal restriction of credit and economic contraction until the nation's balance of payments was once more in equilibrium. Much the same problem assailed the Bretton Woods system although it was assumed that any country with an excessive current account deficit would adjust its economic policies. Indeed, the system managed to survive the major hiccup in the UK of the Wilson government's devaluation of sterling in 1967, as a number of countries moved their reserves into US dollars. However, the final nail in the Bretton Woods system's coffin was the run of US current account deficits caused by the costs of the war in Vietnam in the late 1960s and early 1970s, which flooded the foreign exchange markets of the world with dollars.

Since the collapse of the Bretton Woods system, there have been attempts by governments to manage currency values with varying degrees of success. It has, for example, proved virtually impossible to maintain the parities between the D-mark, the yen and the US dollar for any length of time. The sheer size of the market-place has meant that the central banker is just another player, no longer in a position to dictate to the rest of the market. Intervention has succeeded best when its goals have been limited to smoothing bumps out of a currency's general trend. The first major post-Bretton Woods endeavour to give some order to the international financial system came in September 1985 when five leading industrialized nations (France, Japan, the UK, the USA and West Germany) agreed to act in concert and lower the value of the dollar. The agreement became known as the Plaza Agreement from the location of the meeting in New York's Plaza Hotel. The so-called Group of Five or G-5 (later expanded to Seven, and including Canada and Italy) was established as a "steering committee" for the world economy.

In February 1987, the G-5 countries, together with Canada, reached a second agreement on currency stability. This pact, known as the Louvre Accord, called for a halt to the US dollar's decline and also detailed the economic policies pledged by each participant to re-establish balanced trade and world economic growth. The huge increase in international bond flows in the late 1980s (*see Chapter Three*) was, in large part, a result of the influence of the Tokyo Ministry of Finance on Japanese institutions to buy US bonds to help support the dollar following the Louvre Accord.

The world economy is no longer based solely on the US dollar, although it remains one of the most important currencies. There are two established spheres of influence: a dollar area, which includes all of the Americas; and, in Western Europe, what is effectively a D-mark area under the auspices of the European Monetary System. Despite the strength of the Japanese economy and its position in world trade terms, the yen has yet to become as important an international currency as the dollar and the D-mark. Although much of Asia and Southeast Asia is now economically linked to Japan, the dollar remains the international currency of the two regions.

THE EUROPEAN MONETARY SYSTEM

The basic structure of the European Monetary System (EMS) was set out in 1978 in a resolution by the member states of the European Community and the basic operating structure, the Exchange Rate Mechanism (ERM) was detailed in an agreement between the EC central banks in 1979. The operation of the ERM centred round the creation of an artificial European Currency Unit (ECU), against which all the participating countries in the ERM were given a central rate. Changes to this central rate cannot be made unilaterally but only with the agreement of all the ERM participants.

The ECU is made up of a "basket" of EC currencies and consists of specified amounts of each. The relative weighting of each currency within the ECU is meant to reflect the importance of the individual national economies.

All the Community currencies are now included in the ECU basket, although Greece and Portugal are not members of the ERM. The nine participating currencies are those of the UK (sterling), Germany (D-mark), France (franc), Italy (lira), Netherlands (guilder), Denmark (krone), Ireland (punt), Spain (peseta) and Belgium/Luxembourg (franc). The exchange rate between the Belgian franc and the Luxembourg franc is fixed, with no margin of fluctuation.

Within the ERM, member countries limit their exchange rates in relationship to the other currencies. Seven of the nine member currencies are allowed to fluctuate within margins of up to 2.25 per cent either side of the fixed central rate. The Spanish peseta, which joined in September 1989, and sterling, which joined in October 1990, are the two most recent entries into the ERM. These two currencies are allowed wider margins of 6 per cent either side of their central rates. In practical terms these margins, known respectively as the narrow and wide bands, do not mean that each currency has a total flexibility of 4.5 per cent (narrow band) or 12 per cent (wide band). In practice, a currency is likely to reach its effective limit before it can make full use of this range, owing to the need to remain within these bands against all the other ERM currencies simultaneously. Therefore, a wide band currency cannot be more than 6 per cent above the weakest or 6 per cent below the strongest, making the effective limits in relation to the other currencies significantly less than 6 per cent.

If one currency reaches its limit against another, the central banks of both currencies are obliged to intervene in the market-place during European business hours to buy in order to support the weak currency, and to sell in order to lower the value of the strong currency. This intervention should prevent the exchange rate from moving outside the established limits because traders in the forex market know that they can always get the currency they require from the central banks. Therefore, they will not accept a lower price if they are selling, or a higher price if they are buying. In addition to domestic reserves, the central banks in the ERM have access to credit facilities to assist in financing intervention. Under the most important of these, the Very Short Term Facility (VSTF), each of the ERM central banks makes short-term credit facilities available to each other in their own currencies. This facility is automatically available to each central bank. The VSTF and other facilities within the ERM are overseen by the European Monetary Co-operation Fund, which also issues ECUs to central banks in exchange for deposits by them of 20 per cent of their gold and US dollar reserves. Should intervention by itself not prove to be sufficient to stabilize the currency, the onus is then on the central bank to raise or lower domestic interest rates to bring the currency back into line.

The last resort, should both intervention and interest rates be unable to hold the currencies within their agreed bands, is a wholesale realignment of the system to alter the relative parities of the currencies within it. In fact, given the power and size of the market, except in the short term, intervention is not enough unless the member countries pursue macro-economic policies which are consistent with the established bands. Over its twelve-year existence, owing to the dominance of the D-mark within the system and the Bundesbank's anti-inflationary stance, the ERM has pressured its members' monetary authorities to follow convergent and low-inflationary policies. Although there have been twelve realignments since 1979, they have tended to become less frequent as the member economies have converged and inflation differentials have been reduced. The last major realignment took place in January 1987, though there was a minor change in January 1990 when the Italian lira moved from the wide band to the narrow band.

EUROPEAN ECONOMIC AND MONETARY UNION

The full Economic and Monetary Union (EMU) of EC countries is viewed by many European politicians as the inevitable conclusion of the evolutionary process of economic convergence brought about by the apparent success of the ERM and the development of the single European market. The basic framework of the proposed route to EMU was finalised with the drafting of the European Community Economic and Monetary Union Treaty at Maastricht, in the Netherlands, in December 1991. Under the treaty, which is due to be ratified by March 1992, EC leaders agreed that the second stage of EMU would officially commence on 1 January 1994, with the introduction of a European Monetary Institute (EMI) as a precursor to a future EC central bank. Secondary legislation will ensure that the central bank be independent of national influences, modelled on the German Bundesbank. By the end of 1996 the European Commission and the EMI are to have compiled a report stating whether enough aspiring members of the exchange rate mechanism have met agreed criteria for full currency union.

The timetable introduced at Maastricht puts a strict time limit on the deliberations preceding the introduction of a single European currency. If no single currency is introduced before the end of 1998, EC leaders are to meet to decide by qualified majority vote which economies are strong enough to meet EMU criteria. Those countries would go ahead to the third and final stage of EMU by 1 January 1999 at the latest with no further decisions.

The treaty has protocols which allow two member states, Britain and Denmark, the legally binding right to stay out of the final phase of EMU.

"The United Kingdom shall not be obliged or committed to move to the third stage of economic and monetary union without a separate decision to do so by its government and Parliament," the protocol for the UK says. The opt-out clause for Denmark was inserted because the Danish government says it wants to hold a referendum on participating in stage three of EMU.

However, in another protocol attached to the treaty, all 12 members declare that the drive to a single currency this century is "'irreversible".

Despite the apparently inexorable nature of the EMU process, it is by no means clear that ambitious timetable laid out in Maastricht will be met. The UK has not been alone in its criticisms. In October 1990, Germany's central banker, the then Bundesbank President Karl Otto Poehl, described the Rome communiqué which set out the basic framework agreed at Maastricht as incomprehensible. Although the German government is strongly committed to EMU, the Bundesbank has cooled towards the idea, Poehl had already described German monetary union as a disaster, with regard to the politically-motivated decision to make each Ostmark equal one D-mark. Poehl also suggested that EC monetary policy decisions could only be taken by the European Central Bank, rather than by individual governments, and that legislation was required to preclude the monetary financing of budget deficits by any such central bank.

Although the UK remains out of step with other EC government's on the issue of EMU, political upheaval in the UK and the replacement of Margaret Thatcher as Prime Minister by John Major has resulted in a significantly less combative UK attitude. Many economic analysts believe that commercial integration will force the pace of economic union and make EMU inevitable.

THE THEORY OF EXCHANGE RATE VALUES

The dynamic growth of the forex market over the past twenty years has focussed the attention of many economists on the question of what actually determines the value of a given currency. In the long term, it is the economic fundamentals which count. The most popular theory put forward to explain the linkage of economic fundamentals to exchange rates is that known as "purchasing power parity" (PPP). The basis of the

PPP theory is that exchange rates tend to move towards a point at which the purchasing power of currencies is broadly similar. Thus, PPP theory calculates an exchange rate between two currencies on the basis of the prevailing price levels in the two countries, comparing the movement in prices (i.e. relative inflation) with the movement in the exchange rate.

The importance of inflation in PPP theory is that it renders exports uncompetitive. If, for example, inflation in the USA is running at 10 per cent a year but in Germany is at zero, in one year's time goods from the USA will be 10 per cent more expensive. Unless US productivity improves by 10 per cent or more, purchasers will obviously seek to buy cheaper goods from elsewhere. PPP theory suggests that the value of the dollar should fall by 10 per cent over the same period, leaving the price German customers pay for US goods unchanged in D-marks.

There are two problems associated with the PPP theory in its pure form: first, that of choosing a base year to work from; and, second, deciding which measures of inflation to compare. Both these variables obviously have a major impact on whether a currency is going to be perceived as over-valued or under-valued.

A useful variation of PPP theory is the inclusion of real interest rate differentials in long-term bonds. A "real" interest rate is the rate of interest paid by an investment minus the rate of inflation. This combined theory starts from the premise that investors believe that, over the long term, a currency will return to its PPP level. This level may change according to relative inflation. However, if, after allowing for this change, the real bond yields for two currencies are different, then investors will purchase bonds which offer the higher of the two yields. This requires purchases of the currency in which the bond is denominated and these purchases will force a move in exchange rate values. The differential in real interest rates implies a "forward real exchange rate" and the gap between this and the PPP level is determined by the real bond yield differential. As long as the forward real exchange rate is close to the estimate of the PPP level, investors will hold a currency even if its current rate is significantly at variance with the estimate.

An alternative approach to currency valuation is provided by the fundamental equilibrium exchange rate theory. This theory proposes the use of a model of a national economy to estimate what is described as the fundamental equilibrium exchange rate. Economists use the model to develop a picture of the economy in balance, that is when it is not suffering from either a depression of an excessive boom, and from that can project exchange rate values necessary to achieve this equilibrium.

However, all these economic theories offer only long-term explanations of what currency values are likely to be. The importance of economic fundamentals in short-term currency valuation is undermined by the sheer size of the market. The global currency market is thirty-two times larger than world trade flows and the values of currencies often bear little relationship to the underlying performance of their national economies. In the short term it is what are called "technical" factors which drive the price of a given currency. Technical or chart analysis is the study of the price movements themselves. Technical factors may account for up to 100 per cent of one day's trading moves but have declining influence thereafter. It has been suggested that over a three-month period 50 per cent of price movements are technical and 50 per cent based on the economic fundamentals and that it is not until one looks at a one-year period that economic fundamentals become the best indicator of currency values.

The basic theory behind technical analysis suggests that all the economic fundamentals are already reflected in the value of a currency and that it is the human factor which moves the price on a short-term basis. Technical analysts are, therefore, self-appointed market psychologists, relying on traders in the market to react in similar ways to similar situations. Although it is unlikely that market situations will ever be identical and that participants will act in exactly the same way as in the past, some repetition does occur. It is this repetition that chartists study.

The reading of charts for pattern recognition is a major part of technical analysis but equally important are the definition of trends and the monitoring of positions which appear overbought or oversold, where traders appear to have over-reacted to market conditions and the price has moved much higher or lower than seems warranted. In simple terms, an "uptrend" describes the situation in which prices are rising despite occasional falls, a kind of "two steps forward, one step back" situation. A "downtrend" is simply the reverse of an uptrend. However, despite the apparent straightforward reliance on the production of graphs displaying price movements, technical analysis is not a science. Less charitable economists have likened it to divination—what you believe depends on how you read the entrails. It is certainly true that chart predictions tend to be self-fulfilling.

Charles Henry Dow (*see Chapter One*) is credited with being the first modern technical analyst, formulating the Dow Theory at the turn of the century. Based on studies of the stock market, Dow concluded that emotive elements, hope and fear, played a major part in short-term price movements. While this may now appear self-evident, it was Dow's

FOREIGN EXCHANGE

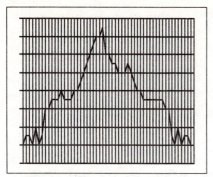

Figure A Head and shoulders

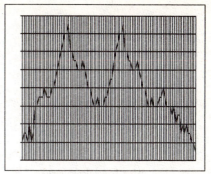

Figure B Double top

rationalization of this and the formulation of his theory which provided the ground rules for technical analysis.

Among the common patterns technical analysts look for are the "head and shoulders" (*see Fig. A*) and "double top/bottom" (*see Fig. B*). A head and shoulders pattern is the pattern on the price chart, showing prices rising dramatically, sinking to find support or buying interest (the left shoulder), then rising sharply higher to new ground before collapsing to the support level (the head). This slide in prices causes a bounce before the price slides again (the right shoulder) to test the support level.

The double top/bottom pattern generally shows when long-term price trends are reversed. The double top formation on the chart appears as twin mountain peaks. The price rises to its first peak, falls back to its support level and then rises once again to the second peak before falling decisively. The base of the peaks is the support neckline, which when broken signals that a top has formed. The double bottom is a mirror image of the double top, appearing on the chart as a W-shape.

CURRENCY MANAGEMENT

Governments attempt to manage exchange rates as tools of overall economic management. The ERM has already been discussed in some detail, but in its early years it did not offer the anti-inflationary discipline with which it is now synonymous. It appeared to operate more as a crawling peg system, with regular devaluations to offset higher inflation than in West Germany. Most of the Latin America nations attempt, with varying degrees of success, to operate a crawling peg against the US dollar.

Not all the world's currencies are freely convertible. Semi-convertible currencies may only be bought or sold through the central bank and then only for specific purposes. Certain countries have more than one set exchange; a notable example of this is South Africa which operates two rates of exchange for the rand, effectively a business rate and a tourist rate. Non-convertible currencies are restricted in circulation to their national boundaries. Eastern European currencies were non-convertible prior to the downfall of the communist regimes, but now most of the new democratic governments are moving steadily towards currency convertibility.

Many governments operate a system of maintaining the value of their currency against a basket of currencies. The obvious example of this is the ERM and the ECU. However, the ECU is not the only "basket currency" and is pre-dated by the Special Drawing Right (SDR), which was originally introduced by the International Monetary Fund (IMF) in 1970 as a reserve asset for IMF members. The value of the SDR was originally linked to gold, which it was intended to replace in the world monetary system. The SDR was first valued equal to 0.89 grammes of fine gold, the same valuation as US$1 when the dollar was linked to gold. Following the break-up of the Bretton Woods system, the SDR was revalued in 1974 as a weighted average of the currencies of the sixteen largest international trading countries. In 1981, the composition of the SDR was changed again with the basket of currencies reduced to those of the G-5 nations. The value of the SDR is revised every five years. Under the latest revaluation in 1990, the weights of each currency in the valuation basket are 40 per cent for the US dollar, 21 per cent for the D-mark, 17 per cent for the Japanese yen and 11 per cent each for the French franc and sterling. Although some bonds and certificates of deposit have been issued denominated in SDRs, the SDR is rarely used by non-governmental bodies.

THE FOREX MARKET

The foreign exchange market does not exist in the sense that a stock market floor exists. It is a market which never closes, has no national boundaries and is, except in very limited terms, beyond the control of governments. The scope for movement in currency rates is much greater than it used to be. This is partly the result of a continuing move towards financial liberalization and partly because the participants have come to regard the forex market as a potential profit centre, rather than simply as a means of facilitating trade or laying off risk.

Foreign exchange trading is dominated by three centres round the world, London, New York and Tokyo, together spanning twenty-four hours of each day and allowing continuous trading. These three centres account for two-thirds of forex market turnover, and of the three, London is by far the most important. According to the BIS survey in 1989, daily market turnover in London amounted to US$187 billion. Although the BIS survey put New York in second place, the trends shown suggest that Tokyo is, by now, likely to have overtaken New York as the second largest centre for forex trading. London remains dominant in the European time zone owing to the relatively liberal financial regime by comparison with the UK's European neighbours. The US dollar is the most heavily traded currency with the dollar/D-mark exchange rate the busiest market, closely followed by the dollar/yen. Third, fourth and fifth place are taken, respectively, by dollar/sterling, dollar/Swiss franc and yen/D-mark.

The growing internationalization of business over the last decade has substantially increased the level of foreign exchange risk to which companies are exposed. At the same time the increased sophistication of the foreign exchange markets has made it unacceptable for companies to blame falling profits on changes in currency values. Indeed, many companies now expect their foreign currency operations to earn a profit in their own right. However, active participation in the forex market can backfire, as witness the £150 million foreign exchange loss registered by the UK foods group Allied Lyons in 1990/91.

Currency exposure is no longer merely a concern of importers and exporters. Most large companies now have foreign operations and the translation of foreign earnings back into their domestic currency is an important concern. Companies whose foreign exchange exposure is limited to exports or imports face critical risk. Their turnover, rather than profits, are exposed and any sudden change in currency rates could put the company out of business. Such companies will sell currencies forward to hedge this risk. Those companies whose exposure is in terms of earnings from foreign assets tend to structure their debt to match the asset base. For example, the UK drinks group Grand Metropolitan earns almost 50 per cent of its profit from US operations. The company issues bonds in the US markets in order to match its dollar assets with liabilities.

Other than the issue of foreign-denominated bonds (*see Chapter Three*), there are two main methods of hedging foreign currency exposure: the forward market, in which companies can contract to buy or sell currencies which they will need or receive in the future at a predetermined rate; and the "over-the-counter" options market, in which call or put options may be purchased, respectively giving the holder the right but not the requirement to buy or to sell a currency at a specified rate. Average daily turnover in the over-the-counter US dollar-based currency options market is estimated to be around US$25 billion. The market in cross-rate options not involving the US dollar is put at between US$5-US$10 billion per day. A network of international banks offers forward contracts and over-the-counter options in an interbank market. There are also established currency contracts on a number of the world's futures and options exchanges. Although options contracts are more expensive than forward or futures contracts, they have grown in importance because they provide a further insurance against exposure (*see Chapter Five*).

EXCHANGE-TRADED FUTURES AND OPTIONS

Exchange trading in currency futures began at the International Monetary Market (IMM) division of the Chicago Mercantile Exchange (CME) on 16 May 1972. The quoted price of the IMM currency futures contract is the US dollar price of one unit of the foreign currency. The value of the contract is that price multiplied by the fixed number of currency units in each contract. For example, the IMM D-mark contract is Dm125,000. If the futures price of the D-mark is US$0.60, the contract value would be 125,000 x 0.60, or US$75,000. Each D-mark contract price change or "tick" of 0.0001 changes the contract value by US$12.50.

Currency futures trading works in the same way as commodity futures trading (*see Chapter Two*). Futures prices are linked to spot prices, in this case the cash exchange rate. The difference, which is due to different delivery times, is the basis (the futures price minus the spot price). The basis tends to move to zero as the delivery day for the futures contract approaches, with the futures delivery effectively becoming a spot delivery. This principle is the essence of the use of futures for the fixing of costs in advance.

Two US exchanges have put forward futures contracts which are not based on US dollar exchange rates and one intends to offer options based on cross rates. Previously, only contracts based on the value of the US dollar against other currencies had been traded. The new cross-rate futures and options on futures contracts are to be offered by the CME and the fledgling Twin Cities Board of Trade in Minneapolis. The requirement for such currency futures not related to the dollar has grown as the yen and the D-mark have gained stature as international currencies. At the same time the Philadelphia Stock Exchange has plans for three cross-currency cash-based options; D-mark/yen and sterling/yen options, based and settled in yen, and D-mark/sterling options based and settled in D-marks.

Currency options were first introduced in late 1982 in Vancouver, Philadelphia and Amsterdam. There are several currency option contracts traded around the world, although turnover and liquidity varies from centre to centre. The Philadelphia Stock Exchange mainly trades "American" style options, which are exercisable at any time, unlike options traded on the CME which are exercisable into the underlying futures contract.

CURRENCY SWAPS

Swaps first came into being as part of the markets which developed following the collapse of the Bretton Woods system. They offer longer-term solutions to foreign exchange exposure than forward and futures contracts, which tend not to be very active beyond one year forward. In the 1970s, for example, US companies suffered unwelcome volatility of earnings from foreign operations and UK companies had difficulty in funding overseas subsidiaries. Both these problems could be tackled by the development of "back-to-back" loan agreements. Under such an agreement, the US firm would make a US dollar loan to the UK company while simultaneously taking an equivalent sterling loan from that UK firm. The principal amounts of the loan were determined by the prevailing spot exchange rate with interest payments on negotiated terms denominated in the currencies of the respective loans. In this instance, the US company received a hedge against its sterling exposure and the UK company obtained dollar funding and a hedge against dollar depreciation. The main drawbacks of this type of loan were the impact on corporate balance sheets and the risk of default by either party.

The invention of the currency swap solved these problems, rewriting the separate loan agreements as a single contract for the exchange of principal and interest payments. The swap, equivalent to a sequence of forward contracts, qualified for off-balance sheet regulatory and accounting treatment and, furthermore, one counterparty would be released from continued obligation in the case of default by the other. Both parties gain by having their debts in a more liquid form, i.e. more readily responsive to changes in the market-place.

At first, swaps were matched case by case, and the market did not really take off until 1981 with a swap between the World Bank and IBM. The prestige of these participants heightened awareness of swaps as a legitimate tool of foreign exchange management and gave potential users confidence in the swaps market. According to the International Swap Dealers Association (ISDA), from a modest US$5 billion in 1981, outstanding swaps contracts reached an estimated US$520 billion notional principal by the end of the decade.

An obvious refinement of the currency swap market was the interest rate swap, defined as having identical currencies on the two sides of the swap. Interest rate swaps first came into vogue in the early

FOREIGN EXCHANGE

1980s owing to the US recession and dollar interest rate volatility. Given that all corporate entities, banks included, tend to be inherently more exposed to interest rate risk than exchange rate risk, the interest rate swap market is substantially larger than the currency swap market. The total notional principal of interest rate swaps outstanding by mid-1990, according to ISDA, reached US$1,900 billion, more than three times the size of the currency swap market. The vast majority of interest rate swaps are fixed/floating. This means a company may exchange a liability for fixed interest rate payments for those made at floating rates which are regularly reset by reference to an agreed market index, usually LIBOR. Financial institutions are the most important users of interest rate swaps, accounting for about 60 per cent of the business.

Although swap activity is concentrated in currencies and interest rates, there are now markets for commodity swaps (*see Chapter Two*) and for equity swaps, in which coupon receipts or dividends may be exchanged.

CHAPTER 5

FINANCIAL FUTURES AND OPTIONS

One of the most remarkable things about financial futures and options, or derivatives as they are also known, has been their explosive growth. Commodity futures developed over a period of more than 150 years. Financial futures trading has mushroomed in little more than a tenth of that time. On the Chicago Board of Trade (CBOT), financial futures trading has soared from a mere 20,125 contracts traded in 1975, the year they were introduced, to over 100 million contracts a year entering the 1990s.

The US futures markets, the CBOT, the Chicago Mercantile Exchange and the Chicago Board Options Exchange, dominate world futures and options trading. Well behind these three, but gradually catching up are the London and Paris markets, LIFFE and MATIF, and in Asia, the Tokyo International Financial Futures Exchange and SIMEX in Singapore. Several other futures markets are also in operation and many more are being developed. For example, already trading in the second rank in Europe are the European Options Exchange in Amsterdam, the Deutsche Terminbörse in Frankfurt and the Swiss futures and options exchange, SOFFEX.

Traders in financial futures are normally required to lodge a deposit with the clearing house of the exchange on which they are trading. This initial or deposit margin is a fixed sum per contract and must be left in place as long as the futures position is maintained. In addition to this, variation margin must be paid to, or is receivable from, the clearing house, as the position held generates losses or profits with movements of market prices. Over and above the clearing house's basic requirements, dealers in the futures markets may require more extensive margining arrangements from their customers.

A financial futures contract is broadly similar to those of commodity futures discussed in Chapter Three, being an agreement to buy or sell a set quantity of a specific financial instrument at a given date in the future at an agreed price. There are three main types of financial futures contract: interest rate futures, currency futures and stock index futures. Currency futures are quoted in the base currency of the contract, and stock index futures are quoted in the underlying index. However, most interest rate futures are quoted on an index basis.

One of the key principles behind many financial futures contracts is "cash settlement". In this process, at the expiry of the contract, a sum of money representing any price changes is paid over, rather than actual physical delivery of the underlying instrument. There is no need to own or deliver the underlying instrument for a contract which is cash settled. However, certain contracts based on cash settlement do not exclude traders who require the option of taking or making physical delivery. This can be achieved through the technique known as Exchange for Physical (EFP). In these situations, the buyer of a cash commodity transfers to the seller an equivalent amount of long futures contracts, or receives from him a corresponding amount of short futures at an agreed price. EFPs are flexible and have become established as an effective means of both pricing physical deals and of price risk management, notably in the International Petroleum Exchange's Brent Blend Futures contract, which is cash settled. They permit the making or taking of physical delivery against a futures position under terms and conditions which can be tailored to meet the needs of industry participants on a one-to-one basis.

Stock index futures

Among the most successful derivative instruments have been stock index futures, giving traders the opportunity for index arbitrage, a trading strategy which allows investors to hedge share portfolios. Stock index futures were first introduced by the US Kansas City Board of Trade in February 1982. The Chicago Mercantile Exchange launched a futures contract on the Standard & Poors 500, now by far the most liquid index futures in the world, just two months later. Stock index futures contracts are now traded around the world, in Australia, Hong Kong, Japan, Singapore, Toronto, the UK, and there are more than half a dozen active contracts in the US markets. Because the index futures contract is a single instrument which mirrors a basket of stocks it opens up a whole range of potential trading strategies for investors.

The holder of a portfolio of stocks which is identical to the make-up of the index or which tracks its performance closely, is thus able to hedge his exposure to price movements in these underlying stocks by selling index futures. Providing the futures market accurately reflects moves in the cash market, any losses made in the latter will be offset by gains in the former. The opposite is also true. Were the hedge to be maintained on a permanent basis, the attractions of investing in stocks would be significantly reduced. However, hedging does become a useful strategy when a portfolio investor in the stock market wishes to lock in his profit because he has become nervous about market conditions. Alternatively, the investor could actively use the futures market, locking in profits at successively higher levels. Hedging cannot guarantee to eliminate all risk and the hedge will be an imperfect one whenever the portfolio of stocks held behaves differently from the underlying index.

Investors holding shares in smaller portfolios or even just in a single stock are also able to reduce their exposure to the vagaries of the market at large by selling index futures. Exposure is thus reduced only to the movements of the individual share itself against general market trends. Such a strategy might be used by merchant banks and the institutional underwriters to a new issue.

Speculation on index futures is much the same as speculation on all futures contracts, with the speculator taking a view on the future performance of the underlying market. Stock index arbitrage is an important part of the business of index futures. In theory, the futures price is determined by prevailing interest rates, dividend rates, the time left to expiry, and relative transaction costs. However, in practice, as in all futures markets, the price differential between the cash market and the futures contract does not hold exactly to the theoretical differential. Stock index arbitrage is designed to take advantage of these instances. This is possible because, whatever the volume of arbitrage activity, the prices will converge at the expiry date, because the settlement price of the futures contract is determined by the cash price.

Thus, if the future is at a sufficient premium to the cash market, the arbitrageur buys a portfolio of shares in the stock market and sells the futures contract. Or, if the future is at a discount to its theoretical value, the arbitrageur buys the futures and sells in the cash market.

One of the most important features of arbitrage is that, in efficient markets, it should bring prices back into line. When the future's premium is too high, arbitrageurs selling the future and buying the underlying index shares in sufficient volume will lower the futures price and raise the cash price until the two are in equilibrium, with the theoretical differential once more established. The same argument applies in reverse when the future is at a discount.

It is important to differentiate between the arbitrageur and the investor. Although both may hold the same shares and be active in the futures market, their motives are quite different. The arbitrageur, unlike the investor, has no direct interest in any given portfolio of shares. At the expiry date of the futures contract, the arbitrageur settles or reverses his transaction in both markets.

Stock index futures are also being used as a substitute for investing in the stock market itself. Criticism of fund managers' failure to outperform stock markets has resulted in many tending simply to buy the whole market and match its performance, prompting the growth of so-called index funds, which are constructed to replicate the index. Two consequences of this development are that, firstly, investors become relatively more interested in events which impact on the market as a whole and, secondly, the investor can just as easily, and indeed more cheaply, buy the index via the futures market.

Most portfolios are not 100 per cent equities but rather a mixture of equities, bonds and cash, with the balance being varied from time to time according to the expectations of prospective market performance and changing risk/return equations. Thus, an investor beginning to feel jittery about the market may decide to reduce the equity in the portfolio in favour of more bonds or a higher cash balance. Traditionally, this has involved the actual sale of equities with the prospect of later repurchase. Portfolio insurance is a trading strategy which involves the use of futures to adjust the *de facto* level of securities and cash in the portfolio without actually having to trade in the stock market itself. The attractions are lower transaction costs, given the smaller margin requirement in the futures market, and the flexibility of retaining the equity itself within the portfolio. Selling index futures in this situation creates a hedged position for part of the portfolio, thereby reducing exposure to risk in the equities held. Conversely, in a rising stock market, buying index futures increases the portfolio's exposure to equities. Because these adjustments are made on a continual basis, portfolio insurance is sometimes referred to as "dynamic hedging".

CURRENCY FUTURES

As well as being used as hedging tools by commerce and industry (*see Chapter Four*), exchange-traded currency futures and options allow for the participation of speculative investors. In fact, the interbank and over-the-counter market in currency forward trading and options is much greater than the exchange-based business. Exchange-traded contracts failed to take off in London and were quietly dropped by LIFFE, and interest in the contracts listed on SIMEX in Singapore is very limited.

"Spread" trading is one of the forms of speculative investment in currency futures used regularly, but the most common is the intermarket spread between the same delivery month of different currencies. This spread can be profitable with either an overall rising or falling currency market because the speculator is only interested in the differential. The spread is calculated by subtracting one currency price from another. Generally, the currencies that are selected share some common economic interests that cause their prices to trend together.

With the exception of a small number of recently introduced cross-rate contracts, currency futures contract value is the US dollar price multiplied by the number of currency units covered. The buyer of a contract, taking a "long" position, agrees to pay the dollar price to receive a fixed amount of the other currency on the contract delivery date, unless the position has been closed out by the sale of a corresponding contract to another party. The holder of a long position will profit if the dollar price of the currency rises after the position is established–that is, if the dollar weakens or the other currency strengthens. Futures prices are closely related to the "spot" or cash rates of exchange with the difference, the basis, being a result of the different delivery times. The basis in foreign exchange reflects the interest rate differential between countries. If there are no restrictions on trade and capital flows between the two countries in question, forward rates of exchange will vary inversely with the interest-rate differential between the two countries. For example, if interest rates are 2 per cent higher in Canada than in the USA, the forward price for Canadian dollars should be at a 2 per cent discount on an annual basis in terms of US dollars.

INTEREST RATE FUTURES

The most important sector of the financial futures markets is that trading in contracts on underlying instruments whose prices are dependent on interest rates. There are two types of interest rate futures, short-term interest rate contracts such as those based on Eurodollars, and long-term interest rate contracts based on government bonds. The most important of these latter markets are the US treasury bond futures contracts in Chicago. Many of these contracts are quoted on an index basis. Eurodollar futures, with contracts traded in Chicago, London and Singapore, are probably the most important financial futures traded, providing participants with the opportunity to hedge or to speculate on movements in short-term interest rates. The rate underlying the Eurodollar contract is the three-month London Interbank Offered Rate (LIBOR).

The price of a Eurodollar contract on LIFFE is quoted base 100 minus the annual interest rate on a three-month time deposit. Each minimum price fluctuation, or "tick", represents US$25, being the interest at a rate of a hundredth of one per cent for three months on US$1,000,000. An increase in the price of the three-month Eurodollar contract from 85.05 to 85.10 represents a change of five ticks, each having a value of US$25, representing a total price move of US$125 for the contract. Such a price change may also be interpreted in terms of interest rate movements, this five tick increase in the value of the Eurodollar contract is equivalent to a fall in interest rates from 14.95 per cent to 14.90 per cent. A trader who purchased ten three-month Eurodollar contracts at 85.05 will be showing a total gain on paper of US$1,250 should the contract price move to 85.10. This is equivalent to the profit he would make by taking a US$10,000,000 deposit for three months at 14.90 per cent and making a similar deposit at 14.95 per cent.

Unlike the Eurodollar futures contracts, many of the bond futures contracts traded round the world, notably the CBOT's Treasury bonds (T-bonds) future, specify settlement through the delivery of actual bonds. Although it is very rare for delivery actually to take place, the fact that the contract is settled in this fashion dictates how it operates. A wide variety of T-bonds are deliverable against the futures contract, which merely specifies a maturity of at least fifteen years. However, because the contract is based on an 8 per cent coupon, the evaluation of the futures position against cash bonds requires a "conversion factor" to be used, which simply converts a given cash bond to an 8 per cent coupon. Obviously, the conversion factor will vary from bond to bond as, therefore, will the basis. In this case the price of the futures contract will track the price of the cash bond which would be the cheapest to deliver against the futures contract.

A recent addition to the interest rate futures sector is the introduction of two futures contracts on interest rate swaps by the CBOT in June 1991. The swaps market has grown explosively in recent years (*see Chapter Four*), although the theory behind it, the hedging of adverse movements in interest rates, is far from new. However, in a swap, the hedge is only as good as the financial health of both parties involved. If one party defaults, the bank responsible for arranging the swap loses its protection from interest-rate risk. By hedging with the CBOT's new contracts, the risk exposure is essentially passed on to risk-takers in the futures market where the transaction is backed by the exchange and the market's clearing house. The CBOT's two contracts are for three-year and five-year fixed/floating swaps and are cash settled.

ASSET MANAGEMENT TOOLS

In a sense, all futures and options contracts are asset management tools, offering investors, portfolio managers and industry the opportunity of managing or reducing the risk in their investments. However, there is a special class of contracts which has been created in the last few years–that of the cash-settled basket contracts. The prices of several underlying commodities are brought together in the form of a proprietary index which then becomes a fungible, or tradeable, instrument in its own right on a cash-settled basis. These contracts operate in a broadly similar way to that of stock index futures contracts. Among the contracts available is BIFFEX (the Baltic International Freight Futures Exchange), which permits hedgers, both ship owners and charterers, to offset the risk of trading on the dry bulk shipping market. The BIFFEX contract is unique in that it is the only futures contract in the world to offer a hedge against shipping. The Baltic Freight Index is based on voyage freight rates and is composed of fourteen representative dry bulk cargo rates, averaged and weighted according to a predetermined formula. There are a number of proprietary commodity indices tracking commodity prices, the New York Futures Exchange trades the Commodities Research Bureau's index and the London FOX trades the MGMI index, a base metal index developed by Metallgesellschaft AG of Germany. The MGMI comprises the prices of the six non-ferrous metals traded on the London Metal Exchange, weighted towards each metal's relative consumption share in the western world.

The boom in financial futures continued in the 1990s with exchanges developing further new products to attract investors. However, the rapid expansion of derivative financial instruments brought problems of its own, as the story of London FOX's property futures contracts demonstrates. The UK property market was estimated to be worth £930 billion in December 1990 and was the largest UK asset base with no hedging vehicle. In May 1991, the London FOX launched four cash-settled futures contracts on UK property. A property futures market in the UK was, in theory, made possible because of well-developed statistics and indices. London FOX used the Investment Property Databank's indices on commercial property capital values and commercial property rent, and the Nationwide Building Society's residential property values index as the basis for three of the contracts. The fourth contract was offered on a mortgage interest rate index created by the exchange itself.

In hindsight, the exchange's decision to launch such contracts at a time when the UK property markets, both commercial and residential, were undergoing a serious recession was over-optimistic. However, this misjudgement was compounded by the exchange authorities' attempts to boost the property futures market by trading on the exchange's own account and by encouraging trading through the issue of indemnities to brokers to protect them against loss. Following the suspension of the property futures contracts in October 1991, it was also revealed that London FOX had been attempting to boost volume in its screen-based arabica coffee, rice and sugar futures contracts in similar ways.

The privatization of the UK's electricity industry and the development of a forward market in electricity for some twenty firms, including all the UK power generators and distributors, holds out the prospect of an electricity futures contract, the first of its kind in the world. The forward market is an extension of the existing market operating around an electricity "pool" set up after the privatization of the industry. The pool, operated by the National Grid, acts as a clearing house to match generators and distributors. The new forward market aims to provide a standard form of contract which would divide the week into twelve standard time periods. London FOX has been investigating the logical development of this forward market into a fully-fledged futures contract. While an electricity futures contract would not be a substitute for existing arrangements, it could provide a complementary risk management medium for major industrial consumers, in which speculators would assume some of the risk currently held within the electricity industry. However, the furore and further revelations following the suspension of the exchange's property futures contracts must cast serious doubt on the coming to market of electricity futures for some time.

The CBOT had planned to launch the world's first insurance futures contract by the end of 1991. However, the launch was postponed to mid-1992 because of problems satisfying the regulators. The first contract to be offered will be on health insurance. The CBOT is also developing contracts on motor, homeowner and ocean marine insurance. The health insurance futures are based on a pool of health policies. A special participating group of at least ten insurance companies are being solicited to become members of the pool. Eligible policies, which are obviously required to be homogenous, will be primary US policies of one-year, fixed-premium terms. The pools will be formed in January and July, and four quarterly contracts are to be traded. Crucial trading information about the claims experience of participating insurers will be collected by the exchange from state regulators for dissemination to the market participants.

OPTIONS TRADING

Unlike futures, options contracts do not put the purchaser under any actual obligation. A standard option contract gives the owner the right but not the obligation to buy or sell a set quantity of a particular instrument (shares, commodities etc.) at a specified price for a specified period of time. An option granting the right to buy is known as a "call option", and an option granting the right to sell is known as a "put option". The specified price of the option at which the option holder may buy or sell the underlying instrument, that is "exercise the option", is known as the "striking price". The buyer or taker of the option will pay a premium to the seller, also known as the grantor or writer. Once the premium has been paid, the option contract is binding only on the seller and may, therefore, be seen as a unilateral contract, in contrast to a futures contract which is a bilateral contract in that the buyer is obliged to buy and the seller obliged to sell.

The effect of this difference between an option and a futures contract is that the option holder has potential known losses which are limited to the value of the premium paid for the option but has, in theory, unlimited scope for profits—the converse is, of course, true of the options writer, who has profits limited to the premium paid and unlimited scope for losses. Against this, the buyer and seller of a futures contract both have equal potential for profit or loss.

In most cases, the options writers will be holding the underlying instrument and making use of the premiums received from writing options to enhance their portfolio return. Options writers not holding the underlying instrument are known as "naked" writers, receiving a fixed premium income but running the risk that the option may be exercised which would immediately force them to deal in the underlying market to cover their exposure.

There are three basic types of option: over-the-counter (OTC) options; dealer options; and exchange-traded options. OTC and dealer options are "traditional" options and are individually-tailored contracts. In OTC contracts the striking price, premium and duration will all be negotiated separately with each taker. The difference between an OTC option and a dealer option is that in the latter case the grantor will have set the striking price and expiry date, leaving only the premium to be negotiated.

Exchange-traded options (ETOs), more commonly known simply as traded options, are a relatively recent phenomenon. ETOs are a logical extension of dealer options in that the market publishes striking prices and expiry dates, thus standardizing the product and allowing for secondary trading. The level of premium is arrived at through competitive pricing by market makers from whom the purchaser buys the ETO. The resale and the exercise of the ETO are guaranteed via the market's clearing mechanism. These traded options were first introduced when the Chicago Board Options Exchange (CBOE) pioneered the listing of equity options in 1973, offering investors the chance to take a view on the future price performance of shares. Ten years later, in 1983, the CBOE was also the first market to establish an exchange-traded stock index option. Throughout the late 1970s and the 1980s, the availability of traded options mushroomed. Although options were introduced on several commodities, in the first instance these were solely options on the underlying commodity, conferring the right to buy or sell a specified amount of that commodity.

Now several exchanges offer options on futures, which are not based directly on the underlying commodity but on the futures contract. Options on futures contracts allow traders to trade their views without committing substantial resources. Through the purchase of an option, the trader has limited his losses if his expectations are not fulfilled but can look forward to profits if he is proved right. However, it should be remembered that, because the underlying instrument in this case is a futures contract rather than a tangible commodity, etc., any potential move in price expected by the trader may well already be discounted in the futures price itself. Hedging through the use of options on futures rather than merely with futures contracts is becoming increasingly popular in the markets because, unlike a futures hedge, the options hedge has not locked the dealer into what might become an adverse position which he must sell at a substantial loss.

Further refinements to options contracts are continuously being tried. Two of the most straightforward variations are "American-style" and "European-style" options. These terms have no geographical significance whatsoever! However, the difference between the two is an important one. An American-style option may be exercised by the holder at any time after it is purchased, until it expires. A European-style option may be exercised only during a specified period, which may be as short as a single business day, prior to expiry.

Among the "exotic options" are "lookback" options which offer the right to buy or sell at, respectively, the lowest or highest price achieved by the underlying instrument over the life of the option. "Knock in/knock out" options only come into being, or cease to exist, if the underlying price falls below a specified level.

It should be obvious, given the unlimited potential of options for profits on the part of the purchaser and losses on the part of the writer, that getting the price, the premium, right is very important indeed. The option premium may be divided into two component parts: intrinsic value and time value. The intrinsic value of the option is merely a reflection of by how much it is "in the money", that is, when the striking price of the option is higher (for a put) or lower (for a call) than the market price of the underlying instrument. Let us take a simple example. If the gold price is US$400/ounce, a put option with a strike price of US$420, giving the right to sell gold at US$20 above the prevailing market price is US$20 in the money. A put option with a strike price of US$395 is "out of the money", one would not, after all, willingly bother to exercise the right to sell gold at a price below that in the general market! A put option with a strike price of US$400 would be said to be "at the money", with the strike price matching that of the current market price.

Staying with the example of gold at US$400, a call option with a strike value of US$395 would be in the money, conferring the right to purchase gold at below the market price; and, of course, a call option with a strike price of US$420 would be out of the money—one would not bother to exercise an option granting the right to purchase at more than the prevailing market price!

It is easy enough to calculate the intrinsic value of an option but it is not such an easy matter to calculate the proper time value of an option. Four main factors affect time value: the duration of the option, i.e. the time remaining until expiration; the historical price volatility of the underlying instrument; the supply of the option; and demand for the option. The longer the remaining duration the higher the time value, because there is greater potential for the option to move into the money. Volatility is the measurement of price change over time. Obviously the more volatile the price of the underlying instrument, the greater is the likelihood that the option will develop or increase in intrinsic value. Finally, the laws of supply and demand affect options in much the same way as they do any other traded instrument—the greater the demand, the higher the premium will go until equilibrium is reached between buyers and sellers.

It should be noted that for European-style options, the limited period of exercisability means that, except when the option is exercisable, the only means of recovering its value is by selling it at its then market price in the secondary market. During the time when a European-style option cannot be exercised it has no intrinsic value and its market price will depend solely on time value, the potential that the option may ultimately be exercisable at a profit.

To demonstrate the performance of a straightforward equity-based call option let us assume that three investors each have US$5,000 to invest and that each anticipates an increase in the price of ABC stock, currently US$50 a share. Investor A invests his money in 100 shares of ABC. Investor B invests US$500 in the purchase of an ABC 50 call (covering 100 ABC shares) at a premium of US$5 a share and invests the remaining US$4,500 in a relatively risk-free investment such as Treasury bonds. Investor C invests his entire US$5,000 in ten ABC 50 calls. For the purposes of this example, it is assumed that all of the options are purchased when they have six months remaining until expiration, and that the risk-free investment undertaken by investor B bears interest at an annual rate of 10 per cent—which means that a US$4,500 investment will earn US$225 in interest over six months.

If the options are sold or exercised immediately before expiry, assuming it is profitable to do so, the following table illustrates the outcome for each investor at a given price of ABC stock at the end of the six-month period.

ABC stock price at expiration of option	Investor A		Investor B		Investor C	
	Profit or loss	% Return	Profit or loss	% Return	Profit or loss	% Return
62	+1200	+24	+925	+18.5	+7000	+140
58	+800	+16	+525	+10.5	+3000	+60
54	+400	+8	+125	+2.5	−1000	−20
50	0	0	−275	−5.5	−5000	−100
46	−400	−8	−275	−5.5	−5000	−100
42	−800	−16	−275	−5.5	−5000	−100
38	−1200	−24	−275	−5.5	−5000	−100

(Table source: The Options Clearing Corporation, Chicago 1987)

The table demonstrates how increased leverage results in both greater profit potential and greater risk of loss. Investor C, as the most leveraged of the three, would realize the highest return if the price rose significantly, but would incur a loss even if the price rose by almost 10 per cent and would lose his investment if the stock price held unchanged or fell.

Options become valueless upon expiration, which means that an options purchaser must not only be right about the direction of the anticipated price change but must also be right about when such a price change will occur.

BETTING

For the pure speculator who is jaded with watching horses and dogs run round in circles and who does not wish to become involved in the complexities of the markets themselves, there are firms of financial bookmakers offering a variety of markets. For example, IG Index in London offers markets in several commodities and derivatives futures and options as well as making "grey markets" in new share issues, notably of the privatized companies. Among the potential attractions to the speculator are the facts that transactions with financial bookmakers are free of capital gains tax and that they may be made with a smaller capital commitment than participation on the actual market might require. However, it should also be borne in mind that the risks remain similar to those incurred when participating in the underlying futures markets.

Unlike a conventional bookmakers, the financial bookmaker does not quote odds, but will quote a price spread against which the punter will bet, either on the price rising above the top of the spread, or falling below the bottom of the spread. "Up bets" are always opened at the higher end of the quotation and "Down bets" at the lower end. When the bet is closed, it is the other way round, with Up bets being closed against the lower price and vice versa. It is also worth remembering that you are not betting on the underlying commodity or derivative itself but on the quotation offered by the bookmaker. The price he offers will depend on the amount of betting he has received and how well he has managed to lay off his risk by hedging on the underlying market.

GLOBEX AND THE DEMISE OF THE TRADING FLOOR

The commencement of trading on the International Futures Exchange (Bermuda) at the end of October 1984 marked the beginning of a new stage of development in the automation of futures markets. Intex was the first completely computerized futures exchange with no trading floor. It is no longer alone in this respect, the New Zealand Futures Exchange also operates without a floor. Several other exchanges have also gone part of the way down the automation route with certain contracts traded on screen and, in some cases, an automated trading session after the official market close. It is likely that the continued internationalization of the world's markets will accentuate the trend towards automation. Truly international markets are disembodied markets, a concept which appears close to fruition with the development of GLOBEX, an international electronic trading system for futures and options, in which orders are matched on time and price priority. GLOBEX is due to be trading by May 1992.

This automated futures and options trading system is the result of a collaboration, initially between the international information provider Reuters and the Chicago Mercantile Exchange (CME). Several futures exchanges will have equal access to terminals and equal trading rights on the system. These partner exchanges retain control, ownership, clearing and responsibility for their own products and may choose what hours their contracts are traded on GLOBEX. The system was originally conceived as an after-hours market-place, after the demonstrable success of after-hours trading in the Sydney Futures Exchange's SYCOM system and the London International Financial Futures Exchange's (LIFFE) APT system. However, the CME is now considering placing some of its less active futures contracts on the electronic market to trade alongside the pit sessions through the day.

Among the exchanges around the world which have already committed themselves to participating in GLOBEX, the CME is being joined by the Chicago Board of Trade and the French financial futures exchange, MATIF. Talks are also at advanced stages with the New York Mercantile Exchange (NYMEX); the Sydney Futures Exchange, which was actually the first non-US market to profess interest in joining GLOBEX; with LIFFE; the Singapore International Monetary Exchange; and the Deutsche Terminbörse.

Individual exchanges are also continuing to develop their own screen-based systems. For example, NYMEX announced plans for its own after-hours electronic trading system in March 1991, to be called Access and due to be launched by the end of 1992. However, the demise, in April 1991, of the London FOX's rubber futures contract, having languished untraded since the previous November, followed by the scandal surrounding the collapse of the property futures contracts, demonstrates that the route to screen-based trading is not necessarily a smooth one. After the suspension of the property futures contracts, the exchange began to review returning most of the remaining screen-based contracts to open outcry pits. In November, the rice futures contract was closed after open interest, the number of contracts outstanding, fell to zero.

CHAPTER 6

PLAYERS AND REFEREES

The players on the world's markets include the banks and brokers who make markets and sell financial services, and the investment institutions, individual investors and companies who use the markets and purchase services. The referees tend to be national bodies; cross-border regulation of markets remains limited, the notable exception being the role of the institutions of the European Community and their growing importance in the regulation of the EC financial markets.

At the centre of the world's financial system are the banks. The national central banks which play an important role in both the regulation of and as participants in the financial markets (*see Chapter Seven*) are relatively modern phenomena by comparison with the origins of commercial banking. The importance of gold as a monetary medium meant that the first bankers were goldsmiths holding gold belonging to others in return for receipts; these receipts were the first "paper" money, the first banknotes.

Among the first bankers in the city of London were Italian goldsmiths from Lombardy, a fact commemorated in the name of Lombard Street in the modern city. However, the banking industry owes rather more of a debt than this to the Italian smiths who settled in London with land grants from King Edward I in the Middle Ages. The word "bank" is an English corruption of the Italian *banco*, meaning bench. Quite simply, the role of the bank is to take deposits and to make loans and, just as simply, the way to make a profit as a bank is to charge a higher rate of interest for the money lent than that paid out on the money received on deposit. There are, of course, a multitude of methods by which these simple business aims are achieved or, in several spectacular cases, not achieved.

From this simple basis there have evolved several types of banking institutions. In the UK, the Banking Act of 1979 defines a bank, for the purposes of regulation by the central bank, the Bank of England, as a deposit-taking institution with a wide range of banking services according to a number of set criteria. The Act also stipulates the net assets a bank must hold to be able to operate. The world's banks settle their debts to each other through a clearing system, similar in concept to that used by the world's trading exchanges. In fact, the operations of banks in the world's money markets may be likened to those of brokers on stock or commodity markets. There is, of course, no established exchange where the banks meet but their dealings in money are settled through a clearing system and they are regulated by the national central banks under the umbrella of the Bank for International Settlements (*see Chapter Seven*).

As well as providing deposit-taking and borrowing facilities for individual and corporate customers, the banks play a major role in several of the markets. The Euromarket is run by the banks and corporate bond issues (*see Chapter Three*) are organized by banks. The over-the-counter foreign exchange market (*see Chapter Four*) is dominated by the major commercial banks.

One of the most notable developments in the banking sector in recent year has been the coming together of the previously separate retail banking and life insurance sectors, a concept known by its French or German title, respectively *bancassurance* or *allfinanz*. Although the idea dates back to the 1940s when the French-Canadian Desjardins banks began selling life insurance, it is only within the last five years that it has become a global phenomenon. The essence of the concept is the provision of a full range of financial services by a single institution to its customers. The two principal areas affected are traditional consumer banking and life insurance, but logically the concept could extend to all personal financial services, including general insurance, as well as to business customers.

In addition to the commercial banks (also known as clearing banks), there are mutual institutions, such as the building societies in the UK and the mutual savings banks (also known as "savings & loans", "S&Ls" or "thrifts") in the USA. These mutual institutions are legally owned by their depositors. Deregulation in both the UK and the USA in the 1970s and 1980s has blurred the distinction between the mutual institutions and the banks, with similar services being offered to customers by both sectors. This deregulation also had the unfortunate effect in the USA of allowing inexperienced mutual bankers to lose massive sums of money on poor investments, making something of a mockery of their nickname "thrifts".

There are three basic models of banks and banking systems operating in the world: the German model; the UK model; and the more fragmented US/Japanese model. In the German model of universal banking, the full range of banking and financial services is provided within a single legal entity. There is no holding company and separate subsidiaries are used only at the convenience of the bank or when required by foreign regulatory authorities for particular activities conducted outside Germany. In most countries with this kind of system, which is broadly similar to that in the Netherlands and Switzerland and, to a lesser extent, that in France and Italy, banks may, and often do, own sizeable equity stakes in commercial companies. However, the opposite is generally not the case, that is to say, manufacturing and other non-financial firms do not typically own and control banks.

The UK-style universal bank differs from the German model in three ways: first, separate legal subsidiaries are more common; second, bank holding of equity in commercial firms is far less common; and third, combinations of banking and insurance firms are also less common.

The more fragmented systems such as those which currently exist in the USA and Japan tend to have rigid legal and operational distinctions between classes of financial institutions, including most notably the separation between commercial and investment banking. However, even between the US and Japanese systems, important differences exist. For example, the bank or financial services holding company is unique to the USA, holding companies do not exist in Japan and, in fact, are strictly forbidden by law. The USA is the only major country which does not have a true national banking system. A crazy-quilt pattern of state and federal laws and regulations currently govern various aspects of interstate banking. In some states in the USA, unit-banking laws stipulate that each bank be a discrete enterprise without branches. With the sole exception of Japan, the USA is the only country with a fragmented banking system that restricts the type of financial products and services which may be offered by particular classes of institutions.

In his 1991 state of the nation address, President Bush announced plans to reform the US banking system. If all the proposals had been adopted they would have resulted in the demise of the 1927 McFadden Act, which limited interstate banking, the 1933 Glass-Steagall Act, which prevents commercial banks from engaging in investment banking and vice versa, and the Bank Holding Act of 1956, which prevents industrial companies from owing banks. The proposals, submitted to Congress in detail by the US Treasury, also called for the regulation of banks and savings and loans to be consolidated, with nationally chartered banks and S&Ls to be regulated by a new Treasury agency to be called the Federal Banking Agency.

The US financial system is in dire need of overhaul, but Congress passed only a significantly watered-down version of President Bush's proposals. Congressional subcommittees reduced the scope of the reform, voting to place strict limitations on US banks' powers to offer securities. Furthermore, the chairman of the Securities and Exchange Commission, Richard Breeden, stated his agency's opposition to the adoption of a universal banking system.

Investment banks, also known in the UK as merchant banks, operate more intimately in the established financial exchanges than the commercial banks. In the US markets, the primary role of the investment bank is the purchase of new issues and the onward placement of these securities with investors. The merchant banks were at one time also known as accepting houses, because of their role in accepting bills of exchange. They may also provide risk capital, deal in gold bullion and in insurance. The merchant banks are active in the Euromarket and the stock market, earning fees through the underwriting of new issues of bonds and shares.

Unlike the clearing banks, these institutions tend not to have a large pool of personal depositors. The main source of their funds is fee income and, in recent years, the main source of this has been merger and acquisition activity in the stock markets. For the successful bidder, a takeover can be an expensive affair, with not only his own costs to meet but also those of the target company. For example, fees to the merchant banks generated by Guinness's acquisition of Distillers in 1986 amounted to £110 million, or 4.4 per cent of the £2.5 billion takeover.

There are two main sources of income for the merchant banks in takeover activity: first, advisory fees; and second, underwriting commissions. Unless the takeover has already been agreed by the management of the target company, the initial bid is likely to be rejected. Both predator and target are then likely to turn to their respective merchant banks, the one to ensure that the offer price is sufficiently attractive to investors in the target, and the other to prove that it is not. Both will try to persuade the shareholders of the target that they offer the best prospect for a long-term investment.

Underwriting commissions in takeover battles have grown in importance with the use of a cash alternative in bids. There are three basic instruments the bidder can offer to shareholders in the target company: cash; shares; and convertible or fixed loan stock. A bid can be made up of any one, two or even all three of these components in varying degrees of importance. Under certain circumstances, the bidding company is required by law to make a cash offer; for example, in the UK, if a person or company acquires a stake of 30 per cent or more of the voting rights of a company, or if a person holding between 30 and 50 per cent acquires more than a further 2 per cent of the voting rights in a twelve month period. In these circumstances the bid, known as a mandatory offer, must be in cash or must include a cash alternative, and be worth not less than the highest price paid in the market by the bidder within the last twelve months.

The cash alternative entails an underwriter agreeing to provide target company shareholders with cash in exchange for which he will receive shares in the bidding company. There is obviously a risk that the latter shares may fall in value, so the underwriter is normally paid a set percentage of the amount underwritten. In a rising or bull market for shares, the merchant bank is virtually assured of making a profit, the value of the bid will be higher and the risk of a fall in the bidding company's own share price will be reduced.

Both advisory fees and underwriting commissions tend to be fixed percentages of the value of the deal involved. The smaller the deal, the higher the advisory fee is likely to be, given that the same amount of resources are likely to be committed, from around 1 per cent for a small deal, the merchant bank's fee is likely to fall to 0.5 per cent for a medium-sized deal and, in certain cases, an advisory fee may be waived if the underwriting commission being generated will itself ensure an adequate return.

Underwriting commission is normally split three ways, with the merchant bank, the lead underwriter responsible for organizing the underwriting of the cash alternative, taking 0.5 per cent, the stock broker involved in the market transactions taking 0.25 per cent, and the investment institutions, the sub-underwriters which provide the cash, 0.5 per cent for the first thirty days, a further 0.125 per cent for each subsequent week and a 0.75 per cent acceptance payment when the takeover is completed. However, towards the end of the 1980s, it became usual for the investment banks to agree to a success-related formula, i.e. taking a higher percentage fee if the bid succeeded but a lower fee if the bid failed. Given that fee income from takeover activity is a percentage of the value of the deal, the increase in large takeovers in the mid- to late-1980s meant a concomitant increase in fee income earned by investment banks, especially in the USA and the UK.

In the world's exchanges themselves, on the trading floors or at the computer screens, are the brokers. Broking firms tend nowadays to be part of much larger companies. Many brokers on the commodity markets are merely the trading arms of primary commodity producers and brokers on the securities and financial markets are usually part of a large financial services company, often but not always a bank.

The London stock market was the world's only major securities market where there was a rigid separation between stockbrokers, acting as agents for clients, and stockjobbers, buying and selling on their own behalf. This distinction went with Big Bang on 27 October 1986 and in its place came market makers, dealers prepared to buy and sell specified securities at all times, thus making a market in them. At one remove from the market are stockbrokers, also known in the USA as commission brokers, who act as agents for client investors in return for a fee or commission. On the futures markets, small dealing companies operating on their own account continue to thrive. These dealers are known as "locals" or "floor traders" to distinguish them from brokers who accept client orders.

All the above may count as investors themselves, but by and large they are more often the purveyors of market/exchange-based financial services to investors.

The growing internationalization of markets and of investment holdings has resulted in an increasing role for the administrators; those who, for example, ensure that a share sold in Tokyo ends up with its purchaser in the USA. These administrators are known as global custodians and it is their job to ensure that international business flows smoothly through the world's financial markets. Estimates of funds held in global custody in 1990 vary from US$830 billion to US$1.7 trillion and the business is estimated to be growing at a rate of around 25 per cent a year.

Quite simply, global custody is the settlement and safekeeping of assets on a global basis. Institutional investors may hold German bonds, UK shares, Japanese government bonds and cash in US dollars. Keeping track of these investments and following the requisite procedures for each is a complex task and one for which the investment institutions call in the experts, the global custodians. The custodian does not take investment decisions but merely ensures that the appropriate procedures are complied with on the sale or purchase of the assets and ensures that funds are remitted correctly.

INVESTORS

The investment community is made up of individual investors and institutions. Individual investors have become less and less important to the financial markets because of the small size of the funds involved. In fact, unless he or she is very wealthy, the individual or "small" investor tends not to invest directly in the financial markets but rather through the institutions. There are four main types of investment institution: the pension funds; the insurance companies; the investment trusts; and the unit trusts. In the UK market, for example, the pension funds are the largest of these four groups, with some £130 billion pounds in assets. They own almost a third of all the shares listed on the UK stock market. Private pension funds account for just over half of all pension fund assets, followed by public sector funds and local government funds.

In the UK, the insurance companies have assets worth some £110 billion. Insurance funds include both those run by large composite insurers and those managed by the life insurance companies.

Investment trusts are publicly-quoted companies whose business is the purchase of shares in other companies. The advantage to the individual investor in purchasing the shares of an investment trust is that he immediately achieves the spread of risk which assembling his own portfolio of shares would also achieve, but at a much lower cost. Investment trusts are "closed-end" funds, that is to say, they have a fixed number of shares in issue.

Unit trusts, also known as mutual funds, are "open-ended" funds. There is no limit to the number of units. These trusts are also a collective form of investment in which the trusts purchase a portfolio of investments to reduce risk. Investors purchase units which fluctuate in value according to the interest and dividends paid on the underlying securities. Unlike investment trusts, the investor does not share in the profits of the organization managing the trust. The unit trust management derives its income from a regular service charge and from the difference between the price at which it sells the units to investors (the offer price) and the price at which it buys the units back (the bid price).

MARKET REGULATORS

The balance between strict regulation and free markets has not always been an easy one to strike. That too strict a regulatory environment stifles business is evident in the fact that the markets in the UK, where "deregulation" took place in the mid-1980s with a major overhaul of the regulatory environment, expanded more swiftly than those elsewhere in western Europe. However, it is also true that stringent regulation can provide great security. Speaking at a seminar on the junk bond market in 1989, Robert L. Clarke, an official with the US central bank, the Federal Reserve, related the following story:

"A friend of mine gave me a book that was published in the United States at the turn of the century. The book was titled *The Business Guide: or Safe methods of Business* ...a banking system free from risk could be devised it argued. And in defence of its position, *The Business Guide* pointed to China, where banks never failed. Why?

"In the words of *The Business Guide*: '...the law in China provides that, when a bank fails, every man connected with it, including the managers and clerks, shall have his head chopped off, and they are all thrown in a heap, together with the books of the firm. This law has had such a beneficial effect that not a single Chinese bank has suspended payment within the last 500 years.'"

The modern approach to the role of finance is more relaxed than the custodial view prevalent in imperial China. The needs of savers and investors to have their investment secure are balanced by the need to provide resources necessary for economic growth. The financial system cannot eliminate risk, rather it is expected to assess and manage risks. Ultimate oversight of the financial markets rests with government ministries and the central banks (*see Chapter Seven*). The UK regulatory environment is reviewed in detail below and the US regime is described in brief.

In the UK, for example, the Treasury and the Department of Trade and Industry (DTI) are the responsible ministries. The Bank of England oversees the banking sector, attempting to ensure that banks have adequate capital, have made appropriate provisions against bad debts and have enough ready cash, or liquidity, to meet likely withdrawals. The Bank is also involved in the supervision of certain other institutions–primarily those operating as brokers and marketmakers in those financial markets where the Bank is itself active, such as gilts, bullion and foreign exchange.

The direct supervision of investment business in the UK falls under the Securities and Investments Board (SIB) and the self-regulatory bodies which report to it. The Financial Services Act 1986 established a comprehensive system of investor protection through the authorization and supervision of those carrying on investment businesses. The SIB was established to oversee the system, under the overall supervision of the DTI. However, the original regulations were heavily criticized as too complex and too expensive to operate, and in 1990 the SIB adopted simplified regulatory rulebooks.

Under the aegis of the SIB are self-regulating organizations (SROs), recognized professional bodies (RPBs) and recognized investment exchanges (RIEs).

The RPBs cover those professions such as lawyers and accountants which may give investment advice and management as a small part of their business.

There were originally five SROs: The Securities Association (TSA) for firms dealing and broking in securities; the Financial Intermediaries, Managers and Brokers Regulatory Association (FIMBRA) for investment brokers and advisers, insurance and unit trust brokers; the Life and Unit Trust Regulatory Organization (LAUTRO) for firms selling or managing life assurance and unit trusts; the Investment

Management Regulatory Organization (IMRO) for companies advising on and managing investments; and the Association of Futures Brokers and Dealers (AFBD) for companies dealing and broking in futures and options. In 1990, the TSA and the AFBD merged, creating the Securities and Futures Authority. The SROs are responsible for ensuring their members follow the guidelines laid down by the SIB and also for monitoring their members' capital adequacy.

The RIEs are trading markets authorized by the SIB to operate in the UK. To be recognized, an exchange must have an established structure, rules and adequate financial resources which offer a fair and efficient market to enable trading. The SIB also recognizes overseas exchanges, describing them as "designated investment exchanges", provided that they are properly regulated in their own country.

In addition to the SIB and the bodies it has authorized, the Department of Trade and Industry also has overall responsibility for competition policy and takes the final decisions to stop or change anti-competitive behaviour. The Office of Fair Trading (OFT) keeps a watch on monopolies and mergers, restrictive agreements and anti-competitive practices. The Monopolies and Mergers Commission (MMC) investigates and reports on potential anti-competitive practices on matters referred to it by the DTI and the OFT. The European Commission, the executive of the European Economic Community, also has powers to act when competition in trade between members of the European Community is affected (*see below*).

These agencies do not generally involve themselves directly in the day-to-day activities of the financial markets. However, the the MMC is asked by the DTI to review certain mergers in the stock market. Mergers are only referred to the MMC if the assets to be taken over are more than £30 million; or a 25 per cent share of a given market is created or increased.

In addition to the statutory bodies, the Takeover Panel, established in 1968, administers the City Code on Takeovers and Mergers. The main aim of the panel is to ensure equality of treatment and opportunity for all shareholders in takeover bids. Although the panel is a non-statutory body, it is supported by the SROs and RIEs which are backed by law.

In the USA, the Treasury Department and the Federal Reserve share responsibility for the oversight of the banking sector and the money markets.

The federal agency responsible for the regulation of the markets in securities is the Securities and Exchange Commission (SEC), established in 1934. The Commodity Futures Trading Commission (CFTC) was set up in 1974 to oversee the conduct of business on the commodity futures exchanges.

The SEC regulates the US stock exchanges, brokers and investment advisers. The US financial markets, like the UK markets, operate a system of self-regulatory organizations. In 1990, twenty-three US equity and futures markets reached agreement on sharing regulatory information concerning mutual member firms considered at risk of falling below the "early warning" capital requirements prescribed by either the SROs or the federal government.

The CFTC, though nominally on a par with the SEC, has been the subject of fierce battles in Congress, where supporters of the Treasury Department and the SEC have been pressing for the agency to be made subordinate to the SEC. The main source of this friction has been the development of futures and options on stock market indices, an area claimed as under their jurisdiction by both the CFTC and the SEC. So far the CFTC has succeeded in maintaining its independence and, under the terms of the 1974 Act which established the agency, supervises "all services, rights, and interests in which contracts for future delivery are presently or in the future dealt in."

In 1990, the chairman of the CFTC, Wendy Gramm, said the agency would focus on breaking down regulatory barriers between US and overseas futures markets and work towards the harmonization of regulations to enhance cross-trading between domestic and international markets.

As well as the national regulation of financial markets, there are international and supranational regulatory bodies. The Bank for International Settlements (*see Chapter Seven*) lays down the broad guidelines on capital adequacy for banks which are followed by the national central banks. There are now attempts to establish international capital adequacy requirements for securities firms. The most advanced of these proposals is the European Commission's Capital Adequacy Directive planned to come into force in 1993. However, the EC's directive applies only to non-bank securities firms in Europe. The Bank for International Settlements is working on extending its capital adequacy regulations and the International Organization for Securities Commissions, a forum for securities regulators and trade associations, is also working to develop international guidelines.

Since September 1990, the EC also has powers to investigate corporate mergers affect the European market. The current threshold for mergers to be investigated by the EC is a combined turnover of ECU 5 billion (around £3.5 billion). This remit is not limited to cross-border takeovers within the European Community but also means the EC may investigate mergers between companies outside the Community if they have significant markets within it. It includes mergers within the Community's national markets as well.

SCANDALS

Dr Johnson said, "There are few ways in which a man can be more innocently employed than in getting money." However, an earlier authority, the *Bible*, claims, "The love of money is the root of all evil." The world's financial markets exist somewhere between these two extremes. The South Sea Bubble (*see Chapter One*) provides us with early examples of attempts to take advantage of man's cupidity. More recently, through the 1980s and into the 1990s there have been numerous examples of boundaries being overstepped.

Investor confidence is affected by the quality and integrity of financial markets and services. There are basically three activities which may seriously impair market integrity: insider dealing; investment fraud and market manipulation. Although all three activities are criminal offences in both the UK and the USA, this is not the case in all of the world's financial markets. Under UK law, the crime of insider dealing is specifically defined in the Companies Securities (Insider Dealing) Act 1985 and the offences of investment fraud and market manipulation are defined in Section 47 of the Financial Services Act.

Insider dealing was first made a criminal offence in the UK in 1980. Prior to that time the London Stock Exchange investigated suspected dealings based on inside information. Although insider dealing was neither a criminal nor a civil offence, if such dealing involved directors of public companies or members of the Exchange, then almost certainly the codes of dealing of the Exchange itself and the Takeover Panel would have been breached. However, the sanctions available were severely limited.

In simple terms, insider dealing involves an individual who knowingly deals in a financial product, usually securities, while in possession of unpublished price sensitive information. Investment fraud means that it is an offence for any person to make a misleading statement, promise or forecast so as to induce another party to enter into an investment agreement, or to exercise any rights conferred by an investment agreement, or to refrain from doing so. Market manipulation is described as being an offence for any person to create a false or misleading impression as to the price or value of an investment with the purpose of inducing others to deal, or to refrain from dealing, in investments. It may also involve misleading investors as to the size or liquidity of a market for the investment concerned.

Although not all the crises which rock financial markets with apparently monotonous regularity can be ascribed to specifically criminal behaviour, most of the scandals described below do exhibit varying degrees of criminality.

The year 1991 proved to be something of a vintage year for scandal in the world's financial markets. In New York, one of the leading US investment banks, Salomon Brothers, was discovered to have been rigging the trillion-dollar US government bond market, buying up huge amounts of certain issues, enabling it to manipulate the price.

In London, the London FOX was revealed to have been creating a false market in certain of its futures contracts. The Bank of England acted to close the Bank of Credit & Commerce International (BCCI) in concert with central banks in the United States, Luxemburg, Cayman Islands, Spain and France. Although BCCI had been viewed with deep suspicion by both regulators and market players for some time, it was only during a probe conducted by auditors Price Waterhouse that a "bank within a bank", created to hide losses on bad trades and loans, was discovered. The bank has been implicated in the laundering of drug money for the Colombian Medellin cocaine cartel. There have also been suggestions of links to terrorists and to the US Central Intelligence Agency. How many of the allegations are true and just how much money has been lost may take some years to uncover.

In Tokyo, several banking frauds were uncovered and a major scandal broke on the stock market involving organized crime and the improper reimbursement of client losses by the leading stock brokerages (*see below*).

In addition to these new scandals, in London the second trial of those involved in the Guinness affair began. Dating back to the takeover of Distillers by Guinness in 1986, the trial centres round a support operation organized for Guinness shares to maintain the value of the company's bid, which was being hotly contested by Argyll.

"Greed Is Good"

In 1985, Ivan F. Boesky wrote a book called *Merger Mania-Arbitrage: Wall Street's best kept money-making secret*. In the book, he sets out to explain "risk arbitrage" as an investment strategy. It is, he said, in essence the calculation of the risk of whether or not a merger will be consummated and the committal of sums of money accordingly. There are many factors to be considered, Boesky claimed, including the value of the deal, timing, cost of money to the investor, fluctuating prices, economic changes, litigation, and government actions. Risks can be limited through careful evaluation; to practise risk arbitrage, said

Boesky, requires constant vigilance. As history shows, however, having inside information can help a great deal too!

Ivan Boesky was known as the "King of the Arbs", "arbs" being short for arbitrageurs. Boesky had already been using inside information before his trading relationship with Michael Milken was established. Dennis Levine, a trader with Drexel Burnham Lambert's New York office had been feeding information to Boesky in return for cash pay-offs. It was Levine's arrest and his co-operation with the authorities which brought Boesky to book. In turn, Boesky bargained with the authorities. Levine was sentenced to two years in a minimum security prison, of which he served seventeen months, and fined US$11.6 million. Boesky received a three-year sentence, of which he served two, and was fined US$100 million. However, Boesky was not asked by the authorities to disclose details of any trades they did not already know about and, in moves which later led to heavy criticism of the District Attorney, was allowed to close out several of his market positions before his agreement to co-operate with the authorities was made public.

In March 1989, Michael Milken was indicted on ninety-eight counts. On 21 November 1990, following plea bargaining, he pleaded guilty to six felonies and was sentenced to ten years in prison–two years each on five of the six counts, to run consecutively-and received a US$600 million fine. Drexel Burnham Lambert itself had already settled separately, paying a US$650 million fine. In February 1990, the firm filed for protection from its creditors to carry out a re-organization of its affairs under chapter 11 of the US Bankruptcy Reform Act 1978.

The actual scope of the insider dealings undertaken by Boesky and Milken did not immediately come into the public domain since virtually all those charged ended up striking some kind of plea-bargaining deal. Milken had been instrumental in the development of the junk bond market (*see Chapter Three*), making both himself and Drexel a great deal of money. Junk bonds and the takeover spree they helped fuel in the US markets in the mid-1980s were and are not illegal.

However, it appears Milken had systematically robbed clients by trading on their confidential information for his own gain and regularly manipulated securities prices to force deals on which he and Drexel would profit from inflated fees. The teamwork of Milken's information and Boesky's buying power can be illustrated by reference to one of the many takeovers in which they were active. In 1985, a Drexel client, the Maxxam Group, made a bid for Pacific Lumber.

Boesky, playing his role as "arb", began buying Pacific Lumber shares. Milken, privy to the bid, knew the price Maxxam was willing to pay to win. Milken shared ownership of the position Boesky built up in

Pacific Lumber, and agreed to cover any possible losses. In declaring his shareholding to the SEC, Boesky did not, of course, mention Milken's involvement. Pacific Lumber resisted Maxxam's initial bid, but when the offer was increased the company, under pressure from Maxxam and the threat apparently posed by Boesky, capitulated.

Milken's scheme earned Drexel some US$20 million in fees from Maxxam. At the same time, he and Boesky made a profit of around US$1 million from their insider trading. Some time later, Pacific Lumber, now controlled by Maxxam, ran into problems from the conservationist lobby by felling tracts of redwood forest to help meet the interest payments on junk bonds obligingly provided by Milken to fund the takeover.

As one further example, Milken's most personally rewarding deal may have been the taking of warrants in Beatrice Co. in connection with the buy-out of the company by Kohlberg Kravis Roberts & Co. in 1986. Milken got the warrants, which gave the right to purchase Beatrice shares at a low price, from Kohlberg Kravis Roberts by arguing that he needed to offer them to clients as an inducement to buy the junk bonds issued by Beatrice to fund the buy-out. Milken actually kept most of these warrants for Drexel, lodging them in his own business. The warrants were ultimately worth an estimated US$650 million.

TOKYO–BROKERS AND GANGSTERS

Throughout the summer of 1991, revelations came from the stock market in Tokyo. Stories of links to gangsters–the *yakuza*, improper reimbursement of client losses by brokers and accusations of share price ramping (the practice of advising favoured clients to buy certain shares and then pushing them strongly at smaller investors as a rising stock to get into) all helped to reveal that much of the Tokyo stock market's strength through the mid- to late 1980s was built on "blue smoke and mirrors".

Once "ambulance" shares rode to the rescue of favoured investors, "political stocks" filled campaign coffers and "finance stocks" defied economic logic and rose. The longer term implications of the truth behind these moves are not easily calculated. Much of the strength of corporate and financial Japan and the entrance, especially, of Japanese financial institutions onto the world markets, was funded through rising share prices and rocketing property values in Tokyo. Japanese banks are now retrenching from some of their global ambitions, having seen their equity and property assets collapse in value.

Yakuza links to corporate Japan have been a known problem for some time, even at the relatively mundane level of quasi-blackmail, using the threat of disruption at annual general meetings. The, to western eyes, unusual practice in which some 3,000 companies all hold their AGMs on the same day is merely an attempt to limit such disruption and reduce corporate vulnerability to the *yakuza*.

However, the stories which appeared in the summer of 1991 proved too strong even for the light regulatory hand of the Ministry of Finance. Share price manipulation is prohibited by the Japanese Securities Exchange Law but the law is vague and has rarely been enforced. As the scandal trickled into the news through the summer, seventeen leading brokerage firms admitted they reimbursed favoured clients to the tune of nearly US$1.3 billion for losses suffered when the stock market fell in 1990. Although such compensation is not actually illegal, unless promised in advance, it does contravene a Ministry of Finance directive. However, the situation was exacerbated when Japanese newspapers uncovered documents showing that the Ministry had known about the practice since 1984 and had taken no action.

The country's biggest brokerage, Nomura, had also been linked to Susumu Ishii, in 1989 boss of the country's second largest crime syndicate. Nomura is said to have helped Ishii buy 27.4 million shares in the railway company Tokyu Corp., and push it artificially high before selling. The brokerage's improper excessive recommendation of shares in Tokyu violated Article 54 of the Japanese Securities and Exchange Law. However, although it uncovered a further US$300 million in payments to leading clients by the big four brokers, the Ministry of Finance says it found no evidence of violations against Articles 58 and 125 which outlaw illegal stock deals and stock manipulation.

As punishment, the Ministry ordered Nomura to refrain from trading stock on behalf of customers and from the investment research business for a period of one month. The other leading Japanese brokerages were also penalized. Nikko and Yamaichi were ordered to refrain from corporate business for a fortnight and Daiwa received a one-week penalty.

Japanese finance minister Ryutaro Hashimoto accepted responsibility for the allowing the scandals to go on and, ultimately, resigned in October 1991.

Three proposals designed to prevent the recurrence of such scandals are being discussed. The first relies only on a reorganization of certain sections of the Ministry of Finance. However, since many observers, including the then Japanese Prime Minister Toshiki Kaifu, believe that part of the problems of the past can be ascribed to the too cosy relationship between the Ministry and the industry it was supposed to be regulating, this idea is unlikely to get off the ground.

Players and Referees

The Ad Hoc Commission on Administrative Reform, reviewing market regulation, recommended the establishment of a semi-independent watchdog agency under the Ministry of Finance's control. Such a body is favoured by the ruling Liberal Democrats but the main opposition parties in the Japanese Diet believe, with perhaps more than a touch of realism, that there is little difference between a semi-independent body and the reshuffling of sections within the Ministry. However, attempts to introduce a fully independent agency along the lines of the US Securities Exchange Commission appear to have been successfully blocked by the Ministry of Finance.

CHAPTER 7

TREASURIES, CENTRAL BANKS AND INTERNATIONAL INSTITUTIONS

The so-called "Group of Seven" (G-7) leading industrialized nations now appears to be the vehicle of choice for the steering of the world economy. It was to this grouping that Soviet President Mikhail Gorbachev turned for aid in the early summer of 1991. The G-7 annual summit meetings trace their origins back to the informal meetings held by Helmut Schmidt of West Germany and Valéry Giscard d'Estaing of France when they were finance ministers. After the two men became heads of state, they invited the leaders of the UK, USA, Italy and Japan to join them in 1975. Canada's prime minister was invited in 1976 and the European Community has attended since 1978.

The G-7, as such, was created at the Tokyo economic summit in May 1986. However, the grouping, previously the Group of Five (G-7, ex-Canada and Italy), had already made its presence felt in the world's markets with the Plaza Agreement, which agreed to accelerate the US dollar's decline in value, in September 1985 (*see Chapter Four*). The Plaza Agreement and the Louvre Accord two years later, which adopted policies aimed at stabilizing the value of the US dollar, stand out as the group's most obviously successful attempts at managing markets.

Since 1981, each delegation has consisted of fifteen members: the head of government, the foreign minister, the finance minister, the personal representative of the head of state (known as the "sherpa"– these are the people who hold pre-summit meetings to prepare the summit agendas), the central bank governors and various other aides.

Although the summit meeting have become elaborate and expensive affairs at which little of substance appears to be achieved, the G-7 now dominates world economic affairs. Even though the summits themselves tend to result only in anodyne communiqués, the continuous process of dialogue between the G-7 nations throughout the year does enable governments to reach consensus on economic issues. No established framework exists for the heads of government summits; it is only decided at the end of each meeting if, when and where the next is to be held.

Ministerial meetings, involving finance ministers and central bank governors, are held three times a year. Two of these meetings are held in conjunction with the semi-annual meetings of the Interim Committee of the International Monetary Fund and the Development Committee of the World Bank and the third is a special surveillance session.

Powers of the G-7 Treasuries (a)

Country	Fiscal policy	Monetary policy	Exchange rate policy	Forex (b) market intervention	Financial market regulation	Structural reform
Canada	D,E	C	D,E/C	C	D,E,C	D/C
Japan	D,E,C	D,C	D,C	D,C	D,E,C	E/C(c)
USA	C	C	D,E/C	D,C	D,E,C	
France	D,E,C	D/C	D,C	C	D,E,C	D/C(d)
Germany	D,E,C	C	D,C(e)	C	D/C	C
Italy	D/C,E	D/C	D,E/C		D,E,C	
United Kingdom	D,E,C	D,C	D,E,C	C	D,C	D/C(f)

C   consultative role only
D   decision-making power
E   executive/implementation powers
D/C decision-making power in consultation with other agencies
E/C   execution/implementation in consultation with other agencies
(a) Judgements are based on interpretation of the exercise of *de jure* mandates.
(b) The European nations are members of the European Monetary System's exchange rate mechanism. Forex intervention is in accord with ERM commitments, consultation procedures vary from country to country.
(c) The Ministry of Finance is responsible for operating the Fiscal Investment and Loan Programme, which channels savings from pension funds and the postal savings system into construction projects through loans at both market and preferential rates.
(d) The Treasury plays a major role in identification and formulation of structural reform.
(e) Under a floating exchange rate, final decisions on market intervention lie with the Bundesbank. Exchange rate realignments in the EMS are the responsibility of the Finance Ministry.
(f) The Treasury plays a major role in identification and formulation of structural reform.
(*Source: Institute for International Economics, Yamaichi International (Europe) Ltd.*)

In each of the G-7 treasuries, one senior official is nominated to represent the ministry at the G-7 deputies meetings. These meetings, which do not involve the central bankers, are more confidential and held more frequently than the ministerial meetings. They are informal and may be held at relatively short notice to monitor and discuss economic performance and foreign exchange market developments.

The G-7 annual summits present attractive photo-opportunities to heads of state and allow troubled politicians a chance to look good away from the daily grind of domestic politics. Real economic policy co-ordination, when it happens, happens as a result of the formal and informal meetings of the treasury ministers, their deputies and the central bank governors.

The treasuries and central bankers in each country have different powers and responsibilities. In general, the role of a treasury ministry is to act as the fiscal agent of government and carry out its goals through:

expenditure and tax policies;
debt management;
regulating domestic financial institutions;
international economic relations;
forming exchange rate policy;
in some cases, forming monetary policy.

UNITED KINGDOM

The central bank of the UK, the Bank of England, was founded in 1694 and is one of the world's oldest central banks. The Bank was established by London merchants to lend money to the protestant King William III, to ensure he had the money he needed to fight the French wars. The city merchants' reasoning was that if the French won, the Stuart dynasty, in the shape of the catholic James II, would be restored and their assets put at risk. The sum of £1,200,000 was raised for the monarch at a perpetual rate of interest of 8 per cent. Given the undercurrent of religious fears which prompted the merchants to assist the crown, it should come as no surprise to learn that many of those subscribing to this fund and, indeed, the first governor of the Bank, were Huguenot, that is, French protestant refugees. In return for assisting the state, the new bank was given the government's account.

The Bank survived its first real crisis in 1720 when the bursting of the South Sea Bubble all but wiped out its credit *(see Chapter One)*. In 1797 the playwright Sheridan called the Bank, "an elderly lady in the City," a phrase picked up by the cartoonist James Gilray and transformed in the nickname which has stuck to this day, "The Old Lady of Threadneedle Street".

The Bank Charter Act of 1844 gave the Bank a monopoly on the issue of bank notes in England and Wales. The Act also accelerated the Bank's withdrawal from ordinary commercial banking to concentrate on its role as banker to other banks and to government, increasing its influence on monetary conditions. The Bank also took on a degree of responsibility for maintaining orderly money and capital markets in London, and for the monitoring of the soundness of the banking system in general. The Bank weathered more market crises through the nineteenth century. However, despite an increasing role in the developing UK financial system through the nineteenth and the first half of the twentieth century, it was not until the passage of the Bank of England Act in 1946 under the post-war Labour administration that the Bank was nationalized and truly became an instrument of state.

The "Old Lady's" main responsibilities now lie in the formulation and execution of monetary policy, and in banking and other financial supervision. In pursuit of the management of the government's monetary policy the Bank is responsible for the issue of government stocks (*see Chapter Three*) and intervention in the forex markets (*see Chapter Four*). The Bank also has day-to-day responsibility for ensuring the liquidity of the domestic money markets. The Bank typically signals changes in base interest rates though its money market operations by changes in its intervention rate, that is, the rate at which it will buy or sell bank bills to the discount houses and the clearing banks. Unlike a number of other central banks, the Bank of England takes no independent policy action but serves to implement strategy and regulations promulgated by the government.

The Bank's supervisory role was only given a legal basis under the Banking Acts of 1979 and 1987 (*see Chapter Six*). Prior to the first of these pieces of legislation, the regulation of financial institutions in the UK was often said to be a matter of how high the head of the Bank of England, the Governor, raised his eyebrows!

The head of government in the UK is the Prime Minister, but this is not actually the title of the office which is held by the individual in question. The office is that of First Lord of the Treasury and the Prime Minister is, therefore, the ultimate authority on all fiscal and monetary decisions as well as being head of government. The Chancellor of the Exchequer is the minister at the head of Her Majesty's Treasury, as the UK's finance ministry is still known, with four junior Treasury ministers to assist him. The Treasury has three main functions: the control of public expenditure; finance; and economic policy.

The heads of government departments submit their spending plans for the next three years to the Treasury each autumn. What each department feels it may require and what the Treasury is prepared to sanction are regularly completely different matters, resulting in protracted negotiations before an agreement is reached. A summary of the agreed expenditure plans is presented in the Chancellor's Autumn Statement and final totals for the coming year are presented to Parliament with the Budget, when revenue plans are announced. It is the Treasury's responsibility to keep track of overall government spending and ensure that it remains within target limits.

There are four main policy areas in domestic finance: the co-ordination of taxation through the Inland Revenue and Customs and Excise; monetary policy, involving interest rates, exchange rates and funding policy; financial regulation; and the maintenance of government funds and accounts.

The four main policy areas at the international level are: overall responsibility for UK policy within the framework of the EC budget, the single European market and towards European economic and monetary union; responsibility for UK policy on international debt; liaison with the International Monetary Fund, the World Bank and the European Bank for Reconstruction and Development; and analysis of the world economy.

UNITED STATES

The US central bank, the Federal Reserve (better known simply as "the Fed"), was established by Congress with the passing of the Federal Reserve Act in December 1913. The decentralized Federal Reserve System was created "to furnish an elastic currency, to afford the means of re-discounting commercial paper, to establish a more effective supervision of banking in the United States". The Banking Act 1935, which revised the reserve system's structure, formally charged the Federal Reserve Board with the responsibility for promoting conditions consistent with business stability and introduced permanent deposit protection insurance.

The Fed, which operates as an agency of the Federal government, is controlled by a seven-member Board of Governors which is directly answerable to Congress. The bank's operations in both the domestic money markets and in the foreign exchanges are overseen by the Federal Open Market Committee (FOMC). The FOMC, which consists of the seven Fed governors and the presidents of the twelve regional Federal Reserve Banks, meets approximately eight times a year.

Although the Fed is an agency of the government, the regional bank presidents are not appointed by government but elected by their own boards of directors. The governors of the Fed, with the exception of the chairman and vice-chairman, serve fourteen-year terms; because of the length of these terms of service and because the Fed funds itself, it is considered to be far more "independent" of the US government than the Bank of England is of the UK government. However, it would still be next to impossible for the Fed to carry on policies which ran counter to those of the government for any length of time.

The Fed is required by law (the Humphrey-Hawkins Act) to provide Congress with details of its monetary policy objectives semiannually. The Humphrey-Hawkins Act, or to give its its full name, the Full Employment and Balanced Growth Act 1978, requires the FOMC to set annual targets for the growth of the US money supply and links these targets to overall economic policy. The Act also requires the Chairman of the Fed to testify before the House and Senate Banking Committees of Congress each February and July.

The Fed commonly regulates monetary policy though adjustments to the Fed Funds rate. Federal funds are non-interest bearing deposits which all US banks are required to keep on reserve with the Fed. Excess deposits above the minimum required are traded on an overnight basis. The rate at which these funds trade is called the Fed Funds rate.

In open market operations, represented by the Federal Reserve Bank of New York, the Fed adds or withdraws cash from the banking system as policy dictates. The Fed manipulates its reserves using repos (*see Chapter Three*) to alter monetary conditions.

The US Treasury shares responsibility for US economic policy with the Council of Economic Advisers, on forecasting, and the Office of Management and Budget, in preparing the annual Federal budget. Domestically, the Treasury is responsible for tax policy, revenue collection, debt management and some financial regulation. Both the Treasury and the Federal Reserve participate in the foreign exchange markets although generally the latter operates at the behest of the former.

There are three main pieces of legislation which have long-term bearing on the US budget process: the Congressional Budget and Impoundment Control Act (1974); the Balanced Budget and Emergency Deficit Control Act (1985), more popularly known as the Gramm-Rudman-Hollings Act; and the Omnibus Budget Reconciliation Act (1990).

The first of these three acts increased Congressional power in budgetary matters, a factor which the cynical may suggest was one of the ultimate causes of the two later acts. Through the first half of the 1980s, the Federal budget deficit grew dramatically, the Gramm-Rudman-Hollings Act was supposed to lead to a balanced budget by gradually enforcing reducing spending patterns. It did not succeed. The Omnibus Budget Reconciliation Act is the latest attempt by the President and Congress to begin to move towards a balanced budget. However, given past performance and the requirement to pander to so many interest groups with separate axes to grind, the process is not going to be easy, or particularly speedy.

The Federal Deposit Insurance Corporation (FDIC) is the third major US government financial agency. It was established in 1934 in the wake of the bank collapses of the Great Depression. The FDIC is funded through "insurance" premiums paid by the banks and aims to protect investors and foster confidence in the American banking system. The FDIC is obliged to pay compensation up to US$100,000 per account (not per individual) should a bank fail. Unfortunately the guarantee resulted in reckless lending by many institutions and a high failure rate which has put heavy pressure on the FDIC's funds. Similar and more serious problems have also occurred in the savings & loans.

Germany

The Bundesbank, the German central bank, is unique in that its independence from the government in its control of monetary policy and foreign exchange market intervention is enshrined in law: "The Deutsche Bundesbank shall regulate the amount of money in circulation and of credit supplies to the economy, using the monetary powers conferred on it by this Act, with the aim of safeguarding the currency..." (*Bundesbankgesetz* 1957).

Subsequent legislation, passed in 1967, says the Bundesbank must aim to ensure stable domestic prices, high employment, a balance of trade and economic growth. With this legislative background, the Bundesbank is the most independent of the G-7 central banks, able to pursue a monetary policy and foreign exchange market intervention in the manner in which it, rather than its political masters, sees fit.

The Bundesbank is based in Frankfurt and there are eleven Lander (state) central banks (LCB). Following the unification of Germany, monetary authority in the five new states of the country rested in fifteen local administration offices, which had been responsible for the introduction of the D-mark into what was East Germany. However, the treaty signed during the reunification process stipulated that decisions be taken on whether and, if so, how many, new state central banks were to be set up. The significance of these decisions rests not solely on the area of authority that the new banks would have but also in the fact that the LCB presidents are automatically members of, and have voting rights on, the Bundesbank Central Council, the main policy-making body. Bank monetary and credit policy is decided at regular fortnightly meetings.

The Bundesbank's philosophy of fiscal rectitude, protecting the external value of the D-mark, maintaining internal economic stability and controlling monetary aggregates, stands as a reaction to the chaos of the runaway inflation which wrecked the German economy in the 1920s. The Bundesbank has four main instruments through which to control monetary policy: the discount rate for normal loans to other banks, the Lombard rate which is used for short-term and overnight funding, open market operations, and reserve requirements. The Bundesbank uses the Lombard and discount rates to make changes in the money markets and interest rates over the long term. Changes to these rates are usually announced following the fortnightly council meetings. Short-term rate moves are signalled through weekly money market operations through the use of repos.

Monetary conditions may also be influenced through the raising or lowering of reserve requirements. As in the USA, German commercial banks are required by law to hold reserve assets against their liabilities. Because the banking system is usually short of these deposits, it must borrow them from the Bundesbank, effectively ensuring that control of the money supply is in the hands of the central bank.

The German Ministry of Finance shares the responsibility for economic oversight with the Economics Ministry and works with the Bundesbank in the regulation of domestic financial markets. The Finance Ministry also makes German policy on the European Monetary System but always takes advice from the Bundesbank.

JAPAN

The Bank of Japan is governed by a policy board of seven members appointed by the Japanese cabinet. The Governor of the Bank is traditionally elected as chairman of the policy board, which is responsible for formulating Bank policy under the influence of the Ministry of Finance. Until 1988, the Japanese financial system was closely regulated. It is only in the last few years that the Bank of Japan has begun to operate in its domestic market in a manner similar to that of the other leading central banks and to use open market operations in the same way the Federal Reserve.

The Bank has three main monetary policy instruments: changes in the official discount rate; credit ceilings (quarterly lending guidelines for the banks); and a special lending facility, which has been in place since 1981 but has yet to be used. The Bank of Japan has largely managed to steer clear of the financial scandals which engulfed the Japanese markets in 1991.

The Japanese Ministry of Finance, like the US Treasury, shares responsibilities. The Economic Planning Agency is responsible for long term forecasting and economic analysis, and the Ministry of International Trade and Industry is closely involved in the economic planning process. However, the Ministry of Finance has a more independent role in budget matters and tax policies, and is also responsible for foreign exchange policy via the central bank. The Ministry of Finance is the agency responsible for regulation in the Japanese markets. The Japanese financial system is broadly similar to that of the USA with a separation of function between banks and securities houses. The US Glass-Steagall Act is mirrored by Article 65 of the Japanese Securities and Exchange Law. In the late 1980s there was much pressure from the banks to reform Article 65 and allow them to enter stockbroking. However, the question of financial reform in Japan is now wide open following the scandals which hit the stock and commodity markets (*see Chapter Six*). In a move which is unthinkable in western governments, the Japanese Finance Minister Ryutaro Hashimoto announced that he would be taking a 10 per cent pay cut for three months as a punishment for the apparent laxity of his ministry! His announcement, early in July 1991, followed revelations of gangster connections to securities houses, and estimates that the Japanese brokerages had improperly compensated clients for their losses to the tune of US$1.3 billion. In October 1991, Hashimoto resigned.

THE BRETTON WOODS INSTITUTIONS

Both the International Monetary Fund (IMF) and the International Bank for Reconstruction and Development (World Bank) were established at Bretton Woods in 1944. The two institutions grew out of international commitment to avoid a repeat of the global depression which had preceded the Second World War.

The IMF is a co-operative institution with more than 150 countries as members. On joining the IMF, a country is required to contribute a quota subscription, the size of which is determined by the Fund, in accordance with the relative wealth and economic performance of the country. The size of the subscription determines both the member's voting and borrowing power. Quotas are reviewed every five years in the light of the Fund's requirements and the state of member countries' economies.

Countries which become members of the IMF are committed to a code of conduct which obliges them to ensure the following: that other members are kept informed of the way in which the country values its currency in relation to other currencies, that foreign exchange transactions are not restricted, that the country pursues economic policies which will benefit its own economy and that of the membership of the IMF at large.

Should it require further funds than are available to it from members' subscriptions, the IMF has lines of credit with several governments and banks called General Agreements to Borrow. The IMF issues its funds to members in the form of Special Drawing Rights (*see* Chapter Four).

The role of the IMF has altered since the organization was created, the Fund is now responsible for supervising an orderly exchange of currencies, providing funds and services to assist members with their external debts and the re-organization of their economies. Within the G-7, the managing director of the Fund assists with the assessment of economic performance and the IMF provides a secretariat. However, the IMF has no authority within the G-7 and the Fund's director does not attend the G-7 discussions on foreign exchange.

The World Bank shares certain characteristics with the IMF, both are owned and directed by their 150-plus member countries. The Bank was originally set up to finance the reconstruction of western Europe in the aftermath of the Second World War and now functions as a global development institution. The World Bank is made up of two organizations, the International Bank for Reconstruction and Development and the International Development Association (IDA). As an investment bank which borrows and lends, the World Bank's equity capital is close to US$100 billion. However, the Bank raises most of its funding through bond issues and is a major borrower in the world's capital markets.

The World Bank gives medium-term (12-15 year) loans to creditworthy governments of developing nations at a nominal rate of interest over the cost of the funds to the Bank. The IDA provides interest-free loans over the long term (35-40 years) to countries with *per capita* gross national product of less than US$850. Affiliated to the World Bank is the International Finance Corporation which lends and makes equity investment in the private sector.

For the fiscal year 1991 the World Bank reported profits of US$1.2 billion. It was the seventh consecutive year the bank made profits over US$1 billion. Although the World Bank is not a commercial institution and does not seek to maximize profits, its aim is to achieve a level of net income adequate to maintain prudent protection against the risks inherent in lending to developing countries. Aid to the successor nations of the Soviet Union is the World Bank's next major challenge. However, the bank is not allowed to lend funds to the Soviet Union until it becomes a full member of the IMF and is allocated a quota. Ironically, the Soviet Union was among the original signatories of the Bretton Woods agreement.

THE BANK FOR INTERNATIONAL SETTLEMENTS

The Bank for International Settlements (BIS) is the oldest international financial institution, having been set up at the Hague Conference of creditor countries in 1930. Based in Basle, Switzerland, the BIS operates as the central banks' bank. The BIS board of directors consists of the central bank governors of eight European countries. The BIS provides the secretariat for the Basle Committee on Banking Supervision which co-ordinates the supervision of global banking. The Bank also acts to assist some eighty central banks to manage and invest their reserves in the international markets.

EUROPEAN INSTITUTIONS

The collapse of the Communist regimes in East Europe at the end of the 1980s led to the creation of the European Bank for Reconstruction and Development (EBRD). The EBRD is virtually the brainchild of one man, its president Jacques Attali, who, while serving as an adviser to President Mitterand of France, proposed the creation of an agency to assist in the regeneration of Eastern Europe. The EBRD, which commenced operations in 1991, has amongst its shareholders all the countries of the EC, of EFTA and the central and Eastern European countries, as well as the USA, Japan, Canada, Australia, New Zealand and others.

In all, a total of thirty-nine countries and two European Community institutions subscribed ECU 10 billion for the bank's capital. The major novelty of the institution is its criteria of eligibility for loans, which depends not only on membership and the viability of projects but also on the ability to satisfy two political tests. These are that the country in question has to be committed to pluralist democracy and to a market economy.

The EBRD, the first pan-European financial institution to be created since the end of the Second World War, says it intends to concentrate on developing "an entrepreneurial spirit at grass roots level by helping the establishment of small enterprises". Some 40 per cent of the EBRD's lending will be to the state sector, 30 per cent of its investments will be made through the purchase of shares in the private sector and project loans will be made to specific private sector projects.

Although presently little more than a set of draft documents, the proposed "Eurofed", as the European Central Bank has been called, is already taking shape in the minds of some. With London winning the battle to be home to the EBRD, the race is already on for the home of the Eurofed, to be created as part of the European Community's drive towards EMU. The rules of the contest are vague and the finishing line a blur on the horizon, but the city of Frankfurt has already pulled ahead of the competition. Europe's central bankers have drawn up a draft constitution for a European Central Bank which stresses the need for

TREASURIES, CENTRAL BANKS AND INTERNATIONAL INSTITUTIONS

a tough, independent bank, but left open the question of where the bank would be based.

Luxemburg, London, Paris and Amsterdam are also in the running but among the attractions of locating the Eurofed in Frankfurt is that such a move might help overcome German suspicion that EMU will replace the strong D-mark with a weaker currency. Frankfurt's claim is also underlined by the fact that Germany has yet to house a major European institution. Militating against the German city, however, is that it is home to the Bundesbank, already a powerful force in European

PART TWO: EXCHANGES AND CONTRACTS

CHAPTER 8

NEW YORK

New York is one of the world's three most important financial centres, vying with Tokyo for the top position in equities trading and for the number two position in foreign exchange dealings. Although the futures markets in New York are overshadowed by those of Chicago (*see Chapter Ten*), three of the four exchanges are only slightly younger than the Chicago markets and the New York Mercantile Exchange's crude oil contract is the world's most actively traded futures contract on a physical commodity.

STOCK MARKETS
New York Stock Exchange (NYSE)

Securities trading in New York began in 1789 when George Washington authorized the issue of US$80 million in government bonds to help finance the costs of the American War of Independence. In 1791, the Secretary of the Treasury, Alexander Hamilton, established the Bank of the United States as the nation's first bank, offering shares to the public. Growing demand for securities led to demand for some kind of formal organization in the market, and in May 1792 a group of twenty-four merchants agreed to give preference to each other in their dealings. This Buttonwood Agreement, named after the tree under which much of their trading activity took place was followed in 1793 with a move into a building at the corner of William and Wall Streets.

In March 1817, the traders adopted a formal constitution creating the New York Stock & Exchange Board, precursor of the New York Stock Exchange. The new market was limited to members only, with membership costing the then not inconsiderable sum of $400. Twice a day, the president of the board read the list of securities, and members shouted bids and offers from the chairs assigned to them. This is the origin of the term "seat" which has become synonymous with the membership of any formal Exchange. In 1863, the market was renamed the New York Stock Exchange. The number of securities traded increased from thirty in 1820 to more than 300 by the end of the American Civil War and now stands at over 1,700. The introduction of the stock ticker in 1867 had revolutionized market communications and as the market-place entered the 1870s, basic listing requirements had been established. Companies wishing to list had to register their shares and provide information about their financial status. At the same time, increasing turnover meant that the original call market method of operation was replaced by continuous trading. With telephones came more business and, in December 1886, daily volume topped one million shares for the first time. In 1903, the NYSE moved to the location of its present home, at the corner of Broad and Wall Streets.

The most significant developments in the market-place in the first half of the twentieth century came in the wake of the crash of 1929 with the passing of the Securities Act 1933 and the Securities & Exchange Act 1934, and the establishment of the Securities & Exchange Commission (SEC). The new federal regulator laid down strict requirements for registration statements, listing applications and financial reporting. Following the Second World War, further advances in communications technology allowed the NYSE to introduce the electronic transmission and storage of trading information in the 1960s. The following decade, the Exchange introduced an electronic Designated Order Turnaround system (DOT) and, in 1984, this was replaced by SuperDot.

Individual investors on the NYSE are catered for by the Exchange's Individual Investor Express Delivery Service (IIEDS) which ensures that individuals receive preferential status. IIEDS speeds investors' orders to execution and guarantees that they are carried out ahead of institutional orders, even programme trading. More than 10,000 US institutional investors with some US$3,500 billion under management make use of the NYSE.

Member firms of the exchange represent buy and sell orders from their customers as well as trading on behalf of their own accounts. Certain members of the market are designated as "specialists" or NYSE-assigned dealers. These specialists are required by the exchange to maintain an orderly market in the securities assigned to them, operating as market makers in a customer-driven system. Assigned dealers perform four functions: quoting prices; executing orders; creating liquidity in the market-place; and matching bids and offers by bringing buyers and sellers together.

The NYSE is governed by regulations set out by the SEC but also functions as a self-regulating organization. The Financial & Operational Surveillance Committee of the NYSE exists to monitor the financial status of members and, in addition, the Exchange maintains continuous surveillance of the market in operation to ensure compliance with rules and guard against manipulation. The NYSE also has its own Enforcement

Division with jurisdiction and powers of prosecution over members, member firms and their employees.

As well as trading some 83 billion shares in more than 1,700 companies, the NYSE lists over 3,000 bonds. These are primarily US corporate bonds although they include foreign corporate and government bonds and US government issues. Most bond trading is conducted through the NYSE's electronic Automated Bond System. Options trading on the NYSE began in the early 1980s and is now served by an electronic order routing system. In 1982, the NYSE authorized its own futures market, the New York Futures Exchange (NYFE–*see below*) to begin trading in stock index futures. The NYSE began trading an Exchange Stock Portfolio in 1989. The portfolio of around 126,000 shares is based on the Standard & Poors 500 index and may be bought and sold in a single transaction which delivers shares in the 500 component companies, including those in the small number of companies in the S&P 500 which are not actually listed on the NYSE.

The best known US market index is the Dow Jones Industrial Average (DJIA), which is composed of thirty NYSE-listed companies and is a simple arithmetical average of the movements in their share prices. The DJIA was first published by the Wall Street Journal on 1 October 1928. However, where the index once did represent the industrial muscle of the US economy, it now includes McDonalds, Coca Cola, American Express and even Walt Disney! There are three other Dow Jones indices, the Transportation Average, the Utility Average and the Composite Average (a combination of the other three indices). Since 1966, the NYSE has produced its own Composite Index and four sectoral sub-indices. The S&P 500, produced by the credit rating agency Standard & Poors, is also a widely regarded index and is the basis for several derivative financial products including the NYSE's stock portfolio trading unit and several futures and options contracts.

Deregulation and Development
Eleven years before London's "Big Bang" of 1986, fixed commissions were terminated in US securities trading in May 1975. Since then, commissions have theoretically been subject to negotiation between broker and client on a competitive basis. However, in practice only commissions on transactions larger than US$100,000 are negotiated.

In the US Securities Acts Amendments of 1975, Congress called for expanding competition among the US stock markets and the creation of a national market system. The basic elements of the national system include fully computerized quotation and transaction reporting and post-trade processing or settlement. A rolling five-day trading account was established with settlement due by the fifth business day after the transaction date. Five clearing corporations operate for securities and one for options. The largest, the National Securities Clearing Corporation, processes about 90 per cent of all equity transactions in New York's three equity markets. The clearing corporations are electronically linked to each other in a network established following the 1975 legislation.

In the same year, the NYSE was instrumental in the inauguration of the Consolidated Tape Association. The term "tape" is a carry over from the days of ticker tape. Dealings on the NYSE are reported on Network A of the Consolidated Tape, and reports of transactions on non-NYSE listed stocks are carried on Network B. Another key element is the Intermarket Trading System although this did not come into operation until 1978, permitting a broker on any of the linked US Exchanges to obtain the best price available in any of the markets for any given stock.

In 1991, in the face of growing competition from the regional markets and from abroad, the NYSE decided to introduce two electronic after-hours trading sessions but share prices remain fixed at the closing prices of the day and orders will only be executed if they can be matched.

New York Stock Exchange
Eleven Wall Street
New York, NY 1005
USA
Tel: (212) 656 3000

American Stock Exchange (AMEX)

Although dealing was formalized on the NYSE several brokers remained outside the market, literally conducting their affairs in the street. These "kerbstone brokers" were the ancestors of the AMEX. Hand signals and distinctive whistles enabled brokers to communicate with their clerks leaning precariously from windows high above the street. The kerb market became one of New York city's tourist attractions as the dealers continued to trade in all weathers. However, on 27 June 1921 the kerbstone brokers marched up Wall Street to a newly-completed building behind Trinity Church. After singing the "Star Spangled Banner", they entered and commenced trading. Each trading-post on the new floor was marked by a street lamp resembling those left behind on Broad Street. Stories abound of many brokers falling ill in the first winter in the market's new home, unused as they were to heated interiors after years of dealing in the cold outdoors. In 1953, the kerb was renamed the American Stock Exchange.

In 1972, the AMEX introduced an automated order handling system and later in the decade, following the launch of options trading in 1975, an options trade processing system was installed. In 1980, the exchange became the first market to trade put options on all the securities underlying its call options. In 1984, the AMEX became the first market to introduce touch-screen technology to a trading floor. The following year, the exchange established another first with the two-way electronic hook-up with the Toronto Stock Exchange, the first link-up between primary equity markets in different countries.

The exchange provides a market-place for stocks and bonds of companies not large enough to qualify for the NYSE. It has less stringent listing requirements and encourages the registration of young companies. The AMEX has also developed a thriving options market and in 1990 launched long-term stock options with expirations of between two and three years, against expirations of up to eight months for the regular-term options which it also trades.

The AMEX is continuing to develop new products for risk management and has plans to trade warrants based on the FT-Actuaries Europe Index, and warrants and options on the Euro Top 100 index. The Exchange is also developing a new market-place for the trading of private placement securities meeting the requirements of SEC Rule 144A, called the System for Institutional Trading of Unregistered Securities.

Trading on the AMEX follows similar practice to that of the NYSE, with specialists acting as market makers to other brokers on the Exchange's 28,000 square-foot floor.

American Stock Exchange
86 Trinity Place
New York, NY 10006
USA
Tel: (212) 306 1000

National Association of Securities Dealers Automated Quotations (NASDAQ)

NASDAQ is the youngest of the USA's equity markets, commencing operations in 1971. It is a nationwide and international screen-based trading system without a central dealing floor. The market was set up by the National Association of Securities Dealers (NASD), a self-regulatory organization responsible for the regulation of NASDAQ and the over-the-counter securities market. The term over-the-counter is now applied only to non-NASDAQ stocks traded through the NASD's electronic bulletin board and printed "pink sheets". The NASD was established under an authority granted by the 1938 Maloney Act amendments to the Securities Exchange Act of 1934. NASDAQ is regulated and operated by the NASD which conducts market and broker surveillance.

In 1971, NASDAQ began as a quotation system, although it also collected and disseminated volume data. A decade later, the NASD adopted higher qualification standards for entry of securities into the NASDAQ system, and in April 1982 the NASDAQ National Market System was launched, offering real-time trade reporting. By the end of 1982, volume in eighty-four NASDAQ/NMS securities exceeded the volume in all 950 AMEX securities.

In 1986, NASDAQ formed a link with the London Stock Exchange for the exchange of quotations and transaction information on 350 issues from each market, and in 1988 the market was the first overseas securities market to be granted full legal status as a recognized investment exchange by the UK Department of Trade & Industry. NASDAQ has developed rapidly and is now the second largest equity market in the USA and the fifth largest in the world, listing securities in over 5,000 companies.

In 1990, the NASD established PORTAL, an electronic vehicle for Rule 144A stocks, offering a foreign company the opportunity to trade not only its American Depository Receipts (ADR) but also its underlying shares, bonds, convertibles or warrants in a range of international currencies as well as the US dollar, without having to meet US disclosure requirements. NASDAQ is already home to more ADRs than any other US market–nearly twice as many as on the NYSE and AMEX combined.

The NASDAQ market has served as a model for the world's newer electronic trading systems. In 1986, the London Stock Exchange's SEAQ and SEAQ International trading systems came into operation, based on the multiple market-maker and electronic quotation system of NASDAQ. Two years later, Singapore's SESDAQ followed and NASDAQ has also provided a role model for STAQS in China and JASDAQ in Japan.

In October 1991, the SEC approved a proposal by the National Association of Securities Dealers to establish a two-year pilot programme for its NASDAQ International Service trading system. NASDAQ International is to operate from London and allow investors, primarily those in the UK and the USA, trade over-the-counter stocks as well as leading issues listed on the NYSE before the start of trading in New York. The new system expands the hours of NASDAQ trading to coincide with trading on the London Stock Exchange.

National Association of Securities Dealers Inc.
1735 K Street,
Washington, DC 20006
USA
Tel: (202) 728-800

ADRs and Rule 144A

American Depository Receipts were originally developed by UK companies in the 1920s as a way round domestic legislation which prevented stocks from going overseas. An ADR is a receipt or certificate, issued by a US bank representing title to a specified number of non-US shares deposited with the bank in the company's country of domicile. Since the ADR is evidence of ownership of the underlying shares, it may be freely traded in the USA without delivery of the actual non-US shares that it represents. Selfridge's department store is said to have been the first ADR, depositing its shares in 1927 with Morgan Guaranty in London, which then created the ADR to trade in the US markets. By 1961, there were 150 ADRs traded. Thirty years later, the number has grown to over one thousand. Much of the recent interest in this form of equity financing is a result of the publicity attached to the UK government's privatization programme. British Gas, British Petroleum and British Telecom have all placed shares with US investors through ADR programmes.

ADRs may be sponsored or unsponsored. Unsponsored ADRs are those initiated by one or more US brokers because of significant US investor interest in the shares of a non-US company. The brokers will ask a depository bank to create ADRs and an exemption will be established for the company from the reporting provisions of the 1934 Securities & Exchange Act. The bank receives its compensation from fees due from the issuance of certificates and deducted from dividend payments prior to their distribution to ADR holders. Unsponsored ADRs may only be traded on an over-the-counter basis.

A sponsored ADR programme involves the active participation of the company. A single depository bank is normally chosen and all future ADRs in the company's shares will be issued through this bank, which assumes sole responsibility for dividend payment, information dissemination and administration. The costs of a sponsored ADR programme are borne by the issuing company rather than by the ADR holder, which is the case with unsponsored ADRs.

Unregistered ADRs may be issued by companies not wishing to register with the SEC, which involves preparing their financial statements in accordance with US Generally Accepted Accounting Principles

(GAAP). Instead, these companies will only provide an English language version of their Annual Report. Unregistered ADRs may only be traded on an over-the-counter basis. Companies desiring to list their ADRs on NASDAQ or one of the traditional floor-based markets require full SEC registration, which involves reconciling their accounts with US GAAP.

ADRs have several advantages both for foreign companies wishing to attract US funds and for US institutional investors looking to increase their international equity holdings. Certain US institutions are prohibited by law from owning anything but American securities. This definition includes ADRs, but excludes the ordinary shares of foreign companies. The ADR also offers investors a potential play on company and currency risk in one package. For foreign companies, ADRs help them to raise capital outside their domestic markets and raise the visibility of the company, its products and its securities in the US market-place.

The liberalization of the private placement market in April 1990 with the adoption of SEC Rule 144A deregulated the issuance and secondary trading of unregistered securities. Under Rule 144A, a market is expected to impose disclosure rules appropriate to the credit of the issuer and the type of securities issued. Securities already listed on a US exchange are not eligible, similarly, if a foreign issuer has listed shares or ADRs, its common and convertible shares are also not eligible for trading under Rule 144A. Sales under the regulation must be made to qualified institutional investors (QIB) only. QIBs include institutional investors that own or have investment discretion over US$100 million of specified securities; banks and savings and loan associations that own or have investment discretion over US$100 million in specified securities and have a net worth of at least US$25 million; and registered broker-dealers that own or have investment discretion over US$10 million in specified securities.

Rule 144A affords foreign companies an opportunity to expedite investment in their shares by US investors. Companies interested in broad retail investment may still pursue a conventional ADR programme. However, if their focus is limited to courting institutional investors, then a private placement of depository shares through the mechanism of Rule 144A is probably a more realistic option.

Futures Markets

In July 1977, New York's four independent commodity exchanges opened a new trading floor in Four World Trade Center under the auspices of a service company called Commodities Exchange Center, Inc. (CEC). CEC manages the 26,500 square-foot trading floor and is also responsible for the computer network which disseminates futures and options price information, telecommunications, security and administration for the four member exchanges. The CEC's member exchanges are: the Coffee, Sugar and Cocoa Exchange, Inc. (CSCE); the Commodity Exchange, Inc. (COMEX); the New York Cotton Exchange (NYCE); and the New York Mercantile Exchange (NYMEX).

All domestic US commodity exchanges are regulated by the Federal Government through the Commodity Futures Trading Commission. All four exchanges in New York operate on the open outcry procedure, although NYMEX has introduced an alternative screen-based trading system in a move prompted partly by concern at the extent to which business has been switching to the much smaller International Petroleum Exchange (IPE) in London.

COMEX and NYMEX have held discussions separately with the IPE on possible joint venture trading. COMEX and NYMEX have also held so far inconclusive talks on a complete merger of the two exchanges. Merger talks between the two markets have been going on in a desultory fashion for more than eleven years.

The CEC is planning to move from the World Trade Center to a new purpose-built location still in Manhattan. Initially the new building will house a 55,000 square foot trading floor, with a further 45,000 square feet of expansion space, compared with the existing 25,000 square foot trading floor at the World Trade Center. The cost of construction of the new facilities, which are scheduled for completion in mid-1994, has been put at $225 million. The CEC's member exchanges will hold a 50 per cent equity interest in the new building.

Commodity Exchange Center, Inc.
Four World Trade Center
New York, NY 10048
USA
Tel: (212) 938 2000

New York Cotton Exchange

The New York Cotton Exchange is the oldest commodity exchange in New York. It was founded in 1870 by a group of cotton brokers and merchants. Since its founding, the NYCE has been an integral part of the cotton industry and is now the world's premier market-place for cotton futures and options trading. However, the NYCE has also introduced several new innovative products. In 1966, the exchange built on its agricultural expertise and expanded its product line through the formation of the Citrus Associates of the New York Cotton Exchange, Inc., an affiliate of the exchange, where frozen concentrated orange juice futures and options are traded. In 1985, the NYCE created the Financial Instrument Exchange division (FINEX®). Under the aegis of FINEX® the NYCE has introduced US dollar index futures and options, five-year US Treasury note futures and options, two-year US Treasury note futures and European Currency Unit (ECU) futures.

In 1988, the New York Futures Exchange, a subsidiary of the New York Stock Exchange, became an affiliate of the NYCE and moved its trading operations into the NYCE. The NYFE's financial products include futures and options on the NYSE Composite Stock Index as well as the Commodities Research Bureau (CRB) Futures Price Index.

Contracts

The NYCE has plans to launch a new World Cotton contract in early 1992 to run in tandem with the existing contract. The Exchange hopes to encourage potential arbitrage between the two contracts.

Market	Contract	Trading unit	Price quotation
NYCE	Cotton futures	50,000 lb (100 bales)	Cents and 1/100 cent
	Options on cotton futures		
Citrus Associates of the NYCE	Frozen concentrated orange juice (FCOJ) futures	15,000 lb orange solids	Cents and 1/100 cent
	Options on FCOJ futures		
FINEX	ECU futures	ECU 100,000	Cents and 1/100 cent per ECU
	US dollar index futures	$500 x index value	Points and increments of 0.01 of a point
	Five-year US Treasury note futures	Five-year US Treasury notes with par amounts such that 0.01 basis point is $100	Points and increments of 0.5 of a point ($50)
	Two-year US Treasury note futures	Two-year US Treasury notes with par amounts such that 0.01 basis point is $100	Points and increments of 0.5 of a point ($50)
	Options on US dollar index futures		
	Options on five-year US Treasury note futures		
NYFE	NYSE composite index futures	$500 x index value	Points and increments of 0.5 of a point ($25)
	US Treasury bond futures	$100,000 x US Treasury bonds with at least fifteen years to maturity	Points and one-half of one thirty-second of a point
	Commodities Research Bureau index futures	$500 x index value	Points and increments of 0.5 of a point ($25)
	Options on NYSE composite index futures		
	Options on Commodities Research Burea index futures		

New York Mercantile Exchange

In 1872, a group of merchants formed the Butter and Cheese Exchange. In 1880, after the obvious addition of eggs, the name was changed to the Butter, Cheese and Egg Exchange. Two years later, the name was changed again to the New York Mercantile Exchange. Futures contracts were introduced on the exchange in the 1920s. In 1941, the Maine potato joined the market, to be followed by yellow globe onions, apples, Idaho potatoes, plywood and platinum. The Maine potato contract was the mainstay of the exchange until the late 1970s. In 1976 and again in 1979, scandal hit the contract, including the failure of delivered stocks to pass inspection. The Maine potato contract was summarily terminated. The exchange's whole future was called into question.

However, the future saviour of the market had already been introduced in 1978 with the launch of the heating oil futures contract. NYMEX has become the world's leading risk management forum for the energy industry and, in the process, has also become the third largest futures market in the USA.

Contracts

The NYMEX energy complex is comprised of heating oil, gasoline (1981), crude oil (1983), propane (1987), residual fuel oil (1989) and natural gas futures contracts, along with options on crude (1986), heating oil (1987) and gasoline (1989). Trading volume on the market continues to rise and the light sweet crude oil contract is the world's

Market	Contract	Trading unit	Price quotation
NYMEX energy complex	Unleaded gasoline futures	42,000 US gallons	Dollars and cents/gallon
	Light sweet crude oil futures	1,000 barrels	Dollars and cents/barrel
	Sour crude oil futures	1,000 barrels	Dollars and cents/barrel
	Heating oil futures	42,000 US gallons	Dollars and cents/gallon
	Natural gas futures	10,000 US gallons	Cents and 1/10 cent/gallon
	Propane futures	42,000 US gallons	Cents and 1/100 cent/gallon
	Residual fuel oil futures	1,000 barrels	Dollars and cents/barrel
	Options on unleaded gasoline futures		
	Options on light sweet crude oil futures		
	Options on heating oil futures		
NYMEX metal	Platinum futures	50 troy ounces	Dollars and cents/troy ounce
	Palladium futures	100 troy ounces	Dollars and cents/troy ounce

most actively traded futures contract on a physical commodity. NYMEX also trades contracts in the precious metals platinum and palladium. In addition to those contracts now trading, NYMEX has received the go-ahead to offer options on its platinum futures contract. There are no price limits in force on current near month contracts. In June 1991, the exchange submitted a sour crude oil futures contract to the Commodity Futures Trading Commission.

Coffee, Sugar & Cocoa Exchange, Inc.

The CSCE was founded as the Coffee Exchange of New York in March 1882 by a group of young coffee merchants reacting to a crisis in their trade. In the wake of uncontrolled speculation and tremendous oversupply that led to the collapse of the market in 1880, they sought to rebuild the coffee trade by establishing an orderly market for the trading of coffee futures. In 1914, sugar futures were added and the exchange's name was changed in 1916 to the New York Coffee & Sugar Exchange, Inc.

In 1925, the New York Cocoa Exchange established the world's first market-place for cocoa futures trading. In 1979, the Coffee & Sugar Exchange, Inc. and the New York Cocoa Exchange merged, forming the Coffee, Sugar & Cocoa Exchange, Inc.

In 1982, the CSCE was the first US futures exchange to introduce trading in options on futures contracts with options on world sugar futures. In 1986, options on cocoa and coffee were introduced. The following year, the exchange instituted the World White Sugar contract and in 1989 the CSCE offered a futures contract based on a new International Market Index. In 1991 the CSCE introduced an electronic trade entry system for its options markets.

Contracts

Market	Contract	Trading unit	Price quotation
CSCE	Sugar no.11 (world) futures	112,000 lb	Cents and 0.1 cent/lb
	Sugar no.14 (domestic) futures	112,000 lb	Cents and 0.1 cent/lb
	World white sugar futures	50 tonnes	Cents/tonne (min. 20 cents/tonne)
	Cocoa futures	10 tonnes	Dollars/tonne
	Coffee "C" futures	37,500 lb	Cents and 0.05 cent/lb
	Options on Sugar no.11 (world) futures		
	Options on cocoa futures		
	Options on coffee "C" futures		

The International Market Index contract failed to attract sufficient interest following its initial launch. The CSCE is reformatting the contract prior to a comprehensive relaunch.

Commodity Exchange, Inc.

Commodity Exchange, Inc. (COMEX), founded on 5 July 1933, is the product of a merger of four older exchanges, the National Metal Exchange, the Rubber Exchange of New York, the National Raw Silk Exchange and the New York Hide Exchange. COMEX is one of the world's two most important metal exchanges and is among the largest commodity futures exchanges in the world.

COMEX is now the leading exchange for gold and silver futures and options trading. The market also trades copper futures and options and is the only US exchange to trade futures in aluminium. COMEX's dominance in gold futures trading is reflected in the fact that the contract's trading volume exceeds the combined volume of all the rest of the world's gold futures almost 100-fold.

The silver contract was introduced in 1963, gold in 1975 and aluminium in 1983, but COMEX has traded copper since its inception in 1933. COMEX is currently upgrading its trade matching and processing system, automating the procedure for the submission of trade data. The exchange is also testing an interactive hand-held transaction entry system to record trades.

Contracts

COMEX has plans to extend the gold futures contract out to five years from its current two-and-a-half years. A similar extension to the options contract on gold futures is also likely. The exchange is seeking regulatory approval of a gold asset participation product and of a five-day gold option and is also considering revamping its copper contract.

Market	Contract	Trading unit	Price quotation
COMEX	Gold futures	100 troy ounces	Multiples of ten cents per troy ounce
	Silver futures	5,000 troy ounces	Multiples of 0.1 of a cent per troy ounce
	Copper futures	25,000 lb grade 1 electrolytic copper	Multiples of 0.05 of a cent per troy ounce
	Aluminium futures	44,000 lb primary aluminium	Multiples of 0.05 of a cent per troy ounce
	Options on gold futures		
	Options on silver futures		
	Options on copper futures		

OTHER MARKETS

The futures markets in Chicago are covered in detail in the following chapter. However, in addition to the exchanges in New York and Chicago, there are several other stock markets and futures markets in the USA. Of these other markets, the most important futures and options exchanges are: the Philadelphia Stock Exchange, which pioneered currency options; in soft commodities, the Kansas City Board of Trade and the Minneapolis Grain Exchange. A new market, the Twin Cities Board of Trade, is being established in Minneapolis-St Paul, bidding to compete with the Chicago Mercantile Exchange's dominance of currency futures trading.

Of the other stock markets in the USA, only the Pacific Stock Exchange (PSE), with trading floors in San Francisco and Los Angeles, operates west of the Mississipi. The PSE sees its future in building links with exchanges throughout the Pacific Rim countries and in 1990 took the first step down this route with the signing of a co-operation agreement with the Taiwan Stock Exchange.

There are five other stock markets in the country: the National Stock Exchange in New York which specializes in smaller companies not listed on any other market; the Philadelphia Stock Exchange, the country's oldest market, founded in 1790; the Boston Stock Exchange; the Midwest Stock Exchange; and the Cincinnati Stock Exchange.

CHAPTER 9

CHICAGO

More than half of the world's and two-thirds of domestic US futures and options trading takes place in the pits of the Chicago markets. Together the Chicago Board of Trade and the Chicago Mercantile Exchange trade ten of the futures industry's twelve most active contracts, with over a quarter of a million contracts changing hands on the two markets every year. Modern futures trading began in Chicago and the markets in the "Windy City" remain the largest and most important centres for futures and options business in the world.

Chicago Board of Trade (CBOT)
The CBOT is both the world's oldest established futures market and its largest, setting a new annual volume record in 1990 with 154,231,583 contracts traded. The CBOT was originally established by a group of eighty-two merchants in 1848 to promote commerce in Chicago. The development of the market owes much to the advances in grain storage technology in the nineteenth century-producers could delay deliveries to wait for better prices and buyers could stockpile grain against shortages. The earliest recorded forward contract in corn was made on 13 March 1851, for 3,000 bushels of corn to be delivered in June. However, the early forward contracts had significant drawbacks, notably their lack of standardization with regard to quality and delivery time.

Therefore, in 1865, the CBOT introduced standard futures contracts and devised a margining system to combat the problem of buyers and sellers defaulting. Although most of the exchange's early records were lost in the Great Chicago Fire of 1871, it has been established that by the mid-1860s the basic principles of structured futures trading as it is now understood had been put in place.

By the end of the 1960s, the CBOT had developed a wide range of agricultural futures contracts. Among the effects of the end of fixed exchange rates in 1971 was a significant increase in the volatility of a wide range of financial assets, such as government bonds. Responding to the demands of this new environment, the CBOT launched the

Market	Contract	Trading unit	Price quotation
CBOT financial	Major market index futures	$250 x index value	Points ($250) and increments of 0.05 of a point
	Tokyo stock index (TOPIX) futures	¥5,000 x index value	Points (¥5,000) and increments of 0.05 of a point
	Mortgage-backed futures	GNMA coupon face value $100,000	Points ($1,000) and thirty-seconds of a point
	Long-term municipal bond index futures	$1,000 x closing value of "The Bond Buyer" municipal bond index	Points ($1,000) and thirty-seconds of a point
	Long-term JGB futures	¥20 million face value	Points (¥200,000) and increments of 1./100 of a point
	US Treasury bond futures	One Treasury-bond, face value at maturity of $100,000 or multiples thereof	Points ($1,000) and thirty-seconds of a point
	Ten-year US Treasury note futures	One Treasury-note, face value at maturity of $100,000 or multiples thereof	Points ($1,000) and thirty-seconds of a point
	Five-year US Treasury note futures	One Treasury-note, face value at maturity of $100,000 or multiples thereof	Points ($1,000) and thirty-seconds of a point
	Two-year US Treasury note futures	One Treasury-note, face value at maturity of $200,000 or multiples thereof	Points ($1,000) and tone-quarter of one thirty-second of a point
	Thirty-day interest rate futures	One contract calling for the daily delivery of interest paid on a principal amount of $5 million overnight Fed funds held for thirty days	100 minus the monthly average overnight Fed funds rate for the delivery month
	Options on TOPIX futures		
	Options on mortgage-backed futures		
	Options on long-term municipal bond index futures		
	Options on long-term JGB futures		
	Options on US Treasury bond futures		
	Options on ten-year US Treasury note futures		
	Options on five-year US Treasury note futures		

world's first financial futures contracts in the value of a non-stock security. The Government National Mortgage Association (GNMA) mortgage-backed certificate futures contract began trading in October 1975. Further financial futures followed this instrument and, in 1982, the next step took place with the introduction of options on futures. The

Market	Contract	Trading unit	Price quotation
CBOT agricultural	Corn futures	5,000 bushels	Cents and 1/4 cents/bushel
	Oat futures	5,000 bushels	Cents and 1/4 cents/bushel
	Soybean futures	5,000 bushels	Cents and 1/4 cents/bushel
	Soybean meal futures	100 tons (2,000 lb/ton)	Dollars and cents/ton
	Soybean oil futures	60,000 lb	Dollars and cents/cwt
	Wheat futures	5,000 bushels	Cents and 1/4 cents/bushel
	Options on corn futures		
	Options on oat futures		
	Options on soybean futures		
	Options on soybean meal futures		
	Options on soybean oil futures		
	Options on wheat futures		
CRCE	CRCE rough rice futures	2,000 cwt	Dollars and cents/cwt
CBOT metal	Kilo gold futures	One gross kg (32.15 troy oz)	Dollars and cents/troy ounce
	100-oz gold futures	100 fine troy oz	Dollars and cents/troy ounce
	1,000-oz silver futures	1,000 troy oz	Dollars and cents/troy ounce
	5,000-oz silver futures	5,000 troy oz	Dollars and cents/troy ounce
	Options on 1,000-oz silver futures		

CBOT's first options contract was on Treasury bond futures. The success of this contract led to the introduction of options on the exchange's agricultural and other financial futures.

The increasing globalization of the futures industry through the 1980s resulted in an expansion of the exchange's trading hours to take account of increasing business interest in the Far East. The CBOT began its first extended hours trading session in April 1987, and now accommodates the morning trading hours in Hong Kong, Singapore, Sydney and Tokyo. The CBOT has a total trading floor area of 51,000 square feet in the forty-five-storey building it has occupied since 1930. There are 1,402 full members of the CBOT, eligible to trade any of the futures or options-on-futures traded on the exchange. In addition, there are around 700 associate members trading only the non-agricultural contracts and a number of membership interests limited to the Index, Debt and Energy Market and the Commodity Options Market.

Chicago

The exchange is linked to two other markets, the CBOE (*see below*) which it founded, and the MidAmerica Commodity Exchange (MidAm). The MidAm market was founded in the 1860s as the Chicago Open Board of Trade, taking its present name in 1972. In March 1986, MidAm officially affiliated to the CBOT. The previous year, the Chicago Rice & Cotton Exchange (CRCE) had affiliated to the MidAm. The CRCE was originally founded in 1871 at the New Orleans Cotton Exchange, moving to Chicago in 1983 as part of the market's growing links with MidAm. The MidAm and the CRCE now trade on the CBOT.

Market	Contract	Trading unit
MidAm	US Treasury bond futures	$50,000 face value
	US Treasury bill futures	$500,000 face value
	US Treasury note futures	$50,000 face value
	Corn futures	1,000 bushels
	Wheat futures	1,000 bushels
	Soybean futures	1,000 bushels
	Soybean meal futures	20 tons (2,000 lb)
	Oat futures	1,000 bushels
	Cattle futures	20,000 lb
	Hog futures	15,000 lb
	NY gold futures	33.2 fine troy ounce
	NY silver futures	1,000 troy ounces
	Platinum futures	25 fine troy ounces
	Sterling futures	£12,500
	D-mark futures	Dm62,500
	Yen futures	¥6,250,00
	Swiss franc futures	SFr62,500
	Canadian dollar futures	C$50,000
	Options on wheat futures	
	Options on soybean futures	
	Options on NY gold futures	

The exchange is in the throes of developing a paperless electronic trading system to maximize the efficiency of the open outcry market. The CBOT electronic trading support system comprises the EOS™ order entry/order delivery system used by brokerages and a hand-held AUDIT electronic trading card for the pit trader. The CBOT is also a partner in the development of the Globex electronic trading system. In 1990, the CBOT and the Chicago Mercantile Exchange (*see below*) began investigating avenues by which the world's two largest futures exchanges could unify their functions. A Futures Exchanges Common Goals committee was set up to look into achieving cost savings and increased efficiency in the following areas: international marketing, systems development, operations and clearing. Since 1925, clearing on the CBOT has been carried out by an independent body, the Board of Trade Clearing Corporation. Each trader reports his trades to one of approximately 135 member firms of the clearing corporation. Member firm accounts are settled at the end of each trading day. The CBOT is regulated by the National Futures Association and the CFTC.

Contracts

The CBOT trades some thirty-four futures and options contracts together with a further twenty-one MidAm contracts and the CRCE's rough rice futures contract. The exchange is actively expanding the number of contracts it offers and in 1992 is to launch the world's first insurance futures contract (*see Chapter Five*). The first such contract to be offered will be on health insurance. The CBOT is also developing contracts on motor, homeowner and ocean marine insurance. The contracts now trading are as tabulated. (NB each options contract is based on a single futures contract).

Chicago Board of Trade
LaSalle at Jackson
Chicago
Illinois 60604-2994
USA
Tel: (312) 435 7217
Fax: (312) 341 3329

Chicago Mercantile Exchange (CME)

On 20 May 1874, a group of South Water Street provisioners established the Chicago Produce Exchange to provide a market-place for farm products. In 1895, dealers dissatisfied with the market pricing established a division within the exchange to establish official quotations. Four years later, this division splintered from the exchange to establish itself as the Chicago Butter and Egg Board. By the end of the First World War, the Board was trading a range of contracts and allowing public participation. In September 1919, the market relaunched itself under the new name of the Chicago Mercantile Exchange and established its own CME Clearing House to guarantee trades. In 1928, the CME moved into a new purpose-built fourteen-storey home with the then huge facility of a 5,000 square-foot trading floor.

Until the end of the Second World War, the CME traded futures on eggs, butter, cheese, potatoes and onions. In October 1945, turkey futures were launched, to be followed four years later by contracts in apples, poultry and frozen eggs. In 1954, futures on iron and scrap steel were added.

However, the market only took off in 1961 with the launch in September of a new futures contracts based on frozen slabs of uncured, unsliced bacon. The pork bellies contract became the world's most heavily traded futures contract and led the CME to introduce further contracts based on meats. In 1964, in a notable departure from accepted practice, that commodities contracts should be written on storable, non-perishable goods, the CME launched a contract on live cattle. This contract was followed, in 1966, by live hog futures and, in 1971, by feeder cattle futures. By the end of the 1960s, the CME was the world's largest trading centre for meat and livestock commodity futures.

The CME also took advantage of the end of the era of fixed exchange rates in 1971. The following year, the CME inaugurated the International Monetary Market (IMM) trading seven contracts on foreign currencies. These were the world's first financial futures instruments and the IMM is now the world's busiest financial futures market. Also in 1972, the market moved to a new 14,000 square-foot trading floor, which was expanded to 23,000 square feet in 1978.

In 1982, the CME launched a second discreet market, the Index and Option Market (IOM) for the trading of indices and options. The IOM's first futures contract was based on the Standard & Poors 500 index, with options being added the following year. In 1983, the CME moved to its present home, the CME Center, with two trading floors, totalling 70,000 square feet. A year later, the trading pits were reorganized to provide facilities for options trading on the existing futures contracts and in 1984 options on D-mark and livestock futures were introduced, to be followed in 1985 by options on sterling, Swiss franc, Live Hogs and Eurodollar futures. The CME has some 2,700 clearing members.

In 1984, the CME established a mutual offset link with the Singapore International Monetary Exchange, allowing dealers to open positions on one market and close them on the other (*see Chapter Fourteen*). However, this mutual offset arrangement is likely to be overtaken by GLOBEX, the electronic trading system being developed by the CME jointly with Reuters (*see Chapter Five*).

In May 1991, the CME introduced a limited ban on the practice of dual trading, whereby brokers trade for their own account as well as for customers. The move is an attempt to stave off more severe federal regulation. The ban, authorized by CME members in April 1990, sprang from the federal undercover probe in the Chicago markets in the late 1980s which stirred public indignation over alleged trading abuses. Most dual trading is now banned in certain contract months of Eurodollar futures and futures-options and D-mark, yen, sterling and Swiss franc futures. Only traders who primarily broker spreads, other members' orders, or have permission from their clients, may continue the practice. There is some concern in the market about whether the ban will have the desired effect of providing further client protection without having serious impact on the liquidity of some of the contracts.

Clearing on the CME is carried out through the exchange's own clearing house. Unlike many other markets, the CME requires gross margining. Margins must be deposited by the clearing member for each open position, rather than for the net position. For example, a firm 99 long and short 100 on the same contract would be required to deposit margin for 199 positions rather than for a single position under the net margining system. The exchange has also established its own Trust Fund for the compensation of customers who incur losses as a result of any clearing member defaulting. The CME is regulated by the Commodity Futures Trading Commission and by the self-regulating National Futures Association.

Contracts
The CME offers a total of thirty futures and options on futures contracts in four sectors, agriculture, currencies, equities and interest rates.

Agriculture: The CME trades futures in four meat contracts: feeder cattle, live cattle, live hogs and frozen pork bellies. All four contracts are priced in US dollars per 100 lbs. Feeder cattle futures are traded in units of 44,000 lbs of 600-800 lbs steers. Live cattle futures are in units of 40,000 lbs made up of choice grade steers weighing 1,050-1,200 lbs per head. The live hog futures contract is for 30,000 lbs of US Department of Agriculture (USDA) grades 1, 2, 3 barrows and gilts, weighing 210-240 lbs per head. The frozen pork belly contract is for 40,000 lbs of USDA inspected 12-14 lb or 14-16 lb pork bellies. The CME offers call and put options on all four meat contracts, the option size being equivalent to one futures contract in each case.

The market also trades "Random Length Lumber" futures, the trading unit is 150,000 board feet, meeting the US Department of Commerce's quality requirements and is priced in US dollars per thousand board feet. Call and put options are also listed on this contract.

Currencies: Call and put options are listed on six of the eight contracts. The contracts are quoted in US dollars at the prevailing exchange rate and the contract sizes are as follows:

Currency	Contract size
Australian dollar	A$100,000
Sterling	£62,500
Canadian dollar	C$100,000
D-mark	Dm125,000
Yen	¥12,500,000
Swiss franc	SFr125,000
French franc	FFr250,000
ECU	ECU125,000

Chicago

There are no options on the French franc or the ECU contract. In May 1991 the CME also became the first futures market to trade cross-rate currency futures. The exchange has introduced three of six planned cross rate contracts. The first three contracts track sterling against the D-mark, the D-mark against the Swiss franc, and the D-mark against the yen. The CME plans to add futures and futures-options on yen/sterling, Swiss franc/sterling and yen/Swiss franc cross rates.

Equities: The CME trades one equity-based contract on futures in the Standard & Poors 500 index, a capitalization-weighted index of 500 stocks. The trading unit of this contract is the index value multiplied by US$500. The market also trades both call and put options on the contract up to twelve months forward.

Interest rates: Three interest rate-based contracts are traded, on Eurodollar time deposits, on ninety-day US Treasury bills, and on the one-month London Interbank Offered Rate (LIBOR). Call and put options are traded on all three contracts. The contract size of the Eurodollar future is ED$1,000,000 and the price is quoted in index points. Treasury bill futures are traded in contracts of US$1,000,000 and the price here is also quoted in index points.

Chicago Mercantile Exchange
30 South Wacker Drive
Chicago
Illinois 60606
USA
Tel: (312) 930 1000

Chicago Board Options Exchange (CBOE)

The CBOE is the youngest of the three markets in Chicago, founded in 1973. The CBOE was originally set up by the CBOT but has always been managed and regulated as a separate exchange. The CBOE revolutionized options trading by creating standardized, listed stock options. The speedy acceptance of this then new concept has resulted in the CBOE becoming the second largest securities exchange in the USA and the largest options exchange in the world. In 1990, over 60 per cent of all US listed securities option trading took place at the CBOE and, in the first seventeen years of its existence, over 1.38 billion options contracts have traded on the market. The CBOE has about 540 member firms and approximately 1,500 traders.

In April 1973, the CBOE began trading call options on sixteen underlying stocks. Put options were introduced in 1977, at which time the rapid growth of the derivative securities market and the multiple listing of some options prompted the Securities & Exchange Commission to place a moratorium on further options expansion pending an in-depth review of market structures and the regulatory environment. A number of improvements in the area of customer protection were made and the moratorium ended in March 1980. The CBOE responded by increasing the number of options on listed stocks to 120, and by taking steps to broaden position limits and reduce strike price intervals. In June 1980, the CBOE merged with the Midwest Stock Exchange's options operations and 411 Midwest members came to the CBOE floor and options on a further sixteen stocks were added. A decade after the first trading of stock options, the CBOE launched its first option on stock indices. The first index option on the CBOE was on the Standard & Poors (S&P) 100 and began trading in March 1983. The CBOE also lists options on the S&P 500. Trading in options on these two indices accounted for more than 90 per cent of the total US index option market in 1990.

In 1984, the CBOE outgrew its trading facilities at the CBOT and moved into its own building with a 45,000 square-foot trading floor. Among the technical innovations on the new floor was the implementation of the Retail Automatic Execution System, which allows small customer orders to be filled automatically at the prevailing price. The CBOE also has an Auto Quote providing updated prices in less active options and an Electronic Book to increase the speed of order execution and reporting. In 1985, the CBOE formed the Options Institute to aid in the education of retail account executives, institutional money managers and pension fund sponsors. In 1989, the CBOE codified its "Firm Quote" programme which applies only to non-broker orders for options expiring in the two near-term trading months. The market-makers are required to fill at least ten contracts of a customer order at the best bid or offer. In conjunction with this programme the CBOE narrowed the spreads allowed under normal market conditions.

Among the newest developments, the CBOE has introduced options on interest rates. Trading in these contracts began in June 1989. There are two option classes, one based on short-term US Treasury bill yields and another based on the longer-term yields to maturity of US Treasury notes and bonds. The underlying value of these options moves on shifts in the US Treasury yield curve. In 1990, the CBOE received approval to trade traditional securities products, including common and preferred stocks, warrants and bonds.

Clearing on the CBOE is by the Options Clearing Corporation, which is jointly owned by the National Association of Securities Dealers and the participating exchanges. All trading on the CBOE is overseen by the Securities & Exchange Commission. Dual trading is prohibited in active, liquid options on the CBOE, although in newly listed options a modified trading system operates. In new options, a designated primary market-maker will make a market and fulfil orders. When the option's liquidity reaches a satisfactory level trading reverts to the normal market-making system. The modified system for new options combines the functions of agency and principal but under open outcry bidding and does not give the primary market-maker priority over other traders or customers.

Most option classes listed are trading under open outcry with certain members of the exchange acting as market-makers while others act as floor brokers, as agents executing orders for customers.

Contracts

In the fiscal year to end-June 1990, the CBOE listed options on 238 stocks. The underlying assets of these options are common stocks listed on the New York Stock Exchange, the American Stock Exchange and qualified over-the-counter markets. The contract size is standardized on 100 shares. The exchange also trades LEAPS (Long-term Equity Anticipation Securities). These are long-term options on stocks trading up to two years in the future.

The exchange lists four options on stock indices. There are options on the Standard & Poors (S&P) 100 index, which is a capitalization-weighted index of 100 stocks, with the contract size being US$100 multiplied by the index level. There a three options contracts on the S&P 500. The settlement of exercising the basic option on the S&P 500 is based on the difference between the closing value of the index on the trading day on which the exercise notice was tendered. The expiration months of this contract are the two near-term months followed by three additional months from the March quarterly cycle, except for January and July, when four additional months are listed. The long-term S&P 500 options have expiration months two years into the future. The S&P 500 opening settlement options differ from the two contracts described above in that the settlement of the option exercise is based on the difference between the opening prices of the underlying stocks in the index on the trading day after the exercise notice is tendered.

In addition to these contracts, the CBOE has plans to introduce options on the London market's FT-SE 100 share index. The contracts will be cash settled, denominated in US dollars, European exercise, and will include trading months up to two years into the future. The exchange has also filed with the Securities Exchange Commission to list an options cap product based on the S&P 100. The proposed caps are European-style vertical spreads, that is, the combination of one long and one short options position with the same expiration.

The short-term interest rate option is based on the most recently auctioned ninety-day US Treasury bill. The new Treasury bill is substituted weekly on the trading day following its auction. The contract size is US$100 multiplied by the composite level, which is ten times the annualized discount rate on the Treasury bill.

The long-term interest rate option is based on a portfolio of government securities; the two most recently auctioned seven-year, ten-year and thirty-year US Treasury bonds, auctioned quarterly. As with the short term option, new issues replace old issues on the trading day following auction. The contract size is the composite level, which is ten times the average yield-to-maturity of the underlying issues.

The CBOE also trades options on US Treasury notes and bonds. The underlying assets of the note options being specific issues of notes with approximately five years to maturity with a contract size of US$100,000 principal amount of the underlying note. The Treasury bond options are based on specific issues of recently issued US Treasury bonds with approximately thirty years to maturity. Again the contract size is of US$100,000 principal amount of the underlying Treasury bond.

Chicago Board Options Exchange
400 South LaSalle
Chicago
Illinois 60605
USA
Tel: (312) 786 5600

CHAPTER 10

TOKYO

The first established markets in Japan were the rice markets in Osaka. In 1688, the Dojima rice market in northern Osaka had more than 1,300 registered dealers. The rice market developed as a forward trading market, enabling growers to sell their crop ahead of harvest. A futures market in rice tickets, receipts for rice stored in warehouses or yet to be harvested, grew up alongside physical trading.

The Japanese financial markets grew from the rice trading in Osaka and the moneychangers in that city and Tokyo; with the currency in Osaka being silver and that in Tokyo, gold, the moneychangers played an important role in the economy, changing rice into money and gold into silver.

However, it was not until the latter part of the nineteenth century and the opening of Japan to "Western" ideas which came with the Meiji Restoration, that Japanese financial institutions began to develop into their current form. Greater private ownership, an end to the feudal system and increasing industrialization meant that national wealth soared in the late nineteenth century. Legislation allowing the formation of limited-liability companies ensured that an owner could separate his company assets and liabilities from his personal wealth. The introduction of limited companies also created the potential for a secondary market in ownership, dealing in company shares. At the same time, banks were being created by the moneychangers. Samurai rice stipends were changed to bonds, and banks took these as deposits and lent money onwards to facilitate industrial expansion.

By 1872, the banks were issuing shares, not yet as a means of raising capital but as a way of dividing up ownership. In fact it was not until well after the Second World War that Japanese companies began to take shares as a means of raising capital seriously, preferring to rely on bank loans and bonds rather than stock offerings. However, the development of the markets continued, although stock trading was considered to be a lowly activity, even within the moneychanging profession itself. The first Japanese stock exchange opened for business in 1878 under the aegis of the Tokyo Stock Exchange Company Ltd. Most of the trading in the early years was limited to bonds but as the Japanese economy grew, so equity transactions also increased.

The driving force of industrialization was the "*zaibatsu*" (the term translates as "financial clique"). In the early twentieth century the *zaibatsu* were to Japan what Rockefeller, Vanderbilt, Carnegie and Morgan had been to the USA in the nineteenth century. However, unlike their US counterparts, the Japanese family firms sought not to dominate in just one industry but across a whole range of enterprises. Instead of one or two firms competing for a dominant market position in each sector of the economy, five companies controlled the entire economy. Although one, Suzuki, fell by the wayside, the remaining four firms controlled virtually all the Japanese economy up to the end of the Second World War, and echoes of their power exist to the present day in equity cross-holdings and shared names. The four were Mitsui, Mitsubishi, Sumitomo and Yasuda. The closest comparison to this hegemony at present is the dominance of the big four brokers in stock and bond trading in the Japanese markets, where Daiwa, Nikko, Nomura and Yamaichi account for more than half of all dealings.

At the end of the Second World War, exchange-based trading was suspended and the *zaibatsu* were broken up. The US-imposed administration believed that the *zaibatsu* had been part of the Japanese war machine and their break-up was viewed as another step in the demilitarization and democratization of Japan.

In 1948, the Securities and Exchange Law, patterned after prewar US securities legislation, was enacted and provided for financial markets broadly based on the US model, with US-style regulations. It is unfortunate in the light of the stock market scandals of the late 1980s and early 1990s that the US-style securities and exchange commission which was established under this law was scrapped by the Japanese authorities shortly thereafter. However, the 1948 Act allowed the re-opening of the Japanese stock exchanges and, in the following year, three markets opened, in Tokyo, Osaka and Nagoya.

Tokyo Stock Exchange (TSE)

Although the TSE is only one of eight stock exchanges in Japan, it is by far the largest, accounting for around 85 per cent of Japanese securities turnover. The meteoric rise of the stock market in the 1980s owed much to the growth of *tokkin* funds, discrete corporate investment funds whose gains may be shown as part of a company's trading profit. The TSE consists of three "sections". The first section, which contains just under 1,200 companies, is for the largest issues in the market. Some 70 per cent of the companies listed in Tokyo's first section are also listed on the Nagoya and Osaka markets. The second section of the market, which comprises just over 400 companies, is similar to the UK's unlisted securities market in that it lists smaller companies, and less stringent listing requirements apply. The third section of the market is the foreign section, which lists all the foreign stocks traded on the TSE.

In addition to the TSE there is a thriving over-the-counter market. Both quoted and unquoted shares are dealt in the OTC market but all OTC issues must be registered with the Japanese Securities Dealers Association. The Japan Over-the-Counter Company acts as an intermediary for OTC issues between securities traders. Because of an effective ban on new equity issues on the TSE from April 1990 into 1991, increasing attention has been focussed on the OTC market. To list on the market, a company is required to have net assets of at least ¥200 million and a minimum of 200 shareholders. However, no trading record is needed and there is no requirement for a dividend to be paid. The OTC market is likely to gain further attention from the introduction of a computerized trading system based on the US NASDAQ market, which is due to be operational by the end of 1991. The use of such a system will increase the transparency of the market and reduce the wide dealing spreads associated with telephone markets.

There are two types of membership on the TSE, regular members, which form the vast majority, and *saitori* members. Regular members are firms which are principally engaged in the trading of securities either as principal or agent. *Saitori* members act only as intermediaries for transactions between regular members. A *saitori* member is not allowed to deal for his own account or for non-members, and is only permitted to deal in a limited number of stocks allocated by the TSE authorities.

Dealings on the TSE are a combination of auction-based and order-driven systems. Trades may be carried out either on the floor of the exchange or through computer. There are two phases of trading: the *itayose* period where opening prices are struck; and the *zaraba* period which begins after the opening prices have been determined.

Trading during *itayose* is on a matched order basis and the deals completed are used to set the opening prices for the day for the commencement of *zaraba*. The *zaraba* session runs from 9.00 am to 11.00 am and from 1.00 pm to 3.00 pm daily and trades during these sessions are executed through an auction. In 1982, the TSE introduced its computerized order routing and execution system, CORES. With the exception of the 150 most active stocks in the first section, all other equities are now traded through CORES.

Since 1972, the Japan Securities Clearing Corporation, which is a wholly-owned subsidiary of the TSE, has been responsible for settlement and clearing on the market. Settlement is normally effected on the third working day after the trade takes place.

The Nikkei Stock Average is the most widely followed Japanese stock index. Like the Dow Jones Industrial Average, the Nikkei is a price-weighted index, It comprises 225 Japanese companies, representing some 19 per cent of first section issues and accounting for around 51 per cent of market value. The index was first calculated on 16 May 1949 and the Nikkei Dow Jones Index, as it was then known, was based at 176.21. At its record high in 1989, the Nikkei was showing a 200-fold increase in some forty years of trading.

However, some of the market's volatility in recent years has been ascribed to the make-up of the index itself. To reduce the Nikkei's own volatility and to limit the impact of futures-related trading on the index, Nihon Keizai Shimbun, the newspaper publisher that administers the Nikkei, is restructuring it in October 1991. This is the first major reform of the index since it was originally quoted and institutes an annual review and the option of dropping and replacing a maximum of six companies each year, should their shares become illiquid or unrepresentative. Previously shares were only dropped from the index because of liquidations and mergers-there were only eight changes to the constituents of the Nikkei in the whole of the 1980s.

There are still limited restrictions in force regarding the foreign ownership of Japanese equity but these were liberalized significantly in 1980 under revisions to the Foreign Exchange and Foreign Trade Control Law. Foreign participation in companies deemed to be of "national interest" is limited to 25 per cent.

Tokyo Stock Exchange
2-1 Nihonbashi-Kabuto
Chuo-ku
Tokyo 103
Tel: 666 0141
Fax: 663 0625

FUTURES MARKETS

The first Japanese futures trading was in rice, the country's staple. For almost 300 years, the government tried to control the price of rice with little success. Only in the mid-twentieth century was the power of the Osaka rice brokers broken with laws enacted banning futures trading. Parts of this legislation remained in place until 1990, and these laws have hampered the development of Japan's futures markets. However, during the early stages of the Gulf crisis in 1990, increased hedging in Euroyen futures briefly turned the small, young Tokyo International Financial Futures Exchange into the second largest market for short-term rate futures after the CME in Chicago.

There are sixteen commodity futures exchanges trading twenty commodities, and two exchanges trading financial futures products in Japan. Turnover in commodity futures hit a new record in the year to March 1991, the fourth year in a row in which volume growth had hit a new high. Precious metals futures accounted for more than a quarter of the total volume of trade.

In December 1990, a new commodities law came into effect, aimed at meeting industry needs for fair and efficient hedging mechanisms, but also moving to internationalize the Japanese commodities markets. Under the new legislation, foreign commodity futures brokers were allowed, for the first time, to become members of the domestic exchanges. The law also simplified the procedures for the listing of new contracts and allowed for the trading of options. Minimum capital requirements were established for brokers and a stricter margin deposit system introduced.

Legislation under discussion in 1991 will, once enacted, allow for the introduction of futures funds and should also go some way to clearing up the regulatory confusion which still exists. At present, the Ministry of Agriculture is responsible for farm product futures, which include soya beans, raw sugar, raw silk, red beans and dried cocoons; the Ministry of International Trade and Industry is in charge of gold, silver, platinum, rubber, cotton and wool yarn; and the Ministry of Finance oversees financial futures. However, the Japanese markets are likely to continue to suffer liquidity problems. Even if futures funds prove popular, most of the trading is likely to be done in more liquid markets elsewhere, where broking commissions are much lower.

Tokyo Commodity Exchange for Industry (Tocom)

Tocom is the largest commodity exchange in Japan, trading futures contracts in six commodities: gold, silver and platinum, which are traded on a screen-based system; and rubber, cotton and wool yarn, which are traded open outcry. Computer-based trading in the precious metals contracts began in April 1991, having been delayed from its original start date in October 1990. The move to automation was intended to boost overseas interest in Tocom. The exchange authorities believed that Tocom's traditional short, open outcry sessions, similar to those on the London Metal Exchange, limited the opportunities for international arbitrage on the exchange. The move has not been as successful as had been hoped, partly because of problems with the new technology. Furthermore, traders in both Hong Kong and Australia say that Tocom would attract more of their business if its trading hours were extended. The exchange authorities are considering this.

Tocom is also considering the introduction of further contracts, partly on the back of the new legislation which allows the trial listing of new contracts to judge industrial hedging requirements. The exchange has asked the Ministry of International Trade and Industry for approval for the introduction of a yen-based futures contract in palladium, a minor metal used mainly in electronic components and dental fillings. The new contract would be traded through Tocom's computer system.

The exchange is also considering the introduction of an aluminium futures contract and options on its gold futures contract. An industry-wide study group on the aluminium futures contract was set up in 1990. However, the feasibility study produced a mixed reception to the idea and the aluminium contract is last on the list of the exchange's potential new instruments. A study is now underway on options to complement Tocom's existing gold futures contract with a forecast date for the introduction of gold options in late 1992. However, Tocom has now plans to introduce options on platinum futures, although the latter is by far the exchange's most successful contract.

Tokyo Commodity Exchange for Industry
Tosen Building 10-8
Horidome 1-chome Nihonbashi
Chuo-ku
Tokyo
Tel: 661 9191

OTHER MARKETS
With the exception of Tocom, most of Japan's commodity futures exchanges presently trade only a couple of contracts with each market specializing in a particular commodity. For example, the Tokyo Grain Exchange trades three soybean contracts, the Kobe Rubber Exchange trades a single crude rubber contract, and the Osaka Textile Exchange trades three cotton yarn contracts, one wool yarn contract and one staple fibre yarn contract. However, in December 1991, the Ministry of Agriculture instructed seven of the country's twelve farm-related commodity exchanges to merge into two large regional markets, one based near Tokyo and the other near Osaka. The move is designed to make the exchanges more internationally competitive.

Tokyo

In the Tokyo area, the Maebashi Dried Cocoon Exchange will be included in a merger between the Tokyo Sugar and Grain Exchanges. In Osaka, the Osaka Sugar Exchange, the Osaka Grain Exchange, the Kobe Grain Exchange and the Kobe Raw Silk Exchange are to merge.

Stock index futures on the Nikkei index were first introduced by the SIMEX, the Singapore futures exchange in 1986. However, in September 1988, index futures contracts were introduced by the Osaka and Tokyo stock exchanges. The Osaka market started trading a futures contract on the Nikkei index and the TSE introduced a contract on the Topix index of 1,100 shares, a wider index than the Nikkei but less well-known. Options on both these contracts were added in June and October 1989 respectively.

On 30 June 1989, the Tokyo International Financial Futures Exchange (TIFFE) opened for business. Trading was initially conducted on a semi-automatic basis under which traders telephoned orders to exchange clerks who then entered trades onto the exchange computer. Users claimed that the system was far too slow and a programme to implement fully automated trading was established in 1991.

TIFFE started trading three contracts: short-term Euroyen interest futures, short-term Eurodollar interest futures and yen/dollar currency futures. The exchange has had only limited success in attracting business. Almost 99 per cent of the market's turnover is in the Euroyen contract, which was the first of its kind in the world. Both the Eurodollar futures and the yen/dollar currency futures are virtually moribund. The TIFFE Eurodollar contract has made little headway against the mutual settlement agreement between SIMEX and the CME. Likewise, the currency futures contract has proved little match for the large Tokyo forward market in foreign exchange. TIFFE's contract looks primitive alongside a variety of tailored over-the-counter packages on offer from the banks.

CHAPTER 11

London

London has a strong, if not indeed overwhelming claim to be the financial centre of Europe. Apart from the sheer size of the banking industry, more than 600 banks from over seventy countries, the city of London is home to the Euromarket (*see Chapter Three*) and is the world's leading centre for foreign exchange trading (*see Chapter Four*). To these must be added a range and diversity of established exchange-based markets second to none in the world.

The city is the leading international centre of expertise in managing global institutional funds, especially in equities, with close on £500 billion in funds under management based in London. Although, in absolute terms, larger sums are managed in both New York and Tokyo, these funds tend to be domestically orientated whereas the London-based funds hold a much higher proportion of their assets internationally. The London Stock Exchange has a 13 per cent share of all cross-border equity trading.

London also remains the centre of the international reinsurance and specialized insurance business through Lloyds of London. In 1688 Edward Lloyd opened a coffee house in Tower Street, close to the Tower of London. Lloyd gained a reputation for providing trustworthy shipping news—one of the most important factors in the successful underwriting of risk. Lloyd's coffee house thus became the recognized home for the marine insurers of the late seventeenth century. Lloyd himself did not take part in any underwriting, his contributions to the development of the world's premier insurance market-place were his name and premises.

In 1720, charters were granted to the Royal Exchange Assurance and London Assurance Corporations, prohibiting marine insurance by any other business. However, the legislation granting these charters deliberately excluded "private and particular persons". It is probably fair to say that Lloyd's owes its existence to this latter omission. The growth of the British Empire through the eighteenth and nineteenth century, founded as it was on maritime trade, provided a major impetus

LONDON

to the development of the market. Lloyds of London now has more than 35,000 members in 376 syndicates managed by underwriters. As well as Lloyds of London, a new London Underwriting Centre is to be established by some ninety specialized reinsurers in 1992. According to the Bank of England, London-based institutions have a 25 per cent share of total cross-border insurance trade. In 1990, according to estimates published by the Central Statistical Office, overall overseas receipts of financial institutions in London rose by 10 per cent to a record £14.1 billion.

However, London's financial pre-eminence in the European time zone is being challenged by Paris and Frankfurt, and the UK's hesitant attitude towards European Monetary Union could result in many of the London markets being sidelined in the future. Against these worries one should set the establishment in London of the European Bank for Reconstruction and Development. Indeed, some optimists whisper that a future European Central Bank could come to London—the argument for this being that not even the French would be happy to see such an institution based in Germany but could be willing to have it established in London as a sop to UK governmental sensibilities!

The 1980s was a period of major change and upheaval for the UK markets with new exchanges, new contracts and new ways of doing business coming thick and fast. Added to this was the impetus to the stock market of the Conservative government's ambitious privatization programme, which raised the profile of UK financial services both domestically and internationally.

STOCK MARKETS

Trading in stocks and shares in London goes back to the seventeenth century (*see Chapter One*) with the main boost to trading coming in 1694 with the founding of the Bank of England. The Bank was set up by King William III and Parliament in 1694 with the express purpose of raising money to fund the war with France. The Bank raised the then substantial sum of £1,200,000 through public subscription and issued loan notes to cover the funds, setting the pattern for UK government funding which continues to this day. Towards the end of the century, the brokers had established their businesses in the coffee houses near the Royal Exchange, notably Garraway's and Jonathan's. The market weathered the bursting of the South Sea Bubble, and by the late 1760s, 150 brokers had formed a subscription club at Jonathan's coffee house, later opening their own room, New Jonathan's, when the old coffee house burnt down. In 1773, the members of New Jonathan's voted to change the name to the Stock Exchange. As the market developed, the need for tighter regulation of business became apparent and a review by an Exchange committee resulted in the 1812 Deed of Settlement, which still underpins many of the market's present regulations.

In 1877, a Royal Commission was established "to inquire into the origin, objects, present constitution, customs and usages of the London Stock Exchange". The commission's report was largely favourable but highlighted the shortage of space in the market, and in 1884 the exchange's premises were expanded. In 1908, rules formalizing the distinction between brokers, trading in the market on behalf of their clients, and jobbers, wholesalers operating in the market on their own account and dealing solely with brokers, were passed. These rules effectively remained in place until Big Bang in 1986.

The exchange weathered the storms of two world wars and the Wall Street crash of the inter-war years. Massive nationalization programmes in the late 1940s and early 1950s provided a significant boost to the market in government stock with gilts to the tune of more than £3.5 billion being issued to fund the buy out of private shareholders. However, it was not until 1959 that restrictions on corporate financing were eased, allowing companies greater freedom to raise funds in the market. In 1965, the process of federation began which led to the amalgamation of the UK's regional stock exchanges under the aegis of the London Stock Exchange in 1973. The preceding year, the construction of a new trading floor and office facility had been completed on the site occupied by the market since 1801.

In 1979, the market took its first step towards automation with the introduction of the computerized TALISMAN clearing system. However, prior to the introduction of TALISMAN, events had already been set in train which would lead to the market's biggest shake-up in its history–Big Bang. Pressure for change was coming from two sources, the lifting of foreign exchange controls in 1979, which exposed the London market to international competition, and the government, which was planning to take the exchange to court over alleged restrictive trading practices. The government's action was the result of the 1976 Restrictive Trade Practices Act, which obliged the exchange to register its rule book with the UK's Office of Fair Trading. The OFT ruled the market guilty of restrictive practices in three areas: fixed commissions; the separation between brokers and jobbers; and limits on membership. The outcome of the government's threat of action was an out-of-court settlement between the exchange and the Department of Trade & Industry, under which the government agreed to drop its legal proceedings, and the market agreed to abolish its system of minimum commissions by the end of 1986.

London

The changes brought about in Big Bang saw the disappearance of the distinction between broker and jobber and the introduction of a system of market makers. However, of greater significance was the relaxation of the restrictions on membership. To enable members to establish the capital base required to compete in international markets, the exchange lifted all restrictions on the control of member firms. For the first time, members of the market could be owned by external corporations; previously control was vested in the hands of individual members. Perhaps unlooked-for, this resulted in a huge influx of foreign banks and brokers seeking market share, resulting in severe overcapacity in the broking business, a situation which persists to this day, despite the withdrawal of several firms in the wake of the crash of 1987.

Big Bang coincided with the 1986 Financial Services Act which established the Securities & Investments Board (*see Chapter Six*) and a new regulatory structure throughout the UK's financial services industry. The new market post-Big Bang witnessed the rapid withdrawal of traders from the exchange's floor with business being transacted on the newly-installed computer terminal-based quotation system, the Stock Exchange Automated Quotations (SEAQ), leaving only the dealers in the London Traded Options Market still on the floor.

However, despite the changes made at the time of Big Bang, the London market is still working to a fixed term account system and paper-based settlement, unlike the New York markets. In May 1992, TAURUS (Transfer and Automated Registration of Uncertificated Stock) is due to come into operation, resulting in the so-called "dematerialization" of the settlement of transactions. Once TAURUS is in operation, shares will be held, recorded, transferred and registered electronically. The only paper to be produced by the system will be notifications to shareholders of any change in their holdings. Shareholders' approval will be required for companies' shares to go paperless and the new system will be run by account controllers. Existing company registrars will become company account controllers and brokers and banks will become commercial account controllers. Investors will have the option of choosing which account controller to use. In the second phase of TAURUS, to be implemented by the end of 1992, the exchange's existing fixed account periods will be done away with and a rolling settlement period introduced, similar to that now operating in the US markets. Under the rolling settlement period, shares purchased would have to be paid for within a set number of working days after the transaction. The exchange's aim is to bring this period down to three working days. TAURUS could have the same kind of impact on back office operations that Big Bang had on the market's method of trading.

London Stock Exchange (LSE)

Effectively, the London Stock Exchange is not one but four stock markets and, in addition, operates the London Traded Options Market (*see below*). The equity markets consist of: SEAQ, trading domestic equity; SEAQ International, trading international equity; the gilt-edged and fixed interest bond market; and the unlisted securities market (USM).

SEAQ's domestic equities market was initially divided into three categories–Alpha, Beta and Gamma. Alpha were the largest, most actively traded stocks, in which market makers were required to show firm, continuous two-way prices. All trades were published within five minutes on the market's TOPIC information system. Trading information on Beta stocks was not published immediately and price quotations in Gamma stocks was allowed to be indicative in the minimum quantity of shares traded. In January 1991, the exchange replaced the Alpha, Beta and Gamma system. Perhaps mistakenly, the three-tier system had become in the minds of both investors and company chairmen a matter of perceived status. The new classification system is based on a company's normal market size (NMS), that is, the number of shares traded in a normal-sized market transaction, and has twelve categories. The main purposes of the new liquidity test are to determine the size of transaction in which market makers have an obligation to deal with each other and on what basis the bargains should be published.

The most widely quoted index in the market is the FT-SE100 share index, which was introduced in January 1984. Based on the top 100 UK companies by market capitalization, it is updated minute-by-minute.

SEAQ International is the exchange's market price information service for leading international stocks, serving as a collection point for bid and offer quotations from competing international market makers. Trading on SEAQ International accounts for more than 60 per cent of all cross-border non-domestic equities trading with the volume of business running almost level with that of domestic UK equities trading and ten times the size of turnover in the next largest non-domestic equity market, NASDAQ. Although some 700 securities from all over the world are quoted on the market, the majority of business on SEAQ International is in European securities. In October 1990, the exchange took the logical step of formulating a market index for these equities, the Eurotrack 100 index. In February 1991, the market added the Eurotrack 200, an amalgamation of the two main indices, the Eurotrack 100 of the leading European shares traded in London and the FT-SE100. In February 1989, SAEF, the SEAQ Automatic Execution Facility, went live, automatically matching buy and sell orders against the best quote already held in the system. SAEF operates on both SEAQ and SEAQ International.

The gilt-edged (UK government bonds) and fixed interest market passed something of a milestone in 1990. It was the first year that the gilt-edged market makers collectively recorded a profit since Big Bang. The market in UK government bonds had marked time through the late 1980s with the government's fiscal surpluses affecting the liquidity of the market-place. The return of government deficits in the 1990s and the issue of new gilts has helped to improve the market's prospects and may also help revive the corporate bond market.

The unlisted securities market was established in November 1980 to provide a separately regulated, cheaper and more flexible market for smaller companies. Over the ten years of the market's existence, 800 companies had raised over £4 billion and more than 150 of them had graduated to a full listing on the exchange. When the USM was started, companies were required to have a five-year trading record to apply for a full listing but needed only a three-year record to list on the USM. Disclosure regulations were also less onerous. However, with the demise of the third market in December 1990 after just under four years of existence, the regulations were altered, reducing still further the disclosure requirements on the USM. At the same time, the record period for companies on the USM and the main market were reduced to two years and three years respectively.

At the bottom of the stock market's equities pyramid are Rule 535 stocks. This is a designation given to companies not quoted on the market but whose shares are traded under the exchange's matched bargain facilities. To obtain this designation, companies must have a trading record of at least one year and must submit an unqualified auditor's report for their last financial year. Private companies with broad shareholder bases use the market and companies which have delisted their shares from quotation occasionally use the 535 facility before rejoining the main market. Quoted shares temporarily suspended may also be traded under Rule 535 after specific exchange permission.

London Stock Exchange
London EC2N 1HP
England
Tel: 071-588 2355

NORDEX

The youngest of the London-based equity markets, NORDEX is an electronic market-place for shares in companies based in the four

Nordic countries–Denmark, Finland, Norway and Sweden. NORDEX, launched in November 1990, is the first public implementation of the *Transvik Market System*, a generic electronic trading system developed by the Transvik unit of the Swedish Kinnevik/Invik industrial and financial group of companies.

The NORDEX system matches bid and offer orders, confirming trades to both counterparties and the market at large immediately. It is integrated, with a centralized clearing and settlement management facility. The core of NORDEX is a central cluster of Digital Equipment Corporation Vax computers.

Although NORDEX has extended trading hours and continues to function after SEAQ International has shut down, it has yet to attract the level of business required to become a fully liquid market-place. The participants are mostly Swedish and Norwegian, although there are active traders based in Amsterdam, London, Luxemburg and New York as well as in Oslo and Stockholm. The market's share listings remain dominated by Swedish and Norwegian equity, with no Danish or Finnish shares listed.

NORDEX
Transvik Ltd
Crown House
72 Hammersmith Road
London W14 8YP
England
Tel: 071-603 4544

FUTURES MARKETS

London's futures markets offer the widest variety of hedging instruments in a single location around the world and reinforce the city's claim to be one of the world's leading financial centres. Although the individual commodity futures markets themselves tend to be smaller than those based in Chicago and New York, they are often more highly regarded within the industries associated with the commodities traded. Most of London's futures contracts are cleared by the International Commodities Clearing House, among the few exceptions are the grain contracts traded on London FOX which are cleared by the Grain and Feed Trade Association.

Developments likely to reinforce London's standing as a centre of futures trading include the merger of the Baltic Futures Exchange with London FOX, and the proposed merger of the London International Financial Futures Exchange with the London Traded Options Market, both moves likely to improve the liquidity and international recognition of the respective markets.

Changes to UK legislation governing derivative products in the last few years have done much to increase the attractions of futures and options to the major investment fund managers. In 1990, trading income from futures and options in the hands of pension funds and authorized unit trusts was exempted from tax. The following year, the government announced it was easing the so-called anti-bond washing rules which discouraged tax exempt institutions from buying or selling equities through the exercise of options, by requiring them to hold the stock for six months or more if they were not to incur a tax charge on dividends paid. The holding period has now been reduced from six months to one month in line with the holding period for equities themselves. Most recently the Securities & Investments Board has allowed futures and options funds to operate in the UK markets.

London International Financial Futures Exchange (LIFFE)

Although LIFFE only opened its doors for the first time in 1982, the site it occupies has been associated with trading for several hundreds of years. Queen Elizabeth I came to the City of London on 23 January 1571, to open Sir Thomas Gresham's Bourse, which had been built in imitation of the main trading centre in Antwerp. She renamed it the Royal Exchange. Many of London's financial markets developed first at the Royal. Queen Victoria opened the present exchange building on the site of Gresham's original exchange in 1844. The Royal Exchange, adjacent to the Bank of England, now houses the London International Financial Futures Exchange. LIFFE was established in 1982 as the first market-place within the European time zone for financial futures contracts. Options were introduced on the market's futures contracts for the first time in 1985. Although LIFFE originally traded a number of currency futures and options, these contracts were suspended by the market owing to poor liquidity.

In November 1989, LIFFE introduced an Automated Pit Trading system (APT). The system was upgraded in 1991 with the launch of a futures contract based on Japanese Government Bonds (JGB), adding order matching capabilities to the system. Traders are now able to lodge orders in APT which will automatically be bid/offered and matched within the system without the need for users to monitor trading continually. The exchange has successfully tested trading terminals in New York and believes it is now operating the most advanced system of its kind in the world. However, with one exception, the APT system only operates after the pit trading sessions have closed.

Volume on LIFFE has grown continuously throughout the exchange's existence, setting a new record in 1990 with a total of 34,169,963 futures and options contracts traded, up 43 per cent on the previous year, representing an average daily turnover of £30.2 billion.

LIFFE is in a toe-to-toe battle with France's Marché à Terme International de France (MATIF–*see Chapter Twelve*) for domination in European financial futures trading. Volumes on the two markets are more or less evenly matched at present although LIFFE would appear to have the edge in the crucial area of non-domestic contracts, i.e. those based on foreign interest rates and financial instruments. Another major deciding factor is likely to be the quality of the exchanges' electronic trading systems. LIFFE's APT proved capable of taking the strain of trading over 2,000 contracts a minute shortly after sterling joined the European exchange rate mechanism in 1990. Against this, some of MATIF's contracts will be available on GLOBEX when it is launched and the French exchange has been given exclusive rights to list ECU-denominated products on GLOBEX.

However, as far as size is concerned in the short term, LIFFE's planned merger with the London Traded Options Market (LTOM–*see below*) to form the London International Financial Futures and Options Exchange is likely to ensure that the London market will remain Europe's leading financial futures exchange through to the end of the century. The merger announcement came in April 1990, and the two markets will form the largest futures and options exchange in Europe and the fifth largest in the world. The merger will be completed by the end of January 1992. Work began on a new trading floor for the exchange in March 1991. However, progress towards the unification of the two markets has been slow, with issues such as stock-lending and the setting up of a unified clearing structure taking months to clarify. It is likely that, even when the two market have merged, there may still be slightly different arrangements for equity products and financial futures. The harmonization of margins is not expected to happen until after the new market is operational.

Matters such as membership rights and structures, and capital requirements have also proved thorny. Furthermore, many smaller firms fear that the proposed move towards screen-based trading for equity options could lead to job losses and the demise of the locals who provide much of the two markets' present liquidity.

Contracts
LIFFE operates a designated broker system on most of its futures and options contracts to ensure liquidity in the market-place. The exchange

trades five short-term interest rate futures and six long-term interest rate futures, with options available on six of these contracts. In addition, LIFFE trades futures in two stock indices, the FT-SE100 and the FT-SE Eurotrack 100. The only contract to be traded exclusively on screen on the APT system through the trading day is that in Japanese Government Bond futures, which was designed by the exchange to facilitate daily roll-over of positions into the Tokyo Stock Exchange's JGB futures contract. The market's newest contract, launched in September 1991, is that based on Italy's Buoni del Tesoro Poiennali (BTPs), domestic government bonds with maturities ranging between four and ten years. It is the first futures contract to be denominated in lira and was developed following reforms to Italian withholding tax legislation early in 1991.

LIFFE's two stock index-based products are both linked to indices produced by the London Stock Exchange. Futures on the FT-SE100 Index began trading on LIFFE in May 1984, and turnover in the futures contract now represents around 50 per cent of the turnover in the underlying equities, making the FT-SE100 futures contract the single most liquid equity instrument in the UK. The newer of the two contracts, D-mark denominated Eurotrack 100 futures, was launched in June 1991, complemented by options contracts to be traded on both the LTOM and the Chicago Board Options Exchange.

The short-term interest rate contracts are: three-month sterling; three-month Eurodollar; three-month Euromark; three-month Euroswiss franc; and three-month ECU. The long-term interest rate contracts are: ECU bonds; Long gilt; German government bond (Bund); US Treasury bond; Japanese Government bond; and Italian Government bond. LIFFE trades options on the three-month sterling, three-month Eurodollar, three-month Euromark, Long gilt, Bund and US Treasury bond contracts. The Bund contract, launched in September 1988, is the exchange's most successful contract, success that the Deutsche Terminbörse hopes to emulate (*see Chapter Twelve*).

London International Financial Futures Exchange
Royal Exchange
London EC3V 3PJ
England
Tel: 071-623 0444

London Traded Options Market (LTOM)

The LTOM, part of the London Stock Exchange, began trading in 1978, offering call options in just ten shares, puts were first introduced in 1981 and by 1983 calls and puts were introduced on all series. Options on the

FT-SE100 index were introduced in 1984, in tandem with the futures contract launched on LIFFE, and options on gilts contracts were launched in the following year. The advent of Big Bang in 1986 opened the market to new firms, removed minimum commission rates and put the London market on an equal footing with the rest of the world. As share trading left the floor of the Stock Exchange, with screen-based market makers operating out of their own dealing rooms, the LTOM, operating an open outcry market, was left as the sole occupant of the Stock Exchange floor.

However, despite continued growth in the number of options traded and the introduction of small number of options based on European equities and on currencies, the LTOM has not recovered from the blow dealt by the stock market crash of 1987. The proposed merger with LIFFE is in part a direct result of the massive reduction in individual investor activity on the LTOM following the crash of October 1987. In preparation for the merger, the LTOM has become operationally independent of the London Stock Exchange's computer systems.

London Traded Options Market
(London Stock Exchange)
London EC2N 1HP
England
Tel: 071-588 2355

London Metal Exchange (LME)
The LME is the oldest of London's futures markets in anything like its present form. The London Metal Exchange Company, precursor of the present LME, was formed in 1876, although a market known as the Lombard Exchange had operated as a forum for metal traders for the previous eight years. The LME's basic dealing practice is little changed from that established in the nineteenth century. In the interests of fair dealing and speed of transaction, the market operated through the open outcry system and traders took their positions around a large chalk circle drawn on the floor of the room to make their bids and offers.

Many of the exchange's features were formalized in its early years. The original three-month forward trading span was established with formal futures contracts. The reason behind this choice of period is that it was approximately the length of time it took to ship copper from Valparaiso, Chile, and tin from Peninsular Malaya to the ports of London and Liverpool. The LME's short five-minute trading periods or "rings" of official dealing were also introduced. Copper and tin were the first metals to be traded, followed shortly by lead and zinc. During the First World War, the LME virtually ceased to operate though trading resumed speedily after the war ended. The inter-war years saw considerable growth in investment activity in the metals industries but also increasing attempts to control the market through cartels. The first attempts to regulate the markets were also made, notably in tin through the Bandung Pool and the International Tin Restriction Scheme. Business ground to a halt again with the Second World War and trading on the LME did not begin again until 1949 with the resumption of trading in tin futures, as government controls over commodities were lifted.

At the turn of the century, the exchange briefly traded a pig iron contract and a silver contract has also traded on three occasions, between 1897 and 1911, again between 1935 and 1939 and most recently between 1968 and 1987. Throughout most of the twentieth century, copper, tin, lead and zinc were the mainstay of the LME's business. Contracts in aluminium and nickel were added in 1978 and 1979 respectively.

The LME has morning and afternoon sessions or rings in which each metal is traded twice, "official" daily prices are published at the end of the morning session. Informal "kerb" trading sessions, so-called because these informal deals were originally conducted out on the street, take place after the end of the ring dealing sessions. In addition, the market trades non-stop through inter-office dealings throughout the day. The LME was originally an independent principals' market but following the collapse of the International Tin Council and the ensuing threat to the market's liquidity in the mid-1980s, the UK government forced the exchange authorities to accept a clearing house operation. The tin contract, which had been suspended in 1985 on the abrupt cessation of the ITC's price support operation, was finally relaunched in 1989.

In 1963, warehouses in Rotterdam became the first official foreign locations for the delivery and acceptance of metal to the LME. The exchange's international profile has risen since then and its importance as a global market-place is underlined by the fact that there are now official warehouses across Europe, in Japan, Singapore and the USA.

Although there are no limits on price movements on the LME, the exchange instituted procedures for monitoring large positions in the market and established position limits in April 1991.

Contracts

The LME's contracts were extended from their original three-month forward span to trade out to fifteen months forward and in June 1991 copper, aluminium and zinc contracts were widened to allow deals to be

Market	Contract	Trading unit	Price quotation
LME	Copper	25 tonnes	£ sterling and £0.5/tonne
	Tin	5 tonnes	Dollars/tonne
	Lead	25 tonnes	£ sterling and £0.25/tonne
	Zinc	25 tonnes	Dollars and $0.5/tonne
	Aluminium	25 tonnes	Dollars/tonne
	Nickel	6 tonnes	Dollars/tonne
Call and put options are traded on all the LME's futures contracts			

struck for up to twenty-seven months ahead. Consideration is being given to extending the contracts further up to thirty-six months forward. The LME has also increased the range of currencies in which contracts can be trade to include the D-mark and yen, although US dollars and sterling remain the only currencies quoted in the official ring dealing sessions.

The exchange is also considering the launch of a secondary aluminium contract, to complement the existing primary aluminium contract.

Although over-the-counter options existed previously, exchange-traded options were first introduced on the LME in 1987 with the move to a centrally cleared market. Following the introduction of options on the tin contract in May 1991, call and put options are now traded on all the LME's futures contracts.

London Metal Exchange
Plantation House
Fenchurch Street
London EC3M 3AP
England
Tel: 071 626 3311

The Futures & Options Exchange (London FOX)
Futures trading in soft commodities sprang from the auction sales of the nineteenth century. At their peak there were as many as fifty or sixty auction sales, where shipments of goods were shown by samples on the spot, every day in the city of London. A special centre for these auctions was created at the London Commercial Sale Rooms in 1811. Rebuilt on the same site in 1890, this remained the headquarters of the soft commodity traders until it was destroyed during the Second World War. The Sale Rooms were the direct predecessor of the London Commodity Exchange which was set up in the 1970s to provide common services to the various Terminal Market Associations whose members owned and

ran the markets. In 1987, the exchange relocated to purpose-built facilities sharing a floor with the International Petroleum Exchange (*see below*), and in June of the that year was relaunched with a new corporate identity as London FOX.

The exchange's new name reflected the addition of a traded options market and the introduction of locals, individual traders dealing on their own accounts, to the exchange's contracts. In 1989, FOX introduced FAST, its proprietary Fast Automated Screen Trading facility. FOX consolidated its position as Europe's leading soft commodity exchange through the merger with London's smallest futures market, the Baltic Futures Exchange (BFE), which took effect in January 1991. The BFE was itself only a relatively new exchange, having been formed in 1987 by those markets located in London's Baltic Exchange, in an attempt to reduce overheads. However, the BFE suffered from limited participation and, initially, no "local" membership. Even a move to merge the trading floors of its five futures markets and the introduction of limited trading licences allowing members to trade on any of the five markets, failed to ensure the BFE an independent future of its own.

FOX has been actively seeking to expand its international profile, collaborating with foreign markets. In August 1990, the exchange announced that it was working with the Tokyo Grain Exchange to create an appropriate arrangement to ensure that contracts would be available to members of each market throughout the entire trading day. In May 1991, FOX began talks with MATIF in Paris, exploring the means of a possible common market for the trading of sugar futures. FOX had also been the front-runner to take over the New Zealand Futures & Options Exchange before the uncovering of a scandal in its (FOX's) property futures contracts (*see below*).

Contracts
Seven new contracts have been launched since the exchange's relaunch under the London FOX name in 1987 not including those which have been brought under FOX's control through the merger with the BFE. However, not all the new contracts have proved successful. In October 1991, barely six months after they were launched, the exchange's four screen-based property futures contracts were suspended after revelations that the exchange had been trading on its own account to boost volumes. In addition, the exchange authorities admitted that financial incentives had been paid to certain traders in other screen-based contracts to increase turnover.

Among the new contracts likely to survive, of particular interest is the MGMI, a metals price index, developed by Metallgesellschaft of

Market	Contract	Trading unit	Price quotation
London FOX	Cocoa Futures	10 tonnes	£ sterling/tonne
	Robusta coffee futures	5 tonnes	Dollars/tonne
	*No.6 raw sugar futures	50 tonnes	Dollars and cents/tonne
	*White sugar futures	50 tonnes	Dollars and cents/tonne
	*MGMI futures	$10 x 10 basis points	Dollars ($100/index point)
	*Rubber Futures	22,222.36 lb	Cents/lb
	*European washed Arabica coffeee futures	37,500 lb	Cents/lb
	†Potato futures	20 tonnes	Pence per tonne
	†Pig futures	3,250 kg	Pence per kilogramme
	†Soyabean meal futures	20 tonnes	£ sterling per tonne
	†Freight futures	$10 per index point	Index points equivalent to $50 a lot
	†Grain futures (wheat/barley)	100 tonnes	Pence per tonne
	Options on cocoa futures		
	Options on robusta coffee futures		
	*Options on raw sugar futures		
	*Options on white sugar futures		
	*Options on MGMI futures		
	*Options on European washed Arabica coffee futures		
	†Options on soyabean meal futures		
	†Options on grain futures		
*These contracts are traded on London FOX's FAST screen-based trading system			
†These contracts originally traded on the Baltic Futures Exchange			

Germany, which is actually based on the prices of contracts on another exchange, the LME. FOX is considering an international cotton index contract, similar in size to the cotton contract traded in New York, and cash settled index futures in electricity. The latter contract, if launched, would initially be confined to UK electricity, but the exchange aims to develop a pan-European electricity contract. However, the scandal surrounding the property futures contracts has cast a shadow over the exchange's development.

In January 1991, after sometimes acrimonious debate, FOX's raw sugar contract moved from open outcry to FAST. Several of the exchange's brokers had expressed concern over the move, which went ahead despite a late attempt by some to bring the coffee, cocoa and raw sugar contracts together onto integrated floor trading in the exchange's pits. The closure of property futures followed by the closure of the rice futures contract early in November 1991 means it is likely that FOX's raw sugar contract will return to the floor at the behest of the traders. Although FAST has screen traders in France, Germany, Singapore and the USA, the prospects of FOX moving steadily away from pit trading to a fully automated screen-based market-place have been much reduced.

London FOX
1 Commodity Quay
St. Katharine Docks
London E1 9AX
England
Tel: 071 481 2080

International Petroleum Exchange (IPE)

The IPE was greeted with a mixture of anticipation and caution when it opened for business in April 1981. The exchange trades futures and options contracts for crude oil and oil-based products. The IPE remains overshadowed by the much higher volume of business on NYMEX, but IPE trading volumes have continued to set new records in recent years and the exchange is firmly established as one of only two futures markets in the world to trade oil-related energy futures contracts. In common with the NYMEX contracts, volume on the IPE began to rise significantly in the mid-1980s as the oil price slumped. These falling values forced the major oil companies to turn to the futures markets to offset their exposure.

In November 1984, the IPE relaunched its gas oil contract. The changes incorporated into the contract at that time ensured its success, and for several years the viability of the market-place rested solely on gas oil futures. The exchange moved to its present premises in May 1987, the move coinciding with the introduction of both pit trading and local membership to improve liquidity in the market-place. Traded options were introduced on the gas oil contract two months later.

After several false starts, including abortive negotiations with NYMEX over proposals to trade the US exchange's light sweet crude oil contract, the IPE finally hit on the right formula for a crude oil contract with the Brent Blend futures contract, launched in June 1988.

The Brent contract has succeeded not by supplanting the existing off-exchange forward market but by complementing it. The forward market for Brent oil was originally little more than a device through which North Sea oil producers could establish a market price in order to determine their tax liabilities. However, the forward market contract size, originally 600,000 barrels but since reduced to 500,000 barrels, effectively barred this market to all but the largest companies. Against this, the IPE's Brent Blend futures contract is only 1,000 barrels and delivery is by cash settlement. Although the health of the forward market is vital to the IPE contract, because the cash settlement is based on an index of forward market prices, the reduced risk and tighter regulatory environment of the futures contract has attracted significant participation.

Contracts

Two of the present five contracts on the IPE have been suspended. They are the contracts for Dubai crude oil and heavy fuel oil. The three contracts traded are gas oil, Brent Blend and naptha, the latter being launched on the market in April 1991. The Brent Blend contract is cash settled but the other two contracts do run to physical delivery. Options are traded on the gas oil and Brent Blend contracts. There are no daily limits to price moves in the IPE's futures contracts.

Market	Contract	Trading unit	Price quotation
IPE	Brent Blend futures	1,000 barrels	Dollars and cents/barrel
	Gas oil futures	100 tonnes	Dollars and cents/tonne
	Naptha futures	100 tonnes	Dollars and cents/tonne
	Options on Brent Blend futures		
	Options on gas oil futures		

Despite the somewhat chequered performance of some of its initiatives over the 1980s, the IPE is continuing to review the potential for new contracts and may relaunch a contract in heavy fuel oil. The exchange is also said to be considering an unleaded gasoline contract.

The International Petroleum Exchange of London
International House
1 St. Katherine's Way
London
E1 9UN
England
Tel: 071 481 0643

OTHER MARKETS

The withdrawal of the silver contract from the London Metal Exchange in the late 1980s left London without a futures contract in the precious metals sector. A London Gold Futures Market was set up in 1982 but closed after just three years, being hit by the bear market in gold and

London

competition from the established contract on COMEX in New York and forward dealing on the established London bullion market. In 1988, at the prompting of the Bank of England, gold trading in London was formalized under the aegis of the London Bullion Market Association (LBMA). All bullion trading in London is undertaken in accordance with the Bank of England's Code of Conduct and the LBMA represents all the main participants in the market.

CHAPTER 12

WESTERN EUROPE

Continental Europe's futures markets are dwarfed by those in the USA and the UK. None of the European commodity markets have succeeded in attracting major international interest and the only financial futures market so far to have established an international presence is France's MATIF (*see below*). In equity trading, the continental European markets are much smaller than the London market. In market capitalization of exchange listed domestic companies, at the end of 1990, expressed in US dollars, the London market, capitalized at US$888 billion, was larger than the two largest markets in Europe put together, France (US$342 billion) and Germany (US$343 billion). The London market accounts for a staggering 93 per cent of cross-border share trading in Europe, worth some £154 billion a year, and regularly accounts for half the domestic equity turnover in German, French and Italian shares.

In 1989, the Federation of European Stock Exchanges set up a Brussels-based company called Euroquote to combine share prices and company news from each national stock exchange and supply them direct to users through a combined electronic feed. However, these efforts to create a unified European securities market failed in July 1991 after the twelve European Community (EC) exchanges refused to co-operate in the funding of Euroquote. Euroquote foundered on national rivalries and doubts about its commercial viability. The Federation of European Stock Exchanges established a working party to examine what kind of information, settlement and support system investors in European shares desire.

However, two projects are still underway, Euro-index, a pan-European index designed for derivatives markets and a halfway house

Market	Proportion of European capitalization 1990 (%)	Proportion of European trading volume 1990 (%)
Germany	22.20	38.90
France	22.10	16.10
Switzerland	10.80	14.00
Italy	9.70	5.30
Netherlands	9.60	10.20
*Rest of Europe	25.60	15.50

*includes Austria, Belgium, Denmark, Finland, Ireland, Luxemburg, Norway, Spain and Sweden.

(Source: Goldman Sachs)

to a pan-European market, named Eurolist is being developed. Given the development of proprietary European indices such as the Eurotrack in London and Eurotop in Amsterdam, with futures contracts already trading, it is difficult to see Euro-index making much headway. Eurolist is designed to harmonize listing requirements for companies across the European exchanges and should begin operation in 1992, initially covering about 150 of the EC's top companies. However, it is not yet clear how Eurolist will work to boost dealing volumes without agreement on a trading system. Regulations governing the multiple listing of shares on European markets have already been established by the EC

In October 1990, Sweden's largest insurance group, Skandia, became the first company in the world to use mutual recognition of listing procedures between EC member states, new EC legislation allowing companies to make multiple listings on several European stock markets, provided that they occur within six weeks of one another. Under these rules, only one prospectus can be used, translated into the appropriate languages and providing considerable savings compared with the costs of separate listings.

The attraction to companies of such internationalized share quotations are the potential for broadening their investor base, given that many institutions are legally restricted from investing in companies not quoted in their domestic market; and also the prospect of cross-border acquisitions in which there are tax advantages in doing so by the use of shares and in which target shareholders would certainly be more amenable to receiving shares that are actively traded and quoted on their domestic market.

Also militating against the development of a pan-European market-place has been the slow speed of development of the EC directives covering capital adequacy requirements for brokerages (*see Chapter Six*).

The main cause of delay here has been the polarization of EC nations into two camps. The first, including the UK, Germany and the Netherlands, is in favour of liberalization to foster competition and to open cross-border trading. The second group, which includes France, Italy, Spain and Belgium, wants to protect domestic exchanges by banning off-market trading and requires the instant publication of trades, customary in order-driven markets but not in quote-driven ones like London. These moves have been interpreted, not incorrectly, as aimed at reining in the influence of London's SEAQ International and the free-wheeling bond market. The intensity of the wrangling is underlined by the fear that if nothing is done, Europe could lose its pre-eminence in international securities dealing completely.

Stock Markets

Perhaps the most striking thing about Europe's stock markets is the fact that many of them are going through some kind of reform at present. Even the Greek stock exchange in Athens, one of Europe's more obsolete securities markets, may finally be dragged into the computer age by 1992. In 1990, the exchange was privatized, a new central depository and a new supervisory board are to be implemented as the next steps in modernizing the market.

The French and German markets, Europe's largest, are discussed in detail separately below. The next three biggest markets, in Switzerland, Italy and the Netherlands are all in the throes of modernizing in order to attract liquidity and, most especially, foreign participation.

Although there is as yet no concerted effort on the part of the authorities to liberalize the Swiss stock markets, some of Switzerland's leading corporations are making more financial information available to investors and are increasing dividend payments. Following the lead set by Nestle SA in 1988, several companies are giving foreign shareholders full voting rights. A patchwork of laws and multiple share structures currently keep Swiss companies under domestic control. There are three classes of stock: registered shares with voting rights; bearer shares with mixed rights; and participation certificates that pay dividends but carry no votes. Foreign investors have little or no change of obtaining significant voting rights because of Vinkulierungspraxis, the registration system which allows companies to refuse to register shares. However, some legislative changes have been proposed. Swiss companies are to be allowed to buy back part of their issued equity and lower the nominal value of their shares to SFr10 from SFr100 and there are plans to reduce the number of regional exchanges from seven to three with the introduction of an electronic trading system by mid-1993.

Italy's stock market reforms have run into problems with the brokers on the floor of the market. The market was hit by strikes through 1990 and 1991 as the floor traders protested against reforms which could cost them their jobs. The brokers' grievances stem from the proposed introduction in 1992 of the Societa di Intermediazione Mobiliare, a new type of broking and fund management operation designed to improve transparency. At the same time, the market will introduce faster settlement procedures and a screen-based trading system.

Being the world's oldest stock exchange has not helped the market in Amsterdam. Indeed the international character of the exchange, together with its relative small size, makes it vulnerable to competition. Half of the companies listed on the market are foreign and

50 per cent of the market's turnover is conducted on behalf of foreigners. This advantage in cross-border trading is counterbalanced by the fact that the market's largest capitalization stocks, such as Philips, Shell and Unilever, are just as easily traded overseas as they are on the domestic exchange. In 1990, the Finance Ministry announced the abolition of stamp duty on market dealings. An experimental open order book for large bond transactions, combining a screen-based quote system with the existing order driven floor market was established in the same year. The bond market order book has since been extended and is likely eventually to cover share trading also as part of a piecemeal "rolling Big Bang" which began in Amsterdam in the mid-1980s.

Among other European exchanges being modernized are the Belgian, Spanish and Swedish equity markets. The liberalization of the Belgian stock exchange, Belgium's "little bang", begun in 1990 has resulted in brokers losing their monopoly of exchange business and made them incorporate as limited liability companies. Lower commission rates were introduced and plans to modernize back office settlement procedures have also been set in motion. The Belgian authorities are also working to set up a futures and options exchange (*see below*).

The modernization of Spain's securities markets was begun in 1989, and will be completed in 1992 with the introduction of a centralized settlement system. The country's four exchanges had originally been set up on the Napoleonic model but when the authorities decided to bring them up to date, the reform framework established was based more closely on the post-Big Bang London market than on the French model. The government forced notaries to become brokers and capitalize themselves. Fixed commissions have been abolished and computerized continuous trading has been introduced. At the same time, a new national securities commission, the Commision Nacional del Mercado de Valores, was established to oversee trading.

In Sweden, the election of a non-Socialist government in September 1991 has provided the impetus for the development of the market in Stockholm. One of the new government's first acts was to propose the abolition of the turnover tax on share trading. The tax, introduced by the Socialists in 1984, drove trading to London and New York; for example, in 1990, 45 per cent of turnover in Swedish equities was conducted outside the country. Other tax changes are being considered. A government commission is considering the elimination of double taxation on dividends and granting individual investors the same right as institutional investors not to pay capital gains tax when the gains are reinvested. The market is also harmonizing its regulations with EC practice to attract greater foreign participation.

Paris Bourse

In January 1991, France's six provincial stock exchanges were integrated into a national market with the Paris Bourse (stock exchange). Previously, the Paris market was already responsible for over 95 per cent of French securities trading. The French equity market is the second largest in Europe behind Germany. Technologically, Paris is probably continental Europe's most advanced market. The Cotation Assiste en Continu (CAC) electronic trading system similar to the CATS system in Toronto and the CORES system in Tokyo, which was introduced in 1988 and has virtually taken over from floor trading. The Relit five-day rolling settlement system, based on delivery against payment, was launched in 1990 and has avoided the back office problems which occurred in London after Big Bang.

In 1988, the Paris market underwent *le petit bang* as it was called, following the review by the Le Porte commission. The reforms instituted following the commission's investigation were the first major changes to the Bourse since its format was established under the Napoleonic system. This first round of reforms allowed outside investors to buy into brokerages for the first time, introduced stricter takeover rules and a clampdown on insider trading. The overall supervision of the French securities markets is undertaken by the Finance Ministry and the following bodies: the Conseil des Bourses de Valeurs (CBV), the French stock exchange council; the Société des Bourses Francaises, the CBV's executive body; and the Commission des Opérations de Bourse, an autonomous agency originally established in 1967 along similar lines to the US SEC.

All securities trading is conducted through one of the forty-five broker members of the exchange (Sociétés de Bourse, previously known as Agents de Change). Prior to 1989, there were restrictions on the ownership of brokerages by foreign firms, limiting their equity holding to 30 per cent. Now more than a dozen of the forty-five brokers have foreign parents.

A second wave of reforms is in train for 1992, with an agreement by regulators to encourage stock brokers to improve their financial security. In January 1992, the CBV will issue separate licences for different aspects of stockbroking activity. This segmentation of functions is the main point of a package of reform proposals which were put to the exchange in the summer of 1991.

The finance ministry is also considering other proposals, including the abolition of turnover tax and the development of trading in large blocks of shares between major institutions off the market. In 1989, the exchange introduced a *contrapartie* market maker system for block trading, but only for matched bargains, with the result that growth in the business has been disappointingly slow.

The Paris market operates a three-tiered trading system, the official list (Côte Officielle), the second market (Second Marché) and the over the counter market (Marché Hors Côte). The Côte Officielle comprises a cash market (Marché au Comptant) in which trading in certain securities is cash-settled within twenty-four hours, and a forward market (Marché à Terme) where settlement is done at the end of the month. The CBV has the power to decide which securities are traded on which of these two markets. Companies quoted on the official list must offer at least 25 per cent of their equity to the public. The second market is for smaller companies and the over the counter market operates along similar lines to Rule 535 in the UK. Shares are traded on the OTC at the request of brokers and companies on the OTC market are not obliged to issue a prospectus and face only minimum disclosure requirements.

The main market index is the CAC General Index, comprising 250 shares. A second index, the CAC-40, was developed as the vehicle for an index futures contract on MATIF (*see below*). It consists of forty of the 100 largest stocks by capitalization on the forward market of the official list.

Settlement is by matched trades which are passed to the settlement and depository system, Sicovam (Société Interprofessionelle pour la Compensation de Valuers Mobilières), and to the Banque de France which maintains accounts for all member firms.

Fixed commissions were abolished in 1989. Brokers are now free to set their own commission rates. Stamp duty amounts to 0.30 per cent of all transactions up to FFr1 million and 0.15 per cent thereafter. A value added tax of 18.6 per cent is charged on the broking commission and a withholding tax on dividends is applied at a rate of 25 per cent for foreign investors.

Paris Bourse
Palais de la Bourse
4 Place de la Bourse
75080 Paris
France
Tel: 140 41 100 00

Frankfurter Wertpapierbörse

The Frankfurt Wertpapierbörse (stock exchange) is one of eight regional stock exchanges operating in Germany, together these exchanges' total market capitalization makes them the world's fourth largest market after Tokyo, New York and London. Frankfurt is by far the largest of the regional markets, its turnover accounts for more than three-quarters of total German equity trading. It is also the oldest of the German markets. Frankfurt has been an important financial centre since the Middle Ages. Trading in bonds and notes began towards the end of the eighteenth century and, by the early nineteenth century, a flourishing bond market had been established. In 1820, the first equities traded in Frankfurt were shares in the Austrian National Bank. However, throughout the nineteenth century the Frankfurt market was dominated by bond trading. Much of the Austrian national debt was financed by bonds on the Frankfurt market and the Northern States of the USA also raised funds in Frankfurt during the American Civil War.

At this time the Berlin Stock Exchange was the most important equity trading centre in Germany. However, Frankfurt established an international presence and just prior to the outbreak of the First World War, out of a total of some 1,500 securities, it listed 388 foreign bonds and 51 foreign shares.

The market suffered badly through both World Wars and in the inter-war period. After the Second World War, the Frankfurt exchange was one of the first German stock exchanges to be reopened in September 1945. Throughout the 1950s and the 1960s, as the Germany economy recovered, the stock market expanded. The liberalization of the capital market permitted the opening of the Currency Exchange in 1953 and, three years later, trading in foreign equities resumed. In 1966, a second trading floor was added to the stock exchange for bond trading. In the late 1980s, a complete redevelopment programme for the New Stock Exchange building, the market's home since 1879, commenced. The work was completed in 1990. The physical remodelling of the stock exchange went hand in hand with reform of the laws governing equity trading and the introduction of electronic trading systems.

The disruption to the development of the market caused by the Second World War and the planned reconstruction of the West German economy which followed it resulted in the equity market being significantly less important to business and industry than in the UK and the USA. Bank lending has historically played a far greater part in business finance and in the equity market itself banks are major shareholders. For example, Deutsche Bank and Commerzbank control more than 50 per cent of Germany's leading department store group, Karstadt.

In 1989, an interbank information system (IBIS) was launched by seven German banks to display two-way indicative prices. IBIS was not a success and, in April 1991, IBIS 2 was introduced. The first "I" in IBIS this time stood for "integrated". The new system also involves brokers and may make more headway than the initial attempt. It is competing again two other price information systems: MATIS, set up by the official brokers and disseminated by Reuters, and GMS, developed by the free brokers and Citicorp's Quotron subsidiary. IBIS 2 is being backed by the stock exchange authorities as part of their plan to create a unified German market-place.

There are three markets for securities on the exchange: the Amtlicher Handel, which is the official market for major blue chip shares and government bonds; the Geregelter Markt, the second or regulated market for smaller companies; and the Freiverkehr, a third market. Trading on the exchange is organized on an auctioneer basis, unlike the market-making system in London and on NASDAQ. Prices are determined by the official brokers (*kursmakler*) and the free brokers (*freimakler*) based on buying and selling orders received from the banks. The official brokers are appointed by the provincial governments and the free brokers operate on behalf of the institutions. Under German law, only the banks are permitted to deal in securities on behalf of clients. Most German shares are easily transferable bearer instruments. The securities traded in Frankfurt are held in the *Kassenverein*, the central depository. Delivery is made on the second working day after a transaction and settlement is effected through book entries from one account to another. There are three stock market indices in Frankfurt. The most important of the three is the newest, the Deutsche Axtienindex (Dax), the first German real-time index of thirty leading shares was launched in the summer of 1988.

The exchange is managed by a Board of Governors, which is responsible for admissions, compliance with the law and controls trading conditions. Dealings are subject to the commission charge payable to the bank and the brokerage fee payable to the *kursmakler*. Bank fees may be negotiable for larger deals but for smaller investors tend to be set around 1 per cent for equity transactions and 0.5 per cent for bonds. Brokerage commissions are currently around 0.06 per cent for equity transactions, although no fee is payable if the shares change hands over the counter and a *kursmakler* is not involved. Turnover tax was abolished in January 1991.

Frankfurter Wertpapierbörse
Börsenplatz 6
Postfach 10 08 11
6000 Frankfurt am Main 1
Germany
Tel: (69) 2197-0

Futures Markets

There are commodity futures markets in seven European countries. However, none of the continental commodity markets have succeeded in establishing much of an international presence. These markets divide into two categories: those formed in the late nineteenth and early twentieth century, more or less at the same time as the commodity futures markets in the USA and the UK were developing; and those established after the Second World War. The oldest of the European commodity markets is the Frankfurt Corn and Produce Exchange in Germany which opened in 1862. Eleven years later, in 1873, the Berne Grain and Produce Exchange in Switzerland and the Vienna Commodity Exchange in Austria were established. In 1875, the Borsa Merci di Padova began trading a variety of agricultural products in Italy. Over the course of the next forty years, a small number of other markets were also established. After the Second World War, the Potato Terminal Market began trading in the Netherlands in 1958 and the Paris Commodity Exchange in France, trading cocoa, coffee and white sugar futures, opened in 1962. There are now two commodity futures markets in Switzerland, in Zurich and in Berne; two in Italy, in Padua and Bologna; three in Germany, in Frankfurt, Duisburg and Worms; and two markets in Amsterdam in the Netherlands.

In 1978, the first derivatives markets were established in Europe: in London, the London Traded Options Market, (*see Chapter Eleven*); and in Amsterdam, the European Options Exchange-Optiebeurs (EOE).

The most internationally important of the continental financial futures markets are the Marché à Terme des Instruments Financiers (MATIF) in France and the Deutsche Terminbörse (DTB) in Germany (*see below*). Several new derivatives markets were established through the 1980s, and three more are in the planning stages. Despite fears that too many competing exchanges may cause liquidity problems, the development of a plethora of market-places is not necessarily misguided. Each country's financial traders want to be able to hedge exposure to local securities which may be unlikely to warrant international interest. Most of these new markets are completely automated and do not have trading floors.

The Options Markand (OM) in Sweden established an options exchange in Stockholm and now operates two exchanges, in Stockholm and London, with a trading and clearing link between the two. In 1987 options trading commenced in Paris with the opening of the Marché des Options Négotiables de Paris (Monep). In the following year Futop, the Danish market for futures and options was established as a part of the Copenhagen Stock Exchange, with trading taking place on the same decentralized electronic system that is used for bonds and equities. Five Swiss banks, together with the three stock exchanges in Switzerland set up the Swiss options and financial futures exchange (Soffex). Soffex began trading options in fifteen Swiss stocks in May 1988, but did not trade a futures contract until November 1990 with the introduction of futures on the Swiss Market Index.

IFOX, the Irish futures and options exchange, trades four futures contracts on a fully automated system introduced in 1989. In the same year, two markets were established in Spain. The first, OM Iberica, was established by Banco Bilbao-Vizcaya and OM, the Swedish option market. The second, Mercado de Futoros Fincancieros SA (MEFF), was set up by Spain's sixteen largest banks and the Barcelona Stock Exchange. In February 1991, the OM Group sold its holding in OM Iberica to the four Spanish stock exchanges and the market was renamed the Mercado de Opciones Financiero Espanol (Mofex).

In 1991, the authorities of Austria's fledgling automated futures and options exchange (OTOB) commenced trading options in five leading Austrian shares and on the new ATX Austrian Traded index of leading shares. In Brussels, the Belgian futures and options exchange (Belfox) is under development and the Italian financial authorities have announced plans for a domestic Italian futures exchange.

In the early 1990s, the establishment of trading links between several of these new markets went some way to improving liquidity and ensuring their further development. The two OM markets linked with the EOE to develop their existing trading technology in tandem. Furthermore several of these markets are discussing the joint listing of contracts, a trend begun with the listing of futures on the EOE-developed Eurotop 100 index on the EOE, Soffex, MATIF and the American Stock Exchange.

Marché à Terme des Instruments Financiers (MATIF)

MATIF, France's financial futures exchange, opened for business in February 1986. Volume on the market has soared from an initial 2,700 contracts a day to over 100,000 contracts a day and, by its third anniversary in February 1989, the MATIF had registered over 33 million contracts.

The Paris market is bidding strongly to compete with LIFFE in London for pre-eminence in Europe in the 1990s. In June 1991, for the first time in more than a year, volume trade on the French market overtook that on LIFFE. However, volume on LIFFE for the whole of the first six months of 1991, at 18.6 million contracts, was still higher than the total of 18.1 million traded on MATIF.

Contracts

The first contract to be traded on MATIF was the *contrat notionnel*, a notional ten-year French government bond. In January 1989, MATIF added the *contrat d'option sur emprunt notionnel*, an option on the government bond futures contract.

MATIF also trades futures on the CAC-40, the share index of the Paris stock market. This contract was launched in November 1988. Earlier in the same year, a contract on the three-month PIBOR (Paris Interbank Offered Rate) had been introduced, superseding a short-term contract on ninety-day Treasury bills which has since been withdrawn. Four-year *billets de trésorie* contracts, linked to Treasury bond interest rates, were launched in June 1989.

A significant expansion of the market's horizon occurred in 1989 with the introduction of the first non-domestic futures contract, the three-month Eurodeutschmark. This contract is similar in concept to the three-month PIBOR, permitting hedging against a variety of Deutschmark deposit rates, as well as offering several arbitraging strategies. The Eurodeutschmark began trading over the counter in April 1989, and was officially introduced the following month.

In October 1990, MATIF launched the world's first ECU bond futures contract. Since March 1991, average daily volumes on this contract have accounted for more than three-quarters of total world trade in ECU bond futures.

MATIF's rivalry with LIFFE increased through 1991 with the two exchanges both introducing futures on Italian government bonds within two weeks of each other in September. The French market has also begun to trade a futures contract on the Eurotop 100 index in competition with LIFFE's FT-SE Eurotrack contract. MATIF has committed itself to linking with GLOBEX, the international electronic trading system being developed by the Chicago Mercantile Exchange and Reuters. A prototype trading system linking the French market to GLOBEX is due to begin testing in July 1992.

MATIF SA
176 rue Montmartre
75002 Paris
France
Tel: 33 (1) 40 28 82 82

Deutsche Terminbörse (DTB)

The DTB began trading in January 1990 with equity options on fourteen German blue chip stocks. The market's first futures contracts, introduced two months behind schedule in November 1990 due to computer software problems, were on the Dax stock market index (*see above*) and on German federal government bonds, known as Bundesanleihen, or Bunds. The DTB does not have a physical trading floor. The market is entirely computer-based. The system, with software based on that designed for Soffex, was developed at a cost of DM60 million.

The development of the market only became possible following changes to German stock exchange law in the Exchange Act of 11 July 1989. Previously, private investors could not be sued for the obligations under futures and options contracts, as they were treated as gambling debts. Now, an investor is held to be liable provided he has been adequately informed of the risks in trading such contracts. Obstacles to the use of futures and options by investment funds and insurance companies were also removed at the same time.

The DTB is Europe's most important stock options market by volume, surpassing the LTOM, the EOE and Soffex in turnover. More than a third of the market's membership is international and the exchange authorities are considering establishing terminals outside Germany. However, the market has had less success in developing its futures contracts.

Volume trading on the Bund future is still only between a fifth and quarter that of the open outcry contract on LIFFE. In April 1991, a group of nine German banks agreed to attempt to improve liquidity in the bund futures contract by making prices on a continuous basis, although they stopped short of instituting a full market-maker system. The agreement is not binding, unlike those involving market-makers in share options, but is on a best effort basis.

The exchange is operated by DTB GmbH, a private firm backed by German banks, which is both the legal body and the clearing agency for the market. However, under the supervisory rules governing Germany's federal stock exchange structure, the DTB's legal supervisory body includes the Minister of Economics in the state of Hesse, where the Frankfurt-based market is located.

Contracts

The DTB trades stock options, futures on the Dax index and on Bunds. In August 1991, the exchange introduced options on the Dax index itself and on the Bund futures contract. The market is also testing futures on medium-term government bonds and options on medium-term government bonds and on the Dax futures contract.

The exchange has also had discussions about listing its Dax index futures and Bund futures on the two Chicago markets and is considering participation in GLOBEX.

Deutsche Terminbörse
Börsenplatz 6
Postfach 10 08 11
6000 Frankfurt am Main 1
Germany
Tel: (69) 2197 0

CHAPTER 13

PRIMARY PRODUCERS

The primary producers are Australia, Canada, the Republic of South Africa and New Zealand. The common denominators between these four countries are developed infrastructure and industry but economies which, despite these attributes and in common with less-developed countries, remain broadly reliant on the export of primary commodities.

In fact, these countries are the world's leading producers of several raw materials and are in the top five producers in the world for others. South Africa is the world's largest producer of gold, gem diamonds and platinum. However, gold's importance to the South African economy has fallen in recent years. In 1989, the value of profits from mining activities other than gold exceeded the value of profits from gold mining for the first time.

Canada is the world's largest producer of nickel and zinc. Australia and New Zealand are among the world's leading exporters of wool and dairy products, and at the same time also have major mineral resources.

Given the importance of primary commodities to the economies of these four countries, it is no surprise that mining companies and commodity producers feature significantly on their respective stock markets and that the performance of these markets is heavily influenced by the performance of natural resource prices. However, that is not say that the commodity producers and miners dominate the markets to the exclusion of other companies, among the largest and most active listed stocks on the Toronto market are communications companies, utilities and banks. However, in Australia over a third of the quoted stocks are mining companies and in South Africa more than half of the market capitalization of all companies is in mineral-related sectors.

STOCK MARKETS
Australian Stock Exchange

Share trading in Australia began in 1828, but only began to grow significantly in importance in the latter half of the nineteenth century, with the demand for capital to support the expansion of mining activities. The first stock exchange was established in Melbourne in 1865, followed over the course of the next twenty-five years by markets set up in Sydney, Brisbane, Adelaide, Hobart and Perth. In 1937, the six exchanges came together to form the Australian Associated Stock Exchanges. However, the markets continued to trade independently of each other until 1987 when they were formed into a single national market, the Australian Stock Exchange, under the Australian Stock Exchange & National Guarantee Fund Act.

Fixed rate commissions were abolished in 1984, and in October 1990 the exchange moved to a fully automated trading system, the Stock Exchange Automated Trading System (SEATS) for all transactions. The old trading floors closed down, with the exception of those facilities which continue to be required for the trading of options.

The quality of regulation of the Australian market was questioned many times in the 1980s, a decade which saw the meteoric rise and equally spectacular fall of a number of entrepreneurs who had borrowed heavily and taken advantage of lax market regulation to expand. The tumbling of the highly-geared corporate dominoes began in the aftermath of the market crash in 1987, and corporate collapses in the late 1980s and into the early 1990s may cost Australian equity investors as much as A$15 billion by the time the shake out has ended.

The exchange authorities and the government have begun to address these problems, and in 1991 the Australian Securities Commission was formed as a national organization reporting to the federal government, replacing the fragmented National Companies and Securities Commission, which reported to individual state governments. At the same time, the budget for the new federal regulator was expanded to A$107 million in its first year of operations, compared with a previous budget for its predecessor of just A$8 million.

In addition to the new market watchdog, disclosure regulations have been tightened up, investors in publicly listed stocks must now disclose holdings of five per cent or more. Previously, the limit above which interest had to be reported was 10 per cent. Furthermore, the Australian Accounting Standards Committee is developing standards to overcome some of the dubious practices which fuelled the entrepreneurs of the 1980s and the market is considering introducing the requirement for quarterly financial statements from listed companies. In October 1991, it was announced that the Australian market was considering the introduction of a fixed settlement period. Under the proposed system, transactions would be settled on the fifth business day after the date of trade. Currently, settlement is by demand, where a seller can determine the day of settlement, by delivering the scrip to the buyer on any day after the date of the trade. It would seem that the authorities are completely serious in their attempts to divest the Australian Stock Exchange of its "wild west" image.

The most widely quoted Australian share index is the All Ordinaries Index, which consists of 250 companies and is calculated on a weighted basis. Industrial companies account for some two-thirds of the index with the remainder being resource-based.

Since 1985, the government has progressively eased the inward control of foreign investment. Acquisition of more than 15 per cent of the voting rights of an Australian company's shares requires the approval of the Treasurer through the Foreign Investment Review Board.

Although there is no established over-the-counter market in Australia similar to that operated by the National Association of Securities Dealers in the USA, there is a Second Board Market not unlike the UK's Unlisted Securities Market. The Second Board was originally established by the Melbourne Stock Exchange in 1984 to offer smaller companies access to new capital.

Australian Stock Exchange Ltd
Level 9, Plaza Building
Australia Square
Sydney NSW 2000
Australia
Tel: 233 5266

Johannesburg Stock Exchange

The Johannesburg Stock Exchange was established in 1886 and is the only formally constituted stock market in South Africa. Owing to the government's post-war policy of apartheid, foreign investment in South African equity has been limited and the exchange has not been successful in establishing itself as an international market-place, hindered further by the fact that most of the international trading of South African shares is done through London where many of the leading companies are also listed. A further hindrance to international investment is the requirement of the South African Exchange Control regulations which obliges foreign investors to channel funds in and out of the country under the "financial rand" exchange rate which is set at a significant discount to the "commercial rand".

The market's barometers are the JSE Actuaries Indices. Shares are categorized into five groups, a separate index being quoted for each group: gold; mining finance; collieries; diamonds and metals; and industrial companies. The indices are weighted to take greater account of the price movements in larger companies' shares.

Developments to end apartheid on the political front have been matched by developments in the market-place. The stock exchange has two subsidiaries, the Development Capital Market and the Venture Capital Market, established in the 1980s, and is now considering the introduction of a Traded Options Market. In 1990, the government successfully privatized the Iron & Steel Industrial Corp Ltd (ISCOR), with trading commencing in ISCOR shares in November.

Modernization of the market and its regulations continued in 1991 with the passage at the start of the year of the Deposit Taking Institutions Act, which brings South African regulations into line with requirements for banks set out by the Bank for International Settlements. At the same time a new Takeovers and Mergers Code was introduced and a Securities Regulation Panel was established, patterned after the UK's Securities & Investments Board.

Further privatizations are planned as the state moves away from the interventionist industrial policies which went hand-in-hand with apartheid. The development of the country's retarded capital markets is likely to follow suit. However, international interest, any political thaw notwithstanding, will remain limited so long as foreign exchange controls remain tightly in place.

Johannesburg Stock Exchange
Diagonal Street
PO Box 1174
2000 Johannesburg
Republic of South Africa
Tel: 833 6580

New Zealand Stock Exchange
Formalized share trading began in the 1870s with markets developing in the four main population centres. However, the exchanges were not regulated until 1902 with the passing of the Sharebrokers Act. The market regulations were further codified in 1908, and many of these early provisions remain in force. The structure of the New Zealand Stock Exchange itself dates back to 1915. Of the four trading floors then operating, the floor in Dunedin was closed in June 1988; however, those in Auckland, Christchurch, and Wellington continued to trade until the introduction of a screen-based system in 1991.

The NZSE is largely self-regulating through the workings of the Stock Exchange Association, although the government established a Securities Commission to oversee the market in 1978. Briefly in the late 1980s, the market ran a second board for the trading of equity in smaller companies. After this second board was abolished, those companies listed on it were transferred to the main market with an NAS (non-standard listing) label. This classification applies to all companies which do not have standard articles of association.

Although dividend payments to both residents and non-residents are subject to a withholding tax, fixed commissions and stamp duties were abolished in 1986.

The NZSE introduced an automatic computer-based screen trading system in July 1991, closing down its three trading floors in Auckland, Christchurch and Wellington. The exchange is using a modified version of the Stock Exchange Automated Trading System (SEATS) developed and used by the Australian Stock Exchange. There are about 130 companies listed on the New Zealand market by comparison with about 1,000 in Australia. Virtually all of the leading New Zealand companies are dual-listed, with quotations on the Australian market as well.

In 1990 the exchange authorities revised the allocations of the weighting given to the forty shares in the market's leading index, the Barclays Share Index, basing the new system on stock available to portfolio investors rather than on total capitalization. The revised index, known as the NZSE-40, was introduced in September 1991 and is quoted continuously during trading hours.

New Zealand Stock Exchange
8th Floor, Caltex Tower
286-292 Lambton Quay
PO Box 2959
Wellington
New Zealand
Tel: 72 75 99

Toronto Stock Exchange

The Toronto Stock Exchange is by far the largest of several markets established throughout Canada, accounting for some three-quarters of total stock turnover. Of the other markets, the two most important are the Montreal Stock Exchange and the Vancouver Stock Exchange; there are also exchanges operating in Calgary and Winnipeg. The Canadian markets have been at the forefront in the development of derivative products. The market in Montreal introduced financial futures contracts in 1975, the Toronto market began trading stock options a year later and Vancouver began options trading in 1982. The Toronto Stock Exchange is the oldest established Canadian stock market. It was formed as an association of traders in 1852, operating as a partnership until incorporation as the Toronto Stock Exchange in 1878. The Montreal market was set up in 1874 and Vancouver in 1907.

All the Canadian markets operate a partly-automated trading system. Each exchange operates as a self-regulating organization and, with the exception of the Vancouver exchange, trading is settled at an independent corporation. Trades in the Vancouver market are settled through a wholly-owned service corporation. There is limited federal regulation of the Canadian securities industry. The regulatory framework for the markets is provided by the provinces in which the exchanges are based, with the lead being taken by the Ontario and Quebec Securities Commissions, governing the Toronto and Montreal markets respectively.

In common with developments south of the border in the US markets, the Canadian stock exchanges introduced limited after-hours trading sessions in June 1991. These one-hour sessions after the official close allow brokers to cross blocks of shares at the day's closing price.

The main market index on the Toronto market is the TSE Composite which was introduced in January 1977, though with a base year of 1975=1,000. The composite index includes some 300 companies and separate indices for a variety of sectors are also calculated. A Toronto 35 index is also produced and options and futures are based on moves in this index. In 1984, the Montreal market launched the Canadian Market Portfolio Index, which consists of the twenty-five largest stocks in all the Canadian markets by market capitalization.

There are few limitations placed on foreign investors, Canada has no system of exchange controls and ownership restrictions are limited.

Toronto Stock Exchange
The Exchange Tower
2 First Canadian Place
Toronto
Ontario M5X 1J2
Canada
Tel: 947 4700

FUTURES MARKETS
New Zealand Futures and Options Exchange (NZFOE)
The futures market in Auckland operates a fully automated trading system which was installed when the exchange began trading in January 1985. The market trades three-year, five-year and ten-year government stock futures, ninety-day bank accepted bills futures, Barclays Share Price Index futures, wool futures and futures on both the US dollar and the NZ dollar. Options are traded on all contracts except US dollar futures. In October 1991, the Barclays Share Index contract was replaced by a contract in the revised NZSE-40.

Following the scandals which hit London FOX in October 1991, the NZFOE rejected a takeover by the London market. The London FOX bid had previously been recommended to shareholders by the NZFOE board. The rejection of the London market's bid left only an approach from the Sydney Futures Exchange on the table (*see below*).

New Zealand Futures and Options Exchange Ltd
PO Box 6734
Wellesley Street
Auckland
New Zealand
Tel: 09 309 8308

Sydney Futures Exchange

The Sydney market is engaged in setting up its own clearing house to take over clearing and settlement of its business from the London-based International Commodities Clearing House. The new clearing house, with procedures and structure modelled on those of the major US futures markets, is expected to be operational by the end of 1991. A partial screen-based system is in operation for out-of-hours trading, the Sydney Computerized Overnight Market (SYCOM), which was introduced in November 1989.

The Sydney market trades futures contracts in ninety-day bank accepted bills, three-year and ten-year Commonwealth Treasury bonds, the All Ordinaries Share Price index, Australian dollars, wool and live cattle. In addition to these contracts, the exchange also offers options on all but the wool and live cattle futures contracts. Both of the bond futures contracts, the ninety-day bills contract and the All Ordinaries contract are also traded on SYCOM.

In 1990, the exchange authorities held discussions with London FOX, considering introducing the latter's base metals index futures contract, the MGMI onto the Sydney market.

The Sydney Futures Exchange is bidding NZ$6 million to take over the NZFOE. An initial cash payment of NZ$1.5 million would be followed by payments of the remainder over a three-year period if NZFOE volume trade projections are met. Although the Sydney bid was not originally favoured by the NZFOE, the rejection of London FOX's bid by the New Zealand market virtually assured the Sydney exchange of success.

Sydney Futures Exchange
30-32 Grosvenor Street
Sydney 2000

Australia
Tel: 02 256 0555

South Africa Futures Exchange (Safex)

The South Africa Futures Exchange opened for business on 30 April 1990. Safex is underwritten by a consortium of twenty-two banks and institutions and has twelve active clearing members, including the Johannesburg Stock Exchange. The market's development has not been without incident. Only a month after it began trading, Safex suffered a broker default and, for most of its first year, the market barely broke even. Trading volumes have been low and foreign participation was not allowed until the beginning of December 1991. The opening of the market to foreign participants followed approval from the Reserve Bank of South Africa for non-resident investors to deal via the financial rand, a second tier currency which fluctuates at a discount to the commercial rand and previously had been primarily used for investment in shares and bonds quoted on the Johannesburg Stock Exchange.

Safex has six futures contracts, including: gold price futures; JSE All Industrial index futures; long bond futures; short-term interest rate futures; JSE All Gold index futures; and JSE All Share index futures. The exchange is planning to launch options on its futures contracts in 1992. All the existing contracts are screen-traded and cash-delivered.

South Africa Futures Exchange
PO Box 4406
Johannesburg 2000
Republic of South Africa
Tel: 836 3311

Winnipeg Commodity Exchange

Although the Canadian stock markets, notably the Vancouver Stock Exchange, trade a number of options contracts, the Winnipeg Commodity Exchange is the only purely futures-based market. It was originally founded in 1887 at the Winnipeg Produce & Grain Exchange, the name being changed in 1972.

The market now trades contracts denominated in Canadian dollars on canola (rapeseed), flaxseed, domestic feed wheat, rye, oats, standard domestic feed barley and western feed barley. The Winnipeg exchange has had a chequered past, unsuccessfully dabbling in livestock, potatoes, financial futures and precious metals. The exchange is to introduce an options contract on canola futures in September 1991, its first venture into options since it withdrew a gold call options contract a decade earlier.

PRIMARY PRODUCERS

The market has had an uphill struggle in the late 1980s and early 1990s to recover from a four-year criminal investigation into trading malpractice. Compliance and public relations resources have been expanded and the exchange is installing a new computerized surveillance system.

Winnipeg Commodity Exchange
500-360 Main Street
Winnipeg
Manitoba
Canada R3B 0V7
Tel: 204 949 0495

CHAPTER 14

TIGERS AND DRAGONS

In economic terms, Asia is the fastest-growing region in the world. Although Japan leads the way it is being closely followed by newly-industrialized countries, notably the four so-called "Tigers": Hong Kong, South Korea, Singapore, and Taiwan. Over the past twenty-five years the average annual economic growth of each of the Tigers exceeded eight per cent. Close behind the Tigers come the four "Dragons": Indonesia, Malaysia, Philippines, and Thailand.

One of the common denominators of all eight countries is high savings ratios, with savings rates ranging from 25 per cent to more than 40 per cent of gross domestic product. These high savings rates suggest that present economic growth is sustainable and that there is huge and relatively untapped liquidity for the financial markets of the region.

The Tigers and Dragons are between ten and fifteen years behind Japan in the process of industrialization with the Dragons now pushing aggressively into heavy industries and moving to reduce their economic reliance on the export of primary commodities. Asia has been likened to a series of waterfalls, with Japan at the top and waves of industry, property investors and tourism moving through from Japan to the Tigers, and then to the Dragons.

Most economic forecasters believe the dynamic growth of the past quarter century will continue through the millennium, potentially making the Asian markets among the most dynamic in the world. However, many of the markets are very young and in their early stages of development, so they are highly volatile. Historical factors have meant that the most advanced and open markets in the region are currently in Hong Kong and Singapore, the traditional international trading centres.

In December 1990, fourteen stock exchanges in Asia, Australia and New Zealand signed the charter of the East Asian & Oceanic Stock Exchanges Federation. Delegates from the markets in Hong Kong, Jakarta, Surabaya, Tokyo, Osaka, Seoul, Kuala Lumpur, Manila, Makati, Singapore, Taiwan, Thailand, New Zealand and Australia agreed to the exchange of information and the promotion of mutual assistance. The charter formalized a loose alliance that had been previously in place.

Tiger Stock Markets
Stock Exchange of Hong Kong (SEHK)

The first stock market established in Hong Kong opened for business in 1891. A second market began trading in 1921. The two exchanges were merged into the Hong Kong Stock Exchange in 1947. However, it was not until the 1960s that the market began to expand. Up to 1962, only sixty-five companies were listed on the exchange. Despite growth through the 1960s, the market remained peripheral to the Hong Kong capital market with little government supervision. The opening of the Far East Stock Exchange in 1969 revolutionized the domestic market, breaking with the London-style business practices of the existing exchange and with trading conducted in Cantonese. Volumes soon surpassed those of the Hong Kong Stock Exchange and two more markets operating along similar lines opened, the Kam Ngan Stock Exchange in 1971 and the Kowloon Stock Exchange in 1972.

In 1973, the Hong Kong government intervened in an attempt to control the mushrooming market, and the Securities Ordinance and the Protection of Investors Ordinance were enacted the following year, establishing, for the first time, a regulatory framework for the securities industry in Hong Kong.

In the late 1970s, prompted by declining market values, the various exchanges began to consider unification and in 1980 the Stock Exchange Unification Ordinance was enacted and, following further legislation in 1985, the Stock Exchange of Hong Kong came into being in April 1986. International dealers had already established presences on the Hong Kong markets prior to unification.

The Hong Kong market was one of the worst casualties of the global market crash in 1987, closing for a week and falling 33 per cent on re-opening. The government had to provide a total of HK$4 billion in rescue packages to the securities and futures markets. Following this *débâcle*, the government appointed a commission to review the industry, resulting in the Securities & Futures Commission Act 1990, which substantially improved and modernized the market's regulatory environment. The seriousness of the situation was underlined by the arrest of three exchange officials in January 1988, including the chairman Ronald Li, who was subsequently jailed for four years, having been found guilt of accepting preferential share allocations as a bribe for approving share listings.

In 1991, resolutions recommended by the exchange's first vice chairman, Philip Wong, that governing council members be given first refusal on newly listed stocks and preferred share allocations were initially passed but later overturned. Dissenting members of the council reported their dissatisfaction to the Securities and Futures Commission and Wong resigned his post. The incident revived memories of 1987 but was held up as an example of the new system's success and the first major test of the market's recently-established watchdog. The exchange is continuing with a modernization process and hopes to have an electronic settlement system in place by the end of 1991. The market has two main indices, the Hang Seng Index, which remains the most widely used barometer, and the more broadly-based Hong Kong Stock Index.

The Hong Kong market remains vulnerable to political events and perceptions of the mood of the Beijing government as 1997 and the handover of the Crown Colony to the People's Republic of China comes closer. A number of the leading companies have taken steps to move their primary listing from the Hong Kong market to end any potential uncertainty about their future after the colony reverts to Chinese sovereignty. The stock market is now considering allowing China-based companies to take up listings. Several Chinese companies have already taken stakes in listed companies in Hong Kong. For example, China International Trust and Investment Corp, Beijing's most westernized company, has some US$2.6 billion in assets in Hong Kong.

There are no regulations limiting foreign participation in the Hong Kong markets.

The Stock Exchange of Hong Kong Ltd
1st Floor Exchange Square
PO Box 8888
Hong Kong
Tel: (852) 5 22 1122
Fax: (852) 5 810 4475

Korea Stock Exchange (KSE)
Organized securities trading in Korea dates back to 1911, but the market in its current form was only established in 1956. As the economy developed through the 1950s and 1960s, a series of reforms were introduced to encourage companies to come to the market and domestic investors to look to the stock market as an avenue of investment. Further revisions to the Commercial Code in the mid-1980s modernized accounting systems and investor protection. The Korea Securities Dealers Association operates a small over-the-counter market. Despite being one of Asia's largest and most modern exchanges, the market

remains tightly regulated under the direct control of the Ministry of Finance and liberalization to allow foreign participation has already been postponed once in 1987. Increasing international pressure, especially from the US and British governments, led to the government promising to allow foreigners to invest directly in Korean equity in 1992. A small number of brokerage licences on the market are also to be made available to foreign dealers. International participation on the Korean market is presently limited to two foreign and eight domestically managed funds and a small number of bond issues.

Korea Stock Exchange
33 Yoido-dong
Youngdeungpo-ku
Seoul 150-010
Republic of Korea
Tel: (82) 2-780 2271
Fax: (82) 2-782 0417

Stock Exchange of Singapore (SES)

The SES in its present form came into being in 1973 following the Malaysian government's unilateral decision to sever the currency link with Singapore. Prior to that time a joint market had existed, the Stock Exchange of Malaysia and Singapore, which had been established in 1964. Share dealing had become a major activity in Singapore early in the twentieth century and in the run-up to independence, as the administrative capital of the British colonies and protectorates in the region, Singapore dominated share trading in Southeast Asia.

Following the Malaysian government's decision in 1973, the stock market was relaunched as the SES and all shares previously listed on the joint exchange were listed on the new market. In 1990, the SES established the Central Limit Order Book (CLOB) International as a computerized over-the-counter market. The main market had moved to electronic trading under CLOB the previous year and a second market had been established, the Stock Exchange of Singapore Dealing and Automated Quotation system (SESDAQ).

The Malaysian government's decision to make companies delist from the SES in 1990 precipitated a huge expansion of SESDAQ under CLOB International. More than half of the Malaysian companies previously listed on the SES listed on CLOB International, although the market is not officially recognized by the Kuala Lumpur Stock Exchange. The SES established a trading link with the US National Association of Securities Dealers in 1988. The Singapore markets are regulated by the central bank and the Monetary Authority of Singapore under the

Securities Industry Act, 1986, which was passed after the collapse of the conglomerate Pan-Electric industries the previous year.

The most important market index is the Straits Times Industrial Index of thirty shares, published by the Straits Times newspaper group, although the SES calculates a number of other indices and the Overseas Chinese Banking Corporation also calculates its own. There are no limits on foreign participation in the Singapore markets although the government does impose a maximum limit on the foreign ownership of certain strategic companies.

Stock Exchange of Singapore Ltd
1 Raffles Place 24-00
OUB Centre
Singapore 0104
Tel: (65) 535 376

Taiwan Stock Exchange

The development of share trading in Taiwan was linked closely to land reform in the 1950s. Following the redistribution of land to farmers, landowners received bonds and shares in state companies. As a result of the growth of the economy, a Securities and Exchange Commission was established in 1960, although the stock market itself was not officially opened until 1962. A major revamp of the market took place through the 1980s and a more modern legal framework for securities and trading was established. In 1982, a small over-the-counter market was launched. There are few potential avenues for domestic investment and the market is, therefore, highly liquid and dominated by individual investors, but foreign participation so far remains limited to a small number of licensed mutual funds.

Taiwan Stock Exchange Corporation
7-10th Floors City Building
85 Yen-Ping South Road
Taipei
Taiwan
Tel: (886) 2-311 4020
Fax: (886) 2-311 4004

Dragon Stock Markets
Jakarta Stock Exchange

A stock market existed in Indonesia prior to independence, having been established in 1912 to meet the requirements of the Dutch business community in what was then Batavia (Jakarta). The market was closed through the Second World War, reopened only in 1952 but closed again in 1958 following the nationalization of Dutch investments in the country. The current stock exchange opened in 1977 as part of President Suharto's attempts to stabilize the economy and create a market economy structure. The Jakarta exchange is overseen by the securities commission (BAPEPAM), which was established at that time. In the late 1980s, the government stepped up a programme of privatizations and gave further encouragement to the development of the still-fledgling capital markets through the introduction of an over-the-counter market, and a second exchange was opened in Surabaya.

As well as the Jakarta exchange's own composite index, there are two proprietary indices of Indonesian shares published, by PT Jardine Fleming Nusantara Finance and by BT Brokerage, part of the Bankers Trust New York Corp group, launched in 1989 and 1990 respectively. Foreign holdings of bonds are not restricted but there are certain limitations on foreign share ownership.

Capital Market Executive Agency (BAPEPAM)
Jalan Medan Merdeka Selatan 13/14
PO Box 439
Jakarta
Indonesia
Tel: (62) 21-36 1460

Kuala Lumpur Stock Exchange (KLSE)
The KLSE in its current form has been in existence only since 1973. Prior to that time the joint exchange with Singapore had been in operation, but the joint market ended when the Malaysian government terminated the interchangeability of currency with Singapore and took the decision to promote Kuala Lumpur as a financial centre in its own right.

The KLSE is a self-regulating body, although the Ministry of Finance, the Bank Negara and the Registrar of Companies also monitor developments in the stock market. The final step in severing the link with Singapore came in January 1990 following the government's announcement that Malaysian incorporated companies should delist from the Singapore market. The move was designed to reduce the KLSE's vulnerability to the Singapore market–many companies had remained cross-listed after the markets went their separate ways in 1973. At the time fifty-four Singaporean stocks were listed on the KLSE and 182 Malaysian stocks were listed on the SES.

There are no overall restrictions on foreign ownership of Malaysian equity but new issues are required to be 30 per cent taken up by native Malay investors and approval is required if foreign holdings rise above 15 per cent of a company's voting equity. The KLSE is continuing with modernization and has plans to move to a completely automated trading system.

Kuala Lumpur Stock Exchange
3rd & 4th Floors Block A
Kompleks Bukit Naga
Off Jalan Semantan
Damansara Heights
Kuala Lumpur 50490
Malaysia
Tel: (60) 3-254 6433

Manila Stock Exchange (MSE)
Share trading in the Philippines began with the launch of the MSE in 1927, patterned on the NYSE. Two other trading floors exist, the Makati Stock Exchange and the Metropolitan Stock Exchange, opened in 1965 and 1974 respectively. The Metropolitan market is moribund but the Makati exchange has grown to rival the MSE. The markets are regulated by a Securities Exchange Commission set up in 1936, also patterned after the US model. Following the overthrow of Ferdinand Marcos in 1986, the Philippines markets have experienced a resurgence of interest, both domestic and international, and there are now plans to expand and automate the markets. There is also a thriving over-the-counter market.

Foreign investment is welcomed and foreign investors may take stakes of up to 40 per cent of a company's equity without prior approval; holdings above this level need the approval of the Board of Investments.

Manila Stock Exchange
Prensa St Cor Muelle de la Industria Binondo
Manila
Philippines
Tel: (63) 2-471125

Securities Exchange of Thailand (SET)
A stock market was first established in Thailand in 1962 when the Bangkok Stock Exchange was set up as a private partnership. The SET itself began operations in 1975 following legislation in 1974–the Securities Exchange of Thailand Act. Government restrictions on foreign ownership are set at two levels: a 40 per cent ceiling in banks and financial companies and 50 per cent in other equity. However, several

companies have lower limits written in to their Articles of Association. The market is regulated directly by the Ministry of Finance.

The Thai market remains sensitive to the country's uncertain political stability. But despite tremors felt by the market following military coups, interest continues to grow and all governments have pushed measures to boost Thailand's capital markets.

Securities Exchange of Thailand
Sinthon Building 2nd Floor
132 Wireless Road
Bangkok 10500 Metropolis
Thailand
Tel: (66) 250 0001 8

Futures Markets

After a sluggish start, the futures industry in the Tigers and Dragons is on the verge of coming of age. So far only one exchange can be termed successful in establishing a place for itself on the international stage, the Singapore International Monetary Exchange. However, the continued economic development of the region and the expanding capital market and growing investment mean that the fledgling industry has a fertile soil in which to grow.

Hong Kong Futures Exchange (HKFE)

Commodity trading in Hong Kong was formalized in 1910 in the self-regulated Chinese Gold & Silver Exchange. Following an approach from traders in 1973, the Hong Kong government banned futures trading pending a review and the introduction of legislation. In 1975, the Legislative Council gave approval in principle to the establishment of a commodity exchange in Hong Kong. The Hong Kong Commodity Exchange opened in 1977, trading cotton and sugar; contracts for soya beans and gold were added in 1979 and 1980. The cotton market was suspended in 1981 and volumes in the other contracts remained low. Following a working party review in the early 1980s, the market was relicensed by the authorities in 1984 and relaunched as the Hong Kong Futures Exchange, with clearing guaranteed by the International Commodities Clearing House.

With the relaunch came the decision to move into financial futures trading and a contract based on the Hang Seng Index was launched in May 1986. The contract proved to be a success, quickly exceeding the other three contracts in terms of value and volume traded. The market came close to collapse in the 1987 crash but was rescued by financial assistance from the government and subsequently restructured following investigation by the Securities Review Committee.

Contracts
The HKFE trades four futures contracts, the Hang Seng Index, soybeans, sugar and gold. The market is now considering the introduction of currency contracts and contracts on sub-indices of the Hang Seng. It is also reviewing the potential for options on its existing contracts.

Hong Kong Futures Exchange Ltd
New World Tower
16-18 Queens Road Central
Hong Kong
Tel: (852) 526 5747
Fax: (852) 810 5089

Singapore International Monetary Exchange (SIMEX)
Futures trading began in Singapore in 1984 with the launch of SIMEX. The market quickly established itself as an important centre through a novel link with the Chicago Mercantile Exchange (CME). The two markets established the first international trading link between exchanges with a mutual offset arrangement, allowing trading positions established on one market to be offset or transferred to the other (*see Chapter Nine*). Deals could, therefore, be opened on one market and closed on the other and still be treated as a single transaction. The move gave the CME access to traders in the Asian time zone and, from the Singapore market's standpoint, allowed SIMEX access to the Chicago market's large liquidity. Four contracts operate under this arrangement, Eurodollar interest rate futures and currency futures in yen, D-marks and sterling. Although the latter three have not been a success, huge volume in the Eurodollar contract ensured SIMEX's place among the world's markets, accounting for more than a third of daily volume in the early years of the exchange's existence. Trading in Eurodollar futures is still responsible for around 25 per cent of the market's daily volume and almost 10 per cent of world volume. However, SIMEX's position as the third leg in the global trading of Eurodollar contracts together with the CME and the London International Financial Futures Exchange is now in question with the introduction of GLOBEX, which could render the mutual offset link outmoded.

Contracts
SIMEX trades eleven financial and energy futures contracts. The Eurodollar, Euroyen interest rates and High Sulphur Fuel Oil (HSFO)

contracts account for close on 90 per cent of the market's volume. Owing to the small size of the domestic market, SIMEX, of necessity, stepped straight on to the international stage and has managed to carve itself a niche in the global market-place.

The market trades futures and options in Eurodollar, Euroyen, yen and D-mark as well as futures in Euromark, Nikkei Stock Average, sterling, gold, fuel oil and Dubai crude oil. However, the currency futures contracts trade only in small volumes because of a very efficient cash market, the gold contract is moribund and the Dubai crude contract did not take off due to lack of liquidity. The exchange introduced a new contract in gasoil futures in 1991. Like the HSFO contract, the gasoil contract is deliverable and has trading practices paralleling those in the physical market.

Simex is to launch a rubber futures contract in 1991 and is considering introducing a new contract in Brent crude to augment the success of the HSFO contract. Others being actively considered include long-term interest rate contracts, ten-year bonds, US Treasury bonds and an ASEAN stock market index futures contract.

Singapore International Monetary Exchange Ltd
1 Raffles Place
#07-00 OUB Centre
Singapore 0104
Tel: (65) 535 7382
Fax: (65) 535 7282

Kuala Lumpur Commodity Exchange (KLCE)
The KLCE was established in July 1980 and trading began in October of that year in Crude Palm Oil futures. The market has had a chequered life with a major trading scandal in palm oil in the mid-1980s which threatened its very existence. The market was restructured in 1985 with regulations being adopted which are similar to those governing the US futures markets. The KLCE is cleared by the Malaysian Futures Clearing Corporation, which is jointly owned by members of the KLCE and domestic banks, and is overseen by the Commodities Trading Commission, an independent national regulatory agency.

A physical market for tin also exists in a separate form under the aegis of the Kuala Lumpur Tin Market. This small market shares facilities and personnel with the KLCE.

Contracts
The KLCE trades six contracts in commodity futures. Two, those in tin and cocoa, are priced in US dollars. The KLCE has long entertained

hopes of some kind of offset arrangement with the London Metal Exchange's tin contract, going so far as to extend its trading hours to overlap with the first tin ring in London. These hopes remain largely unrealized owing to the poor general state of the tin market. The KLCE trades contracts in Ringgit in crude palm oil, SMR20 rubber, RSS1 rubber and refined, bleached and deodorized palm olein. However, although the two rubber contracts are virtually inactive.

Kuala Lumpur Commodity Exchange
4th Floor Citypoint
Dayabumi Complex
Jalan Sultan Hisamuddin
50740 Kuala Lumpur
Malaysia
Tel: (60) 3-2936822
Fax: (60) 3-2742215

OTHER EXCHANGES

A small futures market exists in the Philippines; the Manila International Futures Exchange trades contracts in sugar, coffee, copra and soybean futures but suffers heavily from a lack of international participation. Despite the relatively poor performance of the markets in Malaysia and the Philippines, their experience has not deterred others.

Indonesia, which has had a small physical commodities market trading rubber and coffee since 1985, plans to introduce a futures market to trade rubber and coffee and is also considering contracts in palm oil and cocoa.

Thailand is planning to introduce a commodity exchange for sugar, rubber, maize and farm products, while Taiwan is considering launching futures contracts for rice and pork and South Korea plans contracts for copper, ginseng and red pepper.

The KLCE authorities have viewed the potential developments in neighbouring Southeast Asian countries with some trepidation and have begun to take steps to make their contracts more acceptable to the traders and industries in those countries. They have suggested that, instead of attempting to stop others from introducing contracts, those launched in other countries should be standardized on contracts already trading in Kuala Lumpur. Similar contracts would certainly create opportunities for arbitrage and promote links between the markets.

In the field of financial futures, late in 1990, the Malaysian authorities gave the go-ahead to a private consortium for the formation of a new options and financial futures market, the Kuala Lumpur Options & Financial Futures Exchange (KLOFFE). The move took Malaysia's existing markets, the KLSE and the KLCE, by surprise as both had formulated plans to move into financial futures themselves. The new market is due to be operational by the end of 1991.

CHAPTER 15

DEVELOPING MARKETS I

The development of functional markets in countries throughout Latin America, Asia, the Middle East and Africa has been stultified variously by political instability, political doctrines inimical to capitalism and lack of economic stability. The major problem facing many of these markets is a lack of liquidity with most companies being controlled by a small group of shareholders. Few listed companies are majority-owned or controlled by foreigners. Indeed most of the markets in these areas have complex restrictions on foreign ownership of capital. For example, in the tiny market of Trinidad and Tobago, non-residents are required to be licensed before they can invest and, in extreme cases, a licence may be required for each new capital investment they make, including an application to subscribe to a rights issue on securities already held and for which they are already licensed. There are few futures markets and the equity markets tend to be small and under-capitalized.

However, there is a growing realization that equity markets in particular have an important role to play in stimulating faster economic growth by both encouraging savings and channelling these savings into productive use and by making managers more publicly accountable for their corporate performance. Perhaps most importantly the market can be used as a mechanism to attract foreign capital in a form which does not add to the debt burden already incurred by developing nations.

LATIN AMERICA

In 1990, the leading Latin American stock markets announced plans to create an electronic regional securities trading system that would also include the Spanish markets. The project is being backed by seven stock markets in Latin America as well as the Madrid, Barcelona and Bilbao stock exchanges.

The oldest stock market in Latin America is the Mercado de Valores de Buenos Aires in Argentina. The market was founded in 1854 to trade metals and it was not until 1872 that securities trading began.

Developing Markets I

In 1937, four years after the establishment of the Securities & Exchange Commission in the United States, a Securities Commission along the same lines was established in Buenos Aires. The commission has been an independent government agency since 1969, regulating the issue and trading of securities, including over-the-counter business. The market is Buenos Aires is the largest of five stock markets in the country. Trading is dominated by dealings in government bonds but the government is attempting to boost interest in equities through its privatization programme.

Share trading in Brazil also dates from the mid-nineteenth century when a group of brokers organized themselves on a model of the French market. The most important exchange in Brazil is now the Bôlsa de Valores de São Paulo (BOVESPA), although there are ten stock markets throughout the country. The market in São Paulo established its dominance over the market in Rio de Janeiro, the oldest in the country, with the emergence of São Paulo as Brazil's industrial and financial centre.

The São Paulo and Rio de Janeiro markets account for almost 90 per cent of all Brazilian equity trading. The markets are regulated by the National Monetary Council and overseen by the central bank and the securities commission, the Commissão de Valores Mobiliarios (CVM), the latter created in 1976 by the government to stimulate interest in the markets.

The Brazilian stock markets are the largest in Latin America but progress in developing the markets have been undermined by the country's chronic economic problems and by a lack of liquidity. As an example of the latter problem, the BOVESPA Index, the most widely recognized Brazilian market indicator, although covering eighty-three companies, is heavily weighted towards the government-owned oil producer Petrobras and just five companies account for more than 50 per cent of the index.

Brazil is a rarity among the developing market-places in having established futures and options markets. The oldest of the three main markets, the Bôlsa de Mercadorias de São Paulo (BMSP) has been operating since 1917. Prior to 1983 the market specialized in agricultural products. Since that date the gold contract has become increasingly important.

However, in terms of financial futures, the BMSP has been outstripped by its younger brother, the Bôlsa Mercantil e de Futuros (BM&F), established in São Paulo in February 1986. The BM&F's most successful futures contracts are those on the BOVESPA Index and certificates of deposit. The third major futures market, the Bôlsa

Brasileira de Futuros (BBF) in Rio de Janeiro, began operations in August 1986 but remains very much in the shadow of the São Paulo markets. The exchanges are self-regulating bodies overseen by the CVM. The BM&F operates its own clearing house while the BMSP is cleared by the Caixa Nacional de Liuqidação de Negócios a Termo e Disponível and the BBF by the Camara Brasileira de Compensação, which is jointly owned by five domestic banks and a subsidiary of the International Commodities Clearing House of London.

The first stock exchange established in Chile opened for business in the port of Valparaîso in 1892. However, the market was swiftly overshadowed by the stock market in Santiago which opened the following year. Trading eventually ceased in Valparaîso in 1982, leaving the Bôlsa de Comercio de Santiago as the country's only functioning stock market. Despite having a well-developed market by the late 1940s, economic and political chaos in the following decades saw a gradual decline followed by total collapse in the late 1960s under the Marxist Allende government. Following the military coup in 1973, a series of financial reforms were gradually introduced to boost the market.

The return of democratic government to Chile in 1989 and subsequent revisions to the restrictions on foreign investment, coupled with the Pinochet regime's privatization programme in the 1980s, revived interest in the Chilean market. Activity has increased and a computer system has been installed to disseminate market information throughout the country.

The Bôlsa Mexicana de Valores was established in Mexico City in 1894 and remains the only market of note in Mexico. Until the mid-1970s the market was very much a backwater, even in domestic terms. It was not until the government revamped the powers of the Mexican Securities Commission and issued regulations requiring banks to invest eight per cent of their deposits in shares or bonds that the market took off. Despite these moves the market remains sensitive to the poor state of the Mexican economy and to the muddled politics of the country. However, that being said, it is worth noting that in 1987, the year of Black Monday, in the period January-September, the market's index rose by a staggering 629 per cent in local currency terms, making it the world's top performing market. Unfortunately, the crash was equally as spectacular. The Mexican market now vies with the Brazilian market for first place as the largest in Latin America

Other markets do exist in the region, the best established are in Jamaica, Trinidad and Tobago, Uruguay and Venezuela, but they are very small and generally highly illiquid.

Developing Markets I

Asia and the Middle East

Share trading in India dates back further than any of the other developing markets, largely as a result of the British colonial involvement. Informal share trading began in Bombay some time in the 1830s and official stock exchanges have existed in the country for well over a hundred years. By the number of companies listed, the Indian markets also dwarf other developing markets, with more than 2,000 companies listed on the country's leading market, the Bombay Stock Exchange. There are seven stock markets throughout India although the Bombay market is by far the most important. In the late 1980s, the Indian government passed legislation introducing the Securities & Exchange Board of India (SEBI) to regulate the market. SEBI operates much as the American SEC and the British SIB. However, direct foreign participation in the market remains limited.

In neighbouring Pakistan, the government began to take steps in early 1991 to liberalize financial legislation in order to attract funds into the country to the Karachi Stock Exchange. The government has moved to ease restrictions on the transfer of securities in favour of non-residents and foreign currency accounts, which have been exempted from income, wealth and islamic taxes. The market has also been boosted by privatization and deregulation plans.

The Istanbul Menkul Kiymetler Borsasi in Turkey re-opened in 1986, making the present market, with the exception of those being formed in ex-communist countries (*see Chapter Sixteen*), one of the youngest in the world. Share trading does, however, predate the current market, going back to the mid-nineteenth century and the Ottoman Empire. However, prior to 1986 the stock market which existed was moribund and generated little interest domestically or internationally. The much-publicized revamp was part of the Turkish government's continuing attempts to gain entry to the European Economic Community and develop a modern market economy. Trading is now computerized and several leading international financial institutions, including Chase Manhattan, Citibank and Manufacturers Hanover, have taken up membership of the market.

The market in Kuwait is the only stock market in the Arab islamic countries. Trading began in the 1970s as the country's oil-based wealth exploded but initially the official market was restricted to shares in Kuwaiti companies. An unofficial market in other Gulf shares sprang up in 1978 but two years of boom were followed by a spectacular bust and the government had to step in to rescue investors and restore confidence. Recognizing that the crash owed much to the restrictive regime in place, the government moved to ease legislation through the 1980s. Kuwait had ambitions to become the financial centre of the Gulf, plans which were rudely interrupted by the Iraqi invasion in 1990. The future of the stock market, as with many other Kuwaiti institutions, is uncertain while the country reappraises its direction following the ejection of the Iraqi invaders.

The Tel Aviv Stock Exchange opened for business in Israel in 1953 although share trading in what was then Palestine had begun in 1935. Given the relatively open nature of Israeli society it is only to be expected that the market is one of the most developed of the world's smaller exchanges, with warrants and convertible securities also traded. The market is dominated by mutual funds, there being only a limited private investor base. Direct foreign investment remains limited although there are no real restrictions on foreign ownership of Israeli equity.

AFRICA

The economic, political and social problems of black Africa tend to militate strongly against the development of a viable financial market framework. However, despite the fact that the situation in much of the continent is describable more in terms of drought and mass starvation, in certain countries a functioning economy exists and, as a result, a stock market. There are tiny markets operating in Nigeria, Kenya and Zimbabwe. The importance of these markets is presently limited but is likely to grow as governments progress with their privatization programmes.

CHAPTER 16

DEVELOPING MARKETS II

The doctrine of communism and the state ownership of all means of production effectively precluded the existence of the market mechanism throughout Eastern Europe, the Soviet Union and China for much of the twentieth century. However, the collapse of the communist regimes in Eastern Europe left a vacuum which the emerging democratic governments in the region are struggling to fill. Central to the future development of these countries and to the future of the new democratic processes is the stable economic growth which communism failed to provide. Failure to boost the economy and with it personal income would seriously weaken popular support for any of the new regimes.

Essential to economic transformation is the creation of a real market for capital and efficient allocation of resources. In this context, markets for stocks and shares will play an increasingly important role in the development of the capital markets in Eastern Europe. However, a major conceptual adjustment is also necessary. Only now are the concepts of profit and loss and corporate identity themselves being gradually accepted and understood.

Although the communist party no longer rules in most of Eastern Europe or in what was the Soviet Union, it remains in control in China. However, in all these countries, governments are moving, albeit in some cases cautiously, towards the introduction of a market economy.

EASTERN EUROPE

The first stock market in Eastern Europe was the Budapest Stock Exchange in Hungary, which began trading in June 1990 and had thirty companies listed by the end of that year. Bond trading had already been established in Hungary in 1983. The Budapest market has some forty members, many of them banks. The Hungarian government has plans to privatize most of the state industries, but the stock market has so far played only a minor role in this activity. Hungary also has plans to develop a commodity market. In October 1990, the Chicago Board of Trade and the Chicago Mercantile Exchange signed a memorandum of understanding with the Termenytozade KFT, the Budapest Commodities Exchange, to institute an educational and research exchange programme.

Commodity trading began in Budapest in 1987 and the market there is being used as a model by the Bulgarian authorities. A commodity exchange opened for business in Sofia for the first time in fifty years in July 1991. The market trades basic foodstuffs, such as grain, sugar, meat and butter, once a week. The exchange was founded by thirteen Bulgarian companies each with one broker in the market.

Three markets were also established in Yugoslavia in 1990, in Belgrade, Llubljana and Zagreb. By the end of the year the most successful of the three, the Llubljana market in Slovenia had almost fifty stocks listed. The Llubljana market's capitalization, trade value and volume of business represent over 90 per cent of all stock market activity in Yugoslavia. This dominance is a result of the market-orientated outlook of Slovenia, the most "westernized" of Yugoslavia's six republics. However, the slide into civil war the following year brought the development of the markets to a standstill.

Official share trading began in Poland for the first time since before the Second World War in April 1991, with the opening of a stock market in Warsaw, although trading had commenced unofficially the preceding year and a small private market traded currencies, gold and some bonds. Perhaps to add insult to communist injury, the Warsaw exchange opened for business in what had been the headquarters of the Polish communist party central committee. Trading between seven licensed brokers commenced in the shares of five companies privatized along UK lines. Initial assistance on privatization was given by British financial institutions but future privatizations are to be on a less structured basis, probably through the issue of vouchers and unit trusts, to speed up the process. The exchange itself is modelled on the French markets with advice from the French Société des Bourses and is overseen by a Securities Commission set up under the Public Trading & Securities Act, which became law in October 1990. The organization and powers of the commission are based on the American Securities Exchange Commission.

All the other ex-communist countries also intend to introduce stock markets but plans are most advanced in Czechoslovakia, where regulations enabling the privatization of state industries became law in April 1991. There are proposals to establish two markets, in Prague and Bratislava, and a consortium of eleven domestic banks is raising finance to set up the exchanges. Under the current timetable, dealings are due to commence on the stock markets in early 1992. The Czech stock exchange preparatory committee is in talks with the UK government to help fund research and consultancy work from British institutions. A small number of joint-stock companies already exist and share trading is conducted privately between banks.

RUSSIA

A bust of Lenin still presides over the trading on the Russian Commodities and Raw Materials Exchange in Moscow's former Central Post Office. However, little else remains in the market-place to show the influence of more than seventy years of communism. The collapse of the Soviet economy amid continued bickering between the faltering central government and the governments of the Soviet Republics resulted in the market system gaining ground in the country from the bottom upwards. The price of a seat on the Moscow market has already gone up from 100,000 roubles initially to 250,000 roubles and it has more than 250 members.

The Moscow market began trading in May 1990, but only a year later there were close to 200 so-called commodity exchanges operating throughout the country. These markets bear little resemblance to the received view of commodity exchanges but are the fruits of the collapse of the centrally planned supply system, trading in fabrics, furniture, food, plastics, machinery, automobiles, household supplies and electronics, in effect everything available and anything tradeable. The markets are run like an auction with prices being shouted from a podium.

In November 1990, the Chicago Board of Trade and the Chicago Mercantile Exchange signed memorandums of understanding with the Moscow market and the State Commission of the USSR Council of Ministers on Food and Procurement to begin educational and research exchange programmes. The Moscow market is the largest of the Soviet commodity markets and has ambitions to be the first to list proper futures contracts. The market authorities intend to specialize in oil, grain and construction materials and, following advice from Central Trading Systems of New York, a standardized grain trading contract was introduced in June 1991. The contract, which is not a true futures contract but more similar to the early forward contracts, allows buyers and sellers to negotiate the type of grain, the volume and the delivery period. Each party must put up performance bonds ensuring they will complete the deal.

There are plans to merge the commodity market with the Moscow Central Exchange, which operates a primary market for bonds but has no facility for secondary trading.

In September 1990, Leningrad established the Soviet Union's first stock exchange since the 1920s and, in December 1990, the Peake/Ryerson Consulting Group and Transvik Inc. (operators of NORDEX, *see Chapter Eleven*) signed a letter of intent with the city authorities and officials of the market to form a joint venture to establish and operate the Leningrad Stock Exchange and the Leningrad Commodities Exchange. Under the proposals being put forward by Transvik, the two markets would use a variant of the Transvik Market System, the company's proprietary electronic screen-based trading system.

Early in 1991, Daiwa Securities, one of Japan's big four brokerages, signed a series of deals to provide consultancy and training for the establishment of a stock exchange and to provide advice to the Soviet Ministry of Finance. The nascent Moscow International Stock Exchange trades three shares and fifteen bonds.

The speed of development of the market system across the country took the authorities by surprise and it was only in March 1991 that Russian Federation legislators enacted temporary laws to govern the markets and proposed the institution of a licensing system. Speculation remains a crime, but the law is being honoured much more in the breach than in the letter. Early in 1991, five Soviet republics announced plans to set up an inter-Republican commodity exchange.

THE PEOPLE'S REPUBLIC OF CHINA
With the communist party still effectively in control, the moves towards effective financial markets in the People's Republic of China are heavily politicized. In common with much of the country's political and economic liberalization in the late 1980s, the development of markets in China came to a grinding halt following the events in Tienanmen Square, Beijing, in June 1989. However, by the summer of 1990, reports in the influential newspaper the *China Daily* were once more calling for financial reform and the creation of market structures. The changes proposed by Zheng Hongquing of the State Commission for Restructuring the Economy called for the creation of a shareholding system under which the state would remain the majority shareholder, but managements would have more autonomy to run their businesses.

Following these public comments, the Chinese authorities moved cautiously forward. In October 1990, the country's first futures exchange began trading. The wholesale grain market opened in the Northern city of Zhengzhou, capital of Henan province, a major grain growing region. The market commenced trading wheat and has plans to add contracts for rice, maize and soya beans in the future. The market trades both cash and forward with ceiling and floor prices in place to limit volatility.

Uniform futures contracts are to be introduced at a later date. About 100 state agencies have been authorized to trade but individuals are barred from participating. The market, which was established with technical assistance from the Chicago Board of Trade, is jointly run by the Ministry of Commerce and the Henan provincial government.

The next step forward came just two months later with the formal launch, in December 1990, of a centralized securities trading system, linking eighteen licensed traders in six cities across China. Trading began on the Securities Automated Quotations System (STAQ) in four issues of treasury bonds. More than 1,000 billion yuan (US$190 billion at official rates of exchange) are estimated to be held in savings accounts or stuffed under peasants' mattresses. The new market was largely the product of the government's requirement to fund a ballooning deficit with bond issues. The STAQ system is based on the US NASDAQ market and was modelled on systems used by the international information providers Reuters and Telerate. The electronic market is the first stage in linking the embryonic stock markets in Shanghai and Shenzhen (*see below*) and traders in other cities under one centralized system.

The same month, after a break of forty years, trading officially began on the Shanghai Securities Exchange. Red waistcoated-dealers took their places on the floor of the market in what had once been the Astor Hotel. Although Shanghai was not the first exchange to open, it was the first to be backed officially by the Beijing government. Trading in Shanghai commenced in thirty issues, only eight of which were actually corporate stocks, with strict price movement limits in force. Plans have been drawn up to allow foreign investors to participate in the market through specially designated non-voting shares. The buying and selling of government bonds over the counter had been going on in Shanghai since the mid-1980s.

Share trading in the Special Economic Zone of Shenzhen, next to capitalist Hong Kong, began in 1987 but without formal approval from the central authorities. The Beijing government only allowed the market to operate on a experimental basis; it was not until the spring of 1991 that recognition was forthcoming, and only in July was the market officially opened. By the end of 1991, the exchange authorities believe they will have at least seventeen corporate issues listed. There are also proposals to establish a special class of "B" shares aimed at foreign investors. After receiving official approval, the Shenzhen Securities Exchange decided to install a computerized trading system and launched its own market index, the Shenzhen Stock Price Index, in a move mirroring the launch of the Shanghai market's Jingan Index.

PART THREE: APPENDICES

APPENDIX I

GLOSSARY OF TERMS

allfinanz The concept of retail banking and life insurance operations being run by the same institution.

arbitrage A trading practice which takes advantage of the difference between the value or return on *assets* to make a profit. This may involve the simultaneous purchase and sale of a *security* or *commodity* on separate markets to take advantage of any price difference.

arbitrageurs Also known by the abbreviation "Arbs", this is a term applied to speculators, especially those who buy *shares* in companies which may be subject to take-over bids

assets Anything which has a value or may offer a return on investment.

back-to-back loan Borrowings in one currency set against a loan in another currency, usually arranged between separate companies. It is used to avoid or overcome exchange controls.

backwardation Also known by the abbreviation "Back", this term describes the situation in which the cash or near-term delivery price of a commodity is higher than the forward price. A backwardation may occur as a result of delays in shipment, causing immediate shortages in supplies which would not exist in the long term.

bancassurance This French term corresponds to the German *allfinanz*.

basket currency A created currency unit used to assist in economic management, consisting of several national currencies. There are two well-known basket currencies, *Special Drawing Rights* and *European Currency Units (ECU)*.

bearer bonds These are *bonds* whose proof of ownership is physical possession.

Big Bang The name given to the deregulation of the UK stock market which took effect on 27 October 1986, ending the practice of fixed commissions and the distinction between brokers and jobbers.

billet de trésorie A French unsecured loan note issued for short-term borrowings.

bond Any interest-bearing *security* issued either by companies (corporate bonds are also known as *debentures*) or by governments.

Bretton Woods The location in New Hampshire, USA, of the United Nations Monetary and Financial Conference held in July 1944. The framework for the post-war foreign exchange system which was established at the conference became known as the Bretton Woods system.

buffer stock Part of a scheme of price regulation for commodities, a buffer stock acts to purchase the commodity in times of oversupply to support the price. Conversely stocks held will be sold into the market when there is a shortage. It is not, in theory, the job of a buffer stock to raise the price of the commodity being supported but rather to smooth out the peaks and troughs of price movements.

capitalization The total value at the market price of *securities* issued by a given company, market sector or market as a whole.

Glossary of Terms

cash and carry A trading practice used in *futures* markets when there is a *contango*. If the difference between the cash price and the forward price is greater than the the costs of both insuring and storing the commodity and the interest-rate cost of the money used to purchase it, a dealer will purchase the commodity for cash, sell the futures contract and pocket the excess as profit.

clearing bank Originally used only to describe members of the London bankers' clearing house, this term is now synonymous with commercial bank and is distinguished from an *investment bank* in that the former will have a presence in the retail market dealing with personal customers while the latter does not.

clearing house An organization which exists within a market to ensure that buyers and sellers meet their obligations to each other.

commodity Any raw material. A "primary" commodity is one which has had the minimum of treatment, for example grain rather than bread and metal ingots rather than fabricated products.

contango A *futures* market term describing the normal market condition in which the cash price of the commodity or futures contract is lower than the forward price. The difference between the two prices equates to the cost of storing and insuring the commodity as well as the interest-rate cost of borrowing money to purchase the commodity immediately.

convertible bond This is a bond which entitles the holder to convert it into another form of security under a given set of circumstances. The price at which conversion may occur and the point in time at which the bond may be converted may be stipulated.

corporate issue A *bond* issued by a corporate entity as distinct from those issued by national or local governments.

credit watch A term used by credit-*rating* agencies. These agencies provide credit ratings of *corporate issues* and some government issues to enable purchasers to have a more accurate guide to the value of their *bond* holdings. If a company is placed on credit watch it means the rating agency believes its financial position may be about to deteriorate and, hence, the value of its bonds may decline.

debenture See *bond*.

derivatives Financial instruments which have been "derived" from an underlying security or financial instrument. Options and financial futures are all derivatives.

Eurobond A negotiable *bond* issued by an international syndicate of banks, usually sold to investors who are not domiciled in the country in whose currency it is denominated. Tax is not deducted at source from these bonds.

Eurodollar The first so-called "Euro-" currency, Eurodollars are simply US dollars held in accounts outside the USA.

Euromarket This term describes the international market in currencies and securities outside the countries in whose currency the instruments are denominated. See *Eurobond* and *Eurodollar*.

European Currency Unit A *basket currency* unit consisting of specified weighted amounts of all the currencies of the member countries of the European Economic Community (EC).

European Monetary System A system established in 1978 by the member countries of the EC to manage and regulate the exchange rates of their currencies.

Eurowarrant A certificate linked to a *Eurobond* giving the holder the right to purchase a specified number of *shares* at a pre-determined price at a set time. See *warrant*.

exchange for physical A *futures* market term describing the mechanism through which ownership of a futures contract which does not confer ownership of the underlying commodity is swapped for the same value amount of that commodity. A buyer of the cash commodity will swap this for an equivalent amount of futures contracts or vice versa.

Glossary of Terms

exchange rate mechanism The operating structure of the *European Monetary System* under which the *European Currency Unit* was created and the currencies given a central rate against which their individual fluctuation is limited.

external bonds *Bonds* issued on one domestic market which are denominated in another currency.

The "Fed" The abbreviation used to describe the US central bank, the Federal Reserve.

floating rate note Debt instruments, usually *bonds*, which carry a variable rate of interest, usually calculated at an agreed rate above a specified reference rate, often the *London Interbank Offered Rate*.

force majeure A term used in supply contracts which allows the supplier to break the contract and suspend delivery under certain circumstances. For example, a mining company may call *force majeure* on its contracts to deliver if the workforce at the mine went on strike.

forwardation See *contango*.

Freimakler Free brokers on the German stock market who act as intermediaries between institutions. Under certain circumstances they may act in competition with the *kursmaklers*.

futures contracts Financial instruments which confer on the purchaser the right to buy or sell a security or a commodity at a set price at a specified date in the future.

gilts UK government *bonds*, the certificates were originally issued with gold edging.

global custodians Institutions which specialize in the management of international portfolios, undertaking settlement of funds and management of any potential tax problems arising from international trading.

gold standard The international foreign exchange standard pertaining throughout the Nineteenth century and parts of the Twentieth century under which each national currency had a set value against gold bullion.

hedging The term used in trading, especially but not exclusively of commodity futures, to denote the minimization of potential loss. For example a commodity consumer may purchase commodity futures contracts to ensure continuity of supply at a known price.

indices An index is an artificial creation combining the prices of a number of *shares*, *bonds*, or *commodities* to offer a broad guide to the overall direction of their prices. Indices may be calculated at set intervals or re-calculated every time the price of one of its constituent parts changes. Such indices may themselves be used as as the basis of tradeable instruments.

insider dealing The buying or selling of a financial instrument, usually *shares*, when in possession of information which would affect the price and which is not known in the market-place. This practice is illegal in most markets.

investment bank Also known, especially in the UK, as merchant banks, these institutions operate as financial intermediaries placing new *shares* and bonds with investors and assisting companies involved in take-overs and mergers.

junk bonds These are *bonds* which are issued by companies whose financial position is such that the bonds are not rated by the credit-rating agencies. These low quality *securities* tend to offer a higher rate of return as the attraction to purchase them.

kerb trading Trading carried out after the official close of a market. The term came about because such trading was originally carried on outside the building in which the market was housed, on the pavement kerb.

Kursmakler The *kursmaklers*, the official brokers on the German market, are appointed to serve as ministerial officers by the German lander (provincial state) governments. They act for institutions but do not act for members of the public and are responsible for fixing prices.

Glossary of Terms

local An exchange independent dealer who operates for his own account.

London Interbank Offered Rate The rate of interest offered by commercial banks for funds on the interbank market in London. Known by its acronym LIBOR, this rate of interest is widely used as the base rate for *floating rate note*s and for the *Euromarket*.

margin This the proportion of the full price of a financial instrument or commodity paid by a client to his broker when he purchases them on credit. It is also the initial payment made to the market clearing house by the broker operating on behalf of a client purchasing an instrument. Margin trading is much less common in the UK than in the USA.

maturity The date at which a *bond* or *security* must be repaid. The term is also used to denote the point in time in the future at which a *futures* contract runs out.

mutual funds US term for *Unit trusts*

net margining system This system, used by some US exchanges, involves adding the total margins paid to each broker on the market and results in only the difference changing hands, rather than the full amount of margin paid to each broker being handed over to the clearing house.

open outcry This is the method of business still used in most commodity markets and many derivatives markets in which brokers trade with each other face-to-face and bids and offers must be called out loud for all participants to hear.

options Options confer upon the owner the right but not the obligation to buy or sell a set quantity of a given underlying instrument at a specified price for a specified period of time. An option granting the right to purchase is known as a "call option" and an option granting the right to sell is known as a "put option".

over-the-counter This is a generic phrase used to describe any market for financial instruments between recognized traders which does not operate through a formal exchange-based structure. The term originally came from the USA where, in 1870s, stocks were first purchased across bank counters.

par This is the face or nominal value of the stock certificate, rather than its market price. It is more significant for *bonds* than for *shares* because it describes the value of the bond in terms of what the issuer will repay on *maturity*.

pit trader A dealer operating on the floor of an exchange, usually a *futures* exchange. The "pit" itself is a platform on the trading floor of the exchange, consisting of steps upon which the brokers and dealers stand during *open outcry* trading.

portfolio A collection of investments held by an individual or institution.

preference shares These are *shares* issued by a company which take the form of borrowings rather than ownership. In terms of precedence they rank ahead of ordinary shares but behind bonds in the payment of dividends.

programme trading This has come to mean orders generated by computer programmes faster than a human trader can react once a specific price level has been reached. Its original technical definition is a strategy of switching between underlying *securities* and *options* in response to the change in the premium on the option against the price of the underlying security.

purchasing power parity The most popular theory of currency valuation which seeks to explain the links between economic fundamentals and exchange rates. The basis of the theory is that exchange rates tend to move towards a point at which the purchasing power, i.e. what can be bought for a given sum of money, of separate currencies is broadly similar.

rating This is the classification of the investment grade of *bonds* and borrowings according to risk. The lowest risk bonds are graded AAA, with gradings going down to D for higher risk bonds. Bonds which carry a greater potential for default than D tend to carry a higher rate of interest to attract purchasers to offset the risk of default. Such instruments are known as *junk bonds*.

GLOSSARY OF TERMS

Relit The five-day rolling settlement period of the French stock exchange.

repos This is the abbreviation by which "repurchase agreements" are known. In a repurchase agreement *securities* are sold into the market with an agreement on the part of the issuer to buy them back at a later date. A reverse repo involves the purchase of securities while agreeing to sell them at a later date.

reverse auction In a reverse auction a *bond* issuer wishing to reduce the number of bonds in issue will invite holders to offer prices at which they are willing to sell the bonds back to the issuer. The UK government operated a programme of reverse auctions in the *gilts* market in the late 1980s.

rights issue When a company wishes to raise more funds through the issue of additional *shares* it may decide to do so through giving existing shareholders the right to purchase the new shares on favourable terms, in a given ratio to the number of shares already held. The importance of this form of raising finance is that it gives shareholders the ability to maintain their existing percentage ownership of the company.

saitori These are members of the Tokyo Stock Exchange who act only as intermediaries between the brokers. *Saitori* members of the market are not allowed to deal for their own accounts or for non-members and may be permitted to deal only in a limited number of stocks.

seat Having a "seat" on an exchange has become synonymous with membership of the market. The term came from the New York Stock Exchange where, in the early Nineteenth century, members of the exchange shouted bids and offers for *shares* from the chairs assigned to them.

securities A generic term describing any financial instruments traded on a stock exchange, such as *shares* and *bonds*.

self-regulating organization Under the UK and US legal systems, agencies registered with the financial regulators, the Securities and Investments Board in the UK and the Securities Exchange Commission in the USA, are themselves responsible for monitoring the activities of their members.

shares The ownership of a company is divided between its shareholders according to the percentage of shares held. A shareholder provides money to the company in return for which he receives a proportion of the profits as dividends paid on each share.

sherpa A civil servant representing one of the heads of government of the Group of Seven leading industrialized nations. The sherpas meet before the summit meetings held by these countries to prepare the summit agendas.

Société de Bourse A brokerage member of the French stock exchange.

Special Drawing Right A *basket currency* unit used by the International Monetary Fund, consisting of weighted amounts of the US dollar, D-mark, Japanese yen, French franc and sterling.

spread The difference between the buying and selling price of any financial instrument.

stock A term used in the UK to describe fixed interest-rate bearing *securities* or *bonds* but which is also used to describe *shares*. For example, ordinary shares in the UK are known as common stock in the USA.

straddle A trading position taken in *options* or *futures* in which contracts to buy and to sell at the same point in the future are entered into at the same time. Such a position offers further protection from price fluctuations or the potential for profit from any large price movement.

swap An agreement between two parties to exchange a stream of future payments

tap issues A term used in the UK to describe a situation where the issue of government bonds has not been fully subscribed. In this case, the broker acting for the government retains the unsubscribed stock, releasing it onto the market over a period of time.

Glossary of Terms

terminal market This is another name for a *futures* market in *commodities*, because futures contracts expire on a set or terminal date in the future.

tokkin *Portfolio* trading by investors, particularly companies whose main business is not in the financial markets and who are using their cash surpluses to generate further income, on the Japanese stock market.

tombstone As a matter of record, a tombstone is an advertisement recording the details of a new loan or *bond* issue naming the banks which have underwritten it, that is, guaranteed to purchase the issue if no-one else does.

unit trusts These are savings schemes run by specialist institutions for smaller investors. With the money coming into the scheme the institution purchases *securities*. Investors are allocated units in the trust in proportion to the size of their investment.

vinkulierungspraxis This term describes the situation existing notably on the Swiss stock exchange under which companies can refuse to register the ownership of shares to foreign investors if they do not wish to do so. Effectively it makes it virtually impossible for Swiss companies to be taken over by foreigners.

warrants This is a certificate, usually attached to a *bond*, conferring upon the holder the right to purchase *shares* in a company at a set price on a date in the future.

yearlings These are short-term *bonds*, commonly with a life of just one year, hence the name.

zaibatsu A direct translation of the term means "financial clique". The original *zaibatsu* were the large family-owned conglomerates responsible for the industrialization of Japan in the late Nineteenth and early Twentieth century.

APPENDIX II

ABBREVIATIONS IN TEXT

ADR	American Depository Receipts (USA)
AFBD	Association of Futures Brokers and Dealers (UK)
AGM	Annual General Meeting
AMEX	American Stock Exchange (USA)
APT	Automated Pit Trading (UK)
ATX	Austrian Traded Index
AUD	Australian dollars
BAPEPAM	Securities Commission (Indonesia)
BBF	Bôlsa Brasileira de Futuros (Brazil)
BCCI	Bank of Credit & Commerce International
Belfox	Futures & Options Exchange (Belgium)
BFE	Baltic Futures Exchange (UK)
BIFFEX	Baltic International Freight Futures Exchange (UK)
BIS	Bank for International Settlements
BM&F	Bôlsa Mercantil e de Futuros (Brazil)
BMSP	Bôlsa de Mercadorias de São Paulo (Brazil)
BOVESPA	Bôlsa de Valores de São Paulo (Brazil)
BTP	Buoni del Tesoro Poiennali (Italy)
CAC	Cotation Assiste en Continu (France)
CAD	Canadian dollars
CATS	Computer-Assisted Trading System
CBOE	Chicago Board Options Exchange (USA)
CBOT	Chicago Board of Trade (USA)
CBV	Conseil des Bourses de Valeurs (France)
CD	Certificates of deposit
CEC	Commodities Exchange Center (USA)
CFTC	Commodity Futures Trading Commission (USA)
CIPEC	Council of Copper Exporting Countries
CLOB	Central Limit Order Book
CME	Chicago Mercantile Exchange (USA)
COMEX	Commodity Exchange (USA)
CORES	Computerized Order Routing and Execution System (Japan)
CRB	Commodities Research Bureau (USA)
CRCE	Chicago Rice & Cotton Exchange (USA)
CSCE	Coffee, Sugar and Cocoa Exchange (USA)
CVM	Commissão de Valores Mobiliarios (Brazil)
Dax	Deutsche Aktienindex (Germany)
DEM	Deutschmarks

Abbreviations in Text

DJIA	Dow Jones Industrial Average Index (USA)
DOT	Designated Order Turnaround
DTB	Deutsche Terminbörse (Germany)
DTI	Department of Trade & Industry (UK)
EBRD	European Bank for Reconstruction and Development
EC	European Community
ECP	Eurocommercial Paper
ECU	European Currency Unit
ED	Eurodollars
EFP	Exchange for Physical
EFTA	European Free Trade Area
EMS	European Monetary System
EMU	European Monetary Union
ENEL	Enternazionale per Energia Elettrica (Italy)
EOE	European Options Exchange–Optiebeurs (Netherlands)
ERM	Exchange Rate Mechanism
ETOs	Exchange-Traded Options
FAST	Fast Automated Screen Trading (UK)
FDIC	Federal Deposit Insurance Corporation (USA)
FIMBRA	Financial Intermediaries, Managers and Brokers Regulatory Association (UK)
FINEX	Financial Instrument Exchange (USA)
FOMC	Federal Open Market Committee (USA)
Forex	Foreign exchange
FOX	Futures and Options Exchange (UK)
FRF	French francs
FRN	Floating Rate Note
FT-SE 100	Financial Times-Stock Exchange 100 index (UK)
Futop	Futures & Options Exchange (Denmark)
G-5	Group of Five (France, Germany, Japan, UK and USA)
G-7	Group of Seven (G-5 countries plus Canada and Italy)
GAAP	Generally Accepted Accounting Principles
GBP	Sterling
GLOBEX	Proprietary trading system developed by Reuters plc
GMS	German Market System, operated by Quotron
GNMA	Government National Mortgage Association (USA)
HKFE	Hong Kong Futures Exchange
HSFO	High Sulphur Fuel Oil
IBIS	InterBank Information System (Germany)
ICCH	International Commodities Clearing House (UK)
IDA	International Development Association
IFOX	Futures & Options Exchange (Ireland)
IIEDS	Individual Investor Express Delivery Service (USA)
IMF	International Monetary Fund
IMM	International Monetary Market (USA)
IMRO	Investment Management Regulatory Organization (UK)
Intex	International Futures Exchange (Bermuda)
IOM	Index and Option Market (USA)
IPE	International Petroleum Exchange (UK)
ISCOR	Iron & Steel Industrial Corp Ltd (South Africa)

ABBREVIATIONS IN TEXT

ISDA	International Swap Dealers Association
ISMA	International Securities Market Association
ITA	International Tin Agreement
ITC	International Tin Council
JASDAQ	Japanese Securities Dealers Automated Quotations
JGB	Japanese Government Bonds
JPY	Japanese yen
JSE	Johannesburg Stock Exchange (Rep. of South Africa)
KLCE	Kuala Lumpur Commodity Exchange (Malaysia)
KLOFFE	Kuala Lumpur Options & Financial Futures Exchange (Malaysia)
KLSE	Kuala Lumpur Stock Exchange (Malaysia)
KSE	Korea Stock Exchange (Korea)
LAUTRO	Life and Unit Trust Regulatory Organization (UK)
LBMA	London Bullion Market Association (UK)
LCB	Lander (state) Central Banks (Germany)
LEAPS	Long-term Equity Anticipation Securities
LIBOR	London Interbank Offered Rate (UK)
LIFFE	London International Financial Futures Exchange (UK)
LME	London Metal Exchange (UK)
LSE	London Stock Exchange (UK)
LTOM	London Traded Options Market (UK)
MATIF	Marché à Terme des Instruments Financiers (France)
MATIS	Makler Tele Information System, operated by Reuters plc
MEFF	Mercado de Futoros Financieros SA (Spain)
MGMI	Metallgesellschaft Metals Index
MidAm	MidAmerica Commodity Exchange (USA)
MMC	Monopolies & Mergers Commission (UK)
Mofex	Mercado de Opciones Financiero Espanol (Spain)
Monep	Marché des Options Négotiables de Paris (France)
MSE	Manila Stock Exchange (Philippines)
NASD	National Association of Securities Dealers (USA)
NASDAQ	National Association of Securities Dealers Automated Quotations (USA)
NIF	Note Insurance Facility
NMS	Normal Market Size
NORDEX	Nordic Exchange (UK)
NYCE	New York Cotton Exchange (USA)
NYFE	New York Futures Exchange (USA)
NYMEX	New York Mercantile Exchange (USA)
NYSE	New York Stock Exchange (USA)
NZFOE	New Zealand Futures & Options Exchange
NZSE	New Zealand Stock Exchange
OFT	Office of Fair Trading
OM	Options Markand (Sweden)
OM Iberica	Options Market (renamed Mofex)
OPEC	Organization of Petroleum Exporting Countries
OTC	Over-The-Counter
OTOB	Options Exchange (Austria)
PIBOR	Paris Interbank Offered Rate (France)
PFRN	Perpetual Floating Rate Notes

Abbreviations in Text

RIEs	Recognized Investment Exchanges
RPBs	Recognized Professional Bodies
RUF	Revolving Underwriting Facility
PPP	Purchasing Power Parity
PSE	Pacific Stock Exchange (USA)
QIB	Qualified Institutional Buyer/investor
S&L	Savings & Loans (USA)
S&P	Standard & Poors
SAEF	Stock Exchange Automated Execution Facility (UK)
Safex	South Africa Futures Exchange
SDR	Special Drawing Right
SEAQ	Stock Exchange Automated Quotations (UK)
SEATS	Stock Exchange Automated Trading System
SEBI	Securities & Exchange Board of India
SEC	Securities & Exchange Commission (USA)
SEHK	Stock Exchange of Hong Kong
SES	Stock Exchange of Singapore
SESDAQ	Stock Exchange of Singapore Dealing and Automated Quotation
SET	Securities Exchange of Thailand
SFR	Swiss francs
SIB	Securities & Investments Board (UK)
Sicovam	Société Interprofessionelle pour la Compensation de Valeurs Mobilières (France)
SIMEX	Singapore International Monetary Exchange
SOFFEX	Swiss Options & Financial Futures Exchange
SROs	Self-Regulating Organizations
STAQ	Securities Automated Quotations System (China)
SYCOM	Sydney Computerized Overnight Market (Australia)
TALISMAN	Transfer Accounting, Lodgement for Investors, Stock Management (UK)
TAURUS	Transfer and Automated Registration of Uncertificated Stock (UK)
Tocom	Tokyo Commodity Exchange for Industry (Japan)
TOPIC	Teletext Output of Price Information by Computer
TIFFE	Tokyo International Financial Futures Exchange (Japan)
TSA	The Securities Association (UK)
TSE	Tokyo Stock Exchange (Japan)
UNCTAD	United Nations Conference on Trade and Development
USDA	US Department of Agriculture
VOC	Vereenigde Oost-Indische Compagnie (Netherlands)
VSTF	Very Short-Term Facility
USM	Unlisted Securities Market (UK)

APPENDIX III

TAX AND COMMISSION IN STOCK MARKETS

The table on the following page displays the size of commission, the type of and size of taxation imposed, and the length of settlement period of the major stock markets around the world. In addition to the charges levied on market transactions, international investors may also be liable to a withholding tax. This is a tax deducted on dividends or other income to non-residents by the government in which the stock market is domiciled. Withholding tax is usually levied at the standard rate of income tax in the country concerned.

However, this taxation may be reduced if the country in which the investor is based has a double taxation agreement with the country in which the company is based.

In Australia, withholding tax on dividend payments is charged at a rate of 30 per cent if the shareholder is resident in a country with which there is no tax agreement. In countries where there is a taxation agreement, the tax on dividend payments is reduced to 15 per cent. Withholding tax on interest payable to non-residents is fixed at 10 per cent.

The rate of withholding tax in Canada is 25 per cent, reduced to 15 per cent where there is a tax treaty.

The situation is more complex in France, dividends and interest from French securities are subject to a basic withholding tax of 25 per cent. Rates on interest payable vary up to 51 per cent, although no withholding tax is levied on interest from bonds issued in France since the beginning of 1987. Investors may also be able to claim further tax credits because dividends are paid out of income net of tax.

In Germany, the rates are similar to Canada, with a basic rate of 25 per cent, reduced to 15 per cent in cases where there is a tax treaty. Foreign investors may also be liable to taxation on capital gains on the sale of equity if they hold more than 25 per cent of a German quoted company.

In Hong Kong, as in France, dividends are paid out of after-tax income but there is no further taxation levied. However, because of this

Tax and Commission in Stock Markets

Market	Commission	Tax	Settlement
Australia	Negotiable, normally 0.30%	Transaction tax 0.30%, cannot be avoided by off-exchange trading	No fixed settlement period, set by negotiation (proposals for a trade date +5 business days rolling settlement are being studied)
Canada	Negotiable, normally C$0.04 per share		Trade date +5 business days
France	Negotiable, normally 0.30%	<FFr 1,000,000 0.30%, >FFr 1,000,000 0.15%. Taxes may be avoided by trading ex-country	Monthly account settlement cycle
Germany	Negotiable, normally 0.35%	Börsmumsatz Steuer 0.12% (normally only residents); courtage tax 0.06% (official brokerage fee). Taxes may be avoided by trading ex-country	Trade date +2 business days for domestic dealings; +5 for foreign clients
Hong Kong	Normal commission 0.25%	Stamp duty 0.25%; Exchange Levy 0.050%; Special Levy 0.005%. Levies may be avoided by trading off-market	Trade date +1 business day
Japan	Variable from 1.15% for deals worth <Y1,000,000 to 0.075% + Y785,000 for deals over Y1 billion	Sales tax 0.30%. Taxes may be avoided by trading ex-country	Trade date +3 business days
Singapore	Variable from 1% for the first S$250,000 to 0.50% on amounts above S$1 million	Clearing fee 0.05%; contract stamp duty 0.10%; transfer stamp duty 0.20% (purchases only). Clearing fees and contract stamp duty may be avoided by trading off-market	Trade date +7 calendar days
United Kingdom	Net or negotiable, typically 0.20-0.25%	Stamp duty 0.50% (purchases only)	Settlement is on the second Monday after the end of the two week (sometimes three) account period
USA	Net or negotiable, typically US$0.05-0.08 per share	SEC fee on sale transactions US$0.01 per US$300	Trade date +5 business days

Hong Kong has entered no double taxation agreements and international investors operating through Hong Kong would be subject to the higher levels of withholding tax levied elsewhere.

Withholding tax in Japan is charged at a basic rate of 20 per cent. Where there is a double taxation treaty, this rate is reduced to between zero and 15 per cent. In some cases foreign investors may also be liable to taxation on capital gains on the sale of Japanese stock.

Dividends are taxed at source in Singapore at a rate of 32 per cent and there is no further withholding tax levied. Foreign investors are not liable for tax on capital gains.

In the UK companies are required to pay advance corporation tax on dividends. Where a double taxation treaty exists, investors may claim tax credits against the amount of advance corporation tax paid less a withholding tax of 15 per cent.

Dividends in the USA are subject to a 30 per cent withholding tax, reducing to 15 per cent where there is a treaty and, in certain cases, down to 5 per cent or 10 per cent for larger shareholders.

Sources:
Anatomy of European Markets, Goldman Sachs, 1991
Guide to Global Equity Markets, UBS Philips & Drew, 1991
The GT Guide to World Equity Markets, Euromoney Publications, 1990

Bibliography

Books

Alletzhauser, Albert	*The House of Nomura*, London, Bloomsbury 1990
Andrew, John	*How to Understand the Financial Press*, London, Kogan Page 1990
Bailey, Fenton	*The Junk Bond Revolution: Michael Milken, Wall Street and the "Roaring Eighties"*, London, Fourth Estate 1991
Bannock, G. & Manser, W.	*The Penguin International Dictionary of Finance*, London, Penguin 1989
Beckman, Robert	*Crashes*, London, Grafton Books 1990
Boesky, Ivan F.	*Merger Mania*, New York, Holt, Rinehart & Winston 1985
Bowe, Michael	*Eurobonds*, London, Square Mile Books 1988
de Caires, Bryan & Fletter, Debbie, ed.	*The GT Guide to World Equity Markets*, London, Euromoney Publications 1990
Chapman, Colin	*Selling the Family Silver*, London, Hutchinson 1990
Coggan, Philip	*The Money Machine: How the City Works*, London, Penguin 1986
Coopers & Lybrand	*The Financial Jungle: A Guide to Financial Instruments*, London, Coopers & Lybrand 1987
Corben, E.R., ed.	*A Glossary of Financial and Investment Terms*, London, Bulldog 1990
Corrigan, Daniel; Mackinnon, Neil & Hartnell, Simon	*Gilts–Facing the Challenge*, London, IFR Publishing 1989
Davidson, J.D. & Rees-Mogg, Sir William	*Blood in the Streets*, London, Sidgwick & Jackson 1988
Edwards, Anthony, ed.	*Brazil–A Guide to the Structure, Development and Regulation of Financial Services*, London, Economist Publications 1988.
Fay, Stephen	*Portrait of an Old Lady–Turmoil at the Bank of England*, London, Penguin 1988
Gibson-Jarvie, Robert	*Futures & Options Markets*, Cambridge, Woodhead-Faulkner 1989
Gibson-Jarvie, Robert	*The London Metal Exchange* 3rd ed., Cambridge, Woodhead-Faulkner 1989
Gray, S.J. & McDermott, M.C.	*Mega-Merger Mayhem*, London, Mandarin 1989
Hildreth, Sandra S.	*The A to Z of Wall Street*, Chicago, Longman 1988
Hill Samuel Bank	*Mergers, Acquisitions & Alternative Corporate Strategies*, London, Mercury Books 1989
IG Index	*Dealing Handbook*, London, IG Index 1990
Kay, William, ed.	*The Stock Exchange–A market-place for tomorrow*, London, Sterling Publications 1987
de Keyser, Ethel, ed.	*Guide to World Commodity Markets*, London, Kogan Page 1977
Kleinman, Judith & Sington, Philip, ed.	*Spain–The Internationalization of the Economy*, London, Euromoney Publications 1989
Lake, David & Graham, John	*Investor Relations*, London, Euromoney Publications 1990
Lamont, Barclay W.	*Lamont's Glossary–A Guide for Investors* 5th ed., London, IPS Lamont 1990

BIBLIOGRAPHY

Mansfield, Peter	*Kuwait–Vanguard of the Gulf*, London, Hutchinson 1990
Moffitt, Douglas	*The Family Money Book*, London, J.M. Dent & Sons 1987
Neal, Paula & MacKinnon, Neil	*International Economic Policy*, London, Yamaichi International 1991
O'Connell, Rhona, ed.	*Annual Review of the World Gold Industry*, London, Shearson Lehman Hutton 1989
O'Neill, James	*ECU Bonds–The success story of the 1990s*, London, Swiss Bank Corporation 1990
Reuters	*Reuters Glossary: International Economic & Financial Terms*, Harlow, Longman 1989
Riboud, Jacques	*A Stable External Currency for Europe*, London, Macmillan 1991
Robbins, Peter	*Guide to Non-Ferrous Metals and their Markets* 3rd ed., London, Kogan Page 1982
Roberts, Gerald, ed.	*Guide to World Commodity Markets* 4th ed., London, Economist Books 1985
Stewart, T.H., ed.	*Trading in Futures* 5th ed., Cambridge, Woodhead-Faulkner 1989
Sutton, William	*The Currency Options Handbook*, Cambridge, Woodhead-Faulkner 1988
Tait, Nikki, ed.	*Beginner's Guide to the Stockmarket*, London, Penguin 1986
Tarring ,T. & Pinney ,G., ed.	*Trading in Metals* 2nd ed., London, Metal Bulletin Books 1989
Thomas III, Lee R.	*The Currency-Hedging Debate*, London, IFR Publishing 1990
Valentine, Stuart	*International Dictionary of the Securities Industry* 2nd ed., London, Macmillan 1989
Williamson, John, ed.	*Exchange Rate Rules*, London, Macmillan 1981
Wolff & Co. Ltd,Rudolf	*Wolff's Guide to the London Metal Exchange* 3rd ed., Metal Bulletin Books 1987
Wood, Geoffrey E., ed.	*The State of the Economy*, London, Institute of Economic Affairs, 1991
Yergin, Daniel	*The Prize–The Epic Quest for Oil, Money and Power*, New York, Simon & Schuster,1991

Pamphlets

Brainard, Lawrence J.	*Reform in Eastern Europe: Creating a Capital Market*, London, Amex Bank Review Special Paper 1990
Department of Trade & Industry	*Competition Policy: How it works*, London 1991
Goldman Sachs International	*Anatomy of European Markets*, London 1991
IG Index	*Your Guide to Betting on the World's Financial Markets*, London 1990
KPMG Peat Marwick McLintock	*Global Capital Markets*, London 1988
Macfarlane, Peter, et al.	*Rule 144A: Implications for the ADR Market*, London, Int'l Business Communications 1990
Morgan Guaranty Trust	*World Financial Markets*, New York 1991
Options Clearing Corporation	*Characteristics & Risks of Standardized Options*, Chicago 1987
Philips & Drew Futures	*Understanding Futures & Options*, London 1987
Price Waterhouse	*Privatization: Learning the Lessons from the UK Experience*, London 1989
Securities & Investments Board	*Principles & Core Rules for the Conduct of Investment Business*, London 1991
Securities & Investments Board	*Report of the Securities and Investments Board for 1990/91*, London 1991

BIBLIOGRAPHY

Securities Review Committee	*The Operation and Regulation of the Hong Kong Securities Industry*, Hong Kong, Securities Review Committee 1988
Takeover Panel	*The Takeover Panel–A Guide*, London 1988
Thornton Management (Asia)	*The Case for Investment in Smaller Asian Markets*, London, Thornton Group 1990
UBS Philips & Drew	*Guide to Global Equity Markets*, London 1991
WIDER	*Foreign Portfolio Investment in Emerging Equity Markets*, Helsinki, World Institute for Development Economics Research, 1990

Exchange sources

American Stock Exchange	Introduction to the American Stock Exchange
Chicago Board of Trade	Action in the Market-Place
Chicago Board of Trade	Contract Specifications
Chicago Board Options Exchange	Leadership & Innovation
Chicago Mercantile Exchange	A World Market-Place
Chicago Mercantile Exchange	Futures & Options Facts
Chicago Mercantile Exchange	Spreads in Currency Futures
Chicago Mercantile Exchange	Using Currency Futures & Options
Frankfurter Wetpapierbörse	History/Organization/Operation
International Petroleum Exchange	Introductory Guide to Oil Futures Trading
LIFFE	Futures & Options Accounting & Administration
LIFFE	Futures & Options Funds-New Opportunities
LIFFE	Summary of Futures and Options Contracts
London FOX	Contract Specifications
London FOX	Historical paper
London Stock Exchange	LTOM-London Traded Options Market
London Stock Exchange	Annual Report 1991
London Stock Exchange	Quality of Markets Quarterly (various)
National Association of Securities Dealers Inc	Fact Book 1990
National Association of Securities Dealers Inc	NASD-Fifty Years of Helping Make America Strong
New York Stock Exchange	NYSE-The Capital Market for all Investors
NORDEX	NORDEX- A Transvik Market System

Journals

The Economist
The Financial Times
International Financial Review
Investors Chronicle
Wall Street Journal